John Smeur used to work in the chemical industry and a trade company until his 60th birthday. After that, he was asked by a university college to be a lecturer in the legal field. After one month, the institute asked him to add financial management. Many students had difficulty understanding the then used textbook. After five hours of extra lectures, they understood. This triggered John's ambition to write his own textbook with many exercises.

John Smeur

Financial Management

Austin Macauley Publishers
London * Cambridge * New York * Sharjah

Copyright © John Smeur 2025

The right of John Smeur to be identified as author of this work has been asserted by the author in accordance with sections 77 and 78 of the Copyright, Designs and Patents Act 1988.

All rights reserved. No part of this publication may be reproduced, stored in a retrieval system, or transmitted in any form or by any means, electronic, mechanical, photocopying, recording, or otherwise, without the prior permission of the publishers.

Any person who commits any unauthorised act in relation to this publication may be liable to criminal prosecution and civil claims for damages.

A CIP catalogue record for this title is available from the British Library.

ISBN 9781035829583 (Paperback)
ISBN 9781035829590 (ePub e-book)

www.austinmacauley.com

First Published 2025
Austin Macauley Publishers Ltd®
1 Canada Square
Canary Wharf
London
E14 5AA

The Dutch publication has benefitted from the professional recommendations of the Dutch publisher, Kluwer.

Preface

Financial management is a phenomenon that everybody in a business, be it in marketing, in purchase, in HRM, will have to deal with. In fact, every private person takes multiple decisions based on economic thinking.

Take farmer Jake, who takes his son Gerald aged 14 to the cattle market to buy a cow. Jake walks around and ends up with a dilemma: he can buy Emma II for $ 350 or Anna I for $ 700.

He mumbles to Gerald that he probably should buy Emma because of the price.

Gerald asks both vendors about milk production and finds out that Emma brings 9 Litres daily and Anna 11 Litres per day. Milk can be sold at $ 0.90 per litre. "Dad, you should buy Anna because your annual gains will be much higher compared to Emma" His father, about to ignore his son's interference approaches the Emma vendor, but Gerald pulls at his sleeve and drags him to the nearby pub. He asks the waiter to lend him a calculator and convinces his father that the price difference will be earned back within one year.

Emma: 360 days   X   9 Litres   X $ 0.90   = $ 2 916
Anna: 360 days   X   11 Litres X $ 0.90   = $ 3 564

$ 648

Extra profit $ 648 or: the difference of 2 litres X 360 days X $ .90 = $ 648. Gerald is right: the price difference of $ 350 will be compensated within one year!

Like this example many private persons and business people make similar economic comparisons many times. While private individuals will not encounter economic options on a daily basis, in business there is a daily multitude of such options. **B.E. is the tool to make the right decisions easy.**

Because no businessman can keep all the figures well organized by using his brains and memory only, B.E. comes with a number of supporting instruments that offer instant insight in the business' progress: a balance sheet, a profit & loss statement, a liquidity planning format and, last but not least, ratio formula's to check the company's health at all times.

This book invites the reader to get familiar with all of these formats and with many types of economic options which are essential for a company's continuity.

The first chapter intends to let the student follow a starting business in preparing all of the basic investments for start-up. One will observe how a 45-year-old man, Clark, would very much like to start his own trading company in TV sets and how he finds himself faced with a number of economic options. He will be making a business plan, including an investment budget (chapter 1) and a financing plan (chapter 2).

Once the financing will have been concluded the company can prepare it's opening balance sheet which can be found in chapter 3. From that moment on the company can start it's economic activities.

For demonstrating the period after start-up we shall see Clark operating as an importer and wholesaler looking at his first year's financial results that do not please him. (in Chapter 4). Economic assistance from a friend will help him make substantial improvements for his future profit & loss budgets.

In chapter 5 we will follow the planned annual cash flow in an ice cream saloon and how to deal with temporary cash deficits. And Clark, too, will budget his cash flows. After that, in chapter 6, we will be looking over the shoulders of Clark as he is happily drawing up the first financial year's closing balance sheet. In chapter 7, we will conclude the first year's operations where we will see how simple formulas will help in self analysing the health of a company.

After having closed the first year of operation we will join a company using calculating methods to arrive at the correct full cost price and we also will find which methods there are to calculate annual financial results and how to determine the break even point. We will join a number of managers within a company all being busy to prepare next year's budget. And, finally we will do some exercise to solidly choose from investment options that fit particular types of companies.

Throughout this book we will see modest business people facing a multiple of economic **options and succeed in following a logical step-by-step approach to make the optimal B.E.- choices.**

The mission of this book is to guide through the many economic options a business faces over the years but most of all to make business economics and the formats used **easily accessible**.

Every chapter is concluded by exercises and a final assignment per chapter. Knowing from personal experience the limited time of teachers to prepare tests, every chapter also contains assignments the solutions of which are accessible by teachers and professors only.

After having studied this book and having solved a large number of economic exercises the student can look at himself in the mirror. If he will be looking at a person feeling confident to have understood this economic content, then I, too, will look at myself; positively satisfied about a mission that served it's objective: **make people easily understand the basics of B.E.**

Chapter 1
Start Up of a Business: The Investment Plan

Before we start, we must agree on terminology in this book. British English and American English do have their differences: if a corporation issues a share to a shareholder and receives a higher price than the standard value of such share the British English speaks of" share premium" and American English often uses "additional paid-in capital". We will use this latter expression. In England a "Profit & Loss statement" is prepared periodically. The Americans prefer the words "financial statement". We will use the English terminology.

If a family is moving to a new house, it is logical that this house has to be filled with furniture and equipment to fill their needs. And it is equally logical that this family will do a lot of comparisons between vendors and a lot of financial calculations as to what it can afford. The same applies to a family with three kids planning for a holiday together. Many questions will be addressed: where are we going? When are we going? How are we going there? How long are we going to stay? Which accommodation doe we choose? Which can we do from day to day? How much will all of these cost? Can we afford it?

As soon as somebody contemplates to start his/her own business also he will be facing a number of questions that need to be answered even before the viability of the adventure can be assessed: What would I like to have as a business? Should it be production, or just trade, or, may be, servicing of any kind? In what market(s) would I want to be active? What do I need to know about competitors? Which types of clients will I be aiming at? Which institutes are to be found which can supply market information and financial advice? What material objects (= **assets**) do I need to get started e.g. a building, storing capacity, equipment etc.? How much money will be involved in gathering all of these assets that may be needed? Which % of that money will have to be my own financial input?

As will be clear : these preliminary actions look important enough, not to be taken lightly. Any company can invest it's precious dollars wisely only once! Should it buy the wrong truck no dealer will repay the price originally paid for it. Did it buy the office building instead of leasing it before the whole financial picture is complete it will be too late to undo the purchase.

For the purpose of this book, we will assume that all of the above questions have been studied extensively and that the starting business owner is about to take the step towards the **initial investments** in assets which the company will need at start up date. We will find how the process unrolls of making choices which are economically sound.

Before we are going to follow the process of founding a new business by Clark we have to understand that no business man can record all of his financial decisions and actions in his brain only. He will need recording vehicles from which he can derive data instantly. We will find out what a **balance sheet is, a Profit & Loss budget or –statement and a liquidity format.**

A balance sheet is a large letter T. Left of the vertical, the asset side, will show all of the assets = possessions of a company and right of the vertical we will find all of the resources of finance for these possessions. The total amount left and right shall never get "out of balance".

Below is a simplified drawing of a balance.

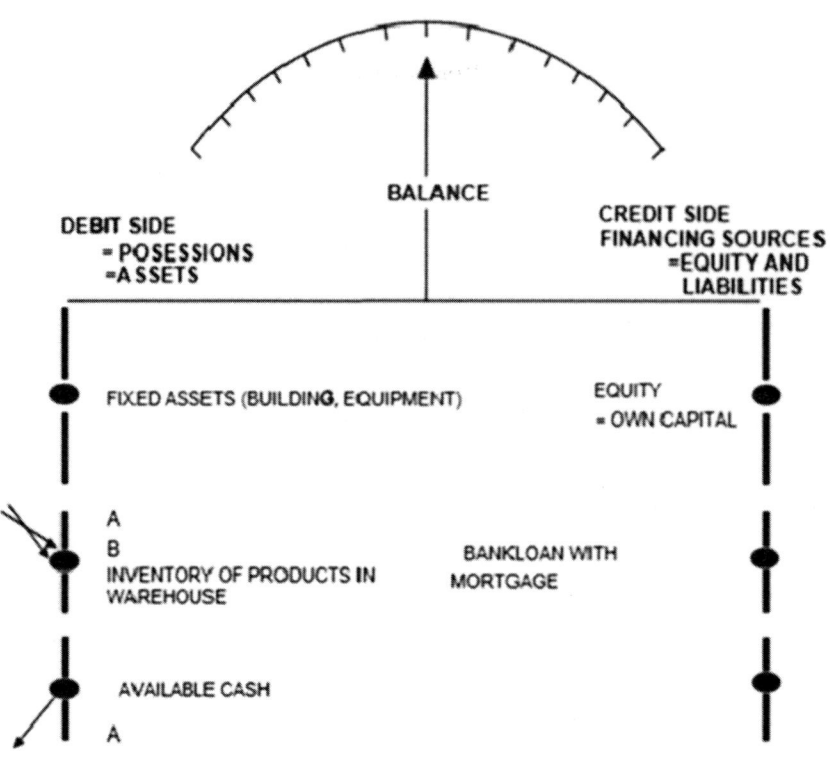

Accounts Receivable	Creditors, e.g. Suppliers
A. Upper arrow left side means inventory purchased for X dollars which were paid in cash (inventory + and cash -). Balance remains "In balance". remains "in balance"	**B.** lower arrow left side means inventory for which the supplier granted a term of payment. (Inventory +, creditors +). Balance

BALANCE SHEET	
DEBIT SIDE **ASSETS**	**CREDIT SIDE** **EQUITY AND LIABILITIES**
Fixed Assets Variable Assets All of the Assets = 100	Equity Long Term Liabilities Current Liabilities All of the Financing Resources = 100

In chapter 3 we will have a closer look at what the purpose of a balance sheet is and how relatively easy it is to translate business decisions into the proper balance positions.

Let us now follow Clark who is about tot start his own company intending to be active in the trade of television sets, imported from Germany. Which assets will his company need? First of all, it will need a warehouse which includes office space. Right from the beginning the starting business will

have to face options from which to make a choice for a building: buy or lease? Assuming that prices of industrial real estate will moderately increase every year, buying would be an attractive option. But will there be enough financial resources to afford the price for such property? If not, that option will have to be left for future consideration.

For the new business the warehouse should have storage racks for orderly storage of the stock of TV-sets of various dimensions, probably a forklift truck, one or more computers with a smart stock- and client system and a delivery van.

We assume that Clark himself can afford $ 560.000 from his savings to invest in his new business. This, plus added future retained earnings is called **"equity"** The remaining amount needed for the start up investments will have to come from outside financial resources, such as bank loans and credit from suppliers.

The crucial meaning of **"outside financial resources"** is that this money is to be paid back always, be it after 60 days to a supplier or in equal annual portions over a period of 30 years for a mortgage.

Banks in general also require that there is a minimum relation (=ratio) between the company's own capital (stock), or equity and outside financial sources. This sounds very logical: **banks, willing to finance will never accept to assume full risk of a business** venture. Depending on the bank's analysis of the business plan and on its knowledge of the market the company intends to enter it's acceptance of the portion of outside financial resources may vary anywhere from 65% to 55% as a maximum. The rest must be funded by the company's founder(s).

For the purpose of this chapter we will assume that a bank is found which will go as far as 65% of outside financial resources With Clark's $ 560.000 in equity this means that this will have to represent 35%. The maximum amount for all of the required assets will, as a consequence, total to ($560.000 : 35) X 100 = $ 1.600.000 Hence, the new company can afford an amount of $ 1.040.000 (= 65%) coming from outside financial resources, such as banks and suppliers of the assets. We will have a closer look at all of the financing resources in Chapter 2

Before we will follow Clarke preparing for business it may be useful to explain the term **"assets"**. Assets are those objects, possessions, acquired by a company and which

a) are essential for a company's economic activities and
b) can be found in the balance sheet.

This b) excludes things like copying paper and ink cartridges for the company's own printer. These types of things will not appear in a balance sheet and are treated as **"operating costs"** or "costs of operation".

Further, in B.E. a distinction is made between those assets that are intended to be used by the company for more than 1 or 2 years and other assets. The assets intended to be used more than 2 years are called: **FIXED ASSETS.**

The other assets that, by nature, vary in balance values frequently, such as **inventory,** outstanding invoices to clients and cash are called **CURRENT ASSETS.** We will discover this extensively in Chapter 3 Let us explore further the difference between fixed and current assets.

There are economical as well as a financial reasons for the distinction between fixed and current assets The main reasons are the following:

Fixed Assets

1. **Financial aspect**

    It is not difficult to get a mortgage on a building, but never will a bank be prepared to grant a mortgage loan on the stock of products in the warehouse. In other words: **long term loans are restricted for the financing of fixed assets.** These assets will be present also next year and the years thereafter and offer a security to banks should the owner no longer be capable of repaying a loan.

2. **Depreciation**

It is common use in business and in BE **to depreciate fixed assets annually** and show its effect in the balance sheet and in the profit & loss statement. It is logical to assume that electric equipment, racks, computers etc. will lose economic value over time. A motor car bought a year ago for $ 5.000 will have lost value which loss is proportionate with time. A car will be depreciated in a period of 3-5 years in equal annual amounts, large machinery in about 10 years and computers in 2-3 years. Buildings, by almost all companies in the world are depreciated in 25-30 years. Contrary to other fixed assets, possessed by a company, however, many buildings grow in market value from year to year! Depreciation will show its financial advantages later in this book

There is scarcity of technically good buildings, both industrial and private. And when something is scarce its price will go up. We will find out that this presents a financial opportunity to business under certain circumstances.

3. **Fiscal advantages of depreciation**

In most countries a company's net profit at the end of a financial year is taxed by corporate tax. Percentages vary from country to country. In Holland it now is 25%. Ireland shows the lowest rate: approximately 13%. U.K. applies 30% and the U.S.A. 40%

The amount of **depreciation is treated as an operating cost** by all companies. The net profit will be lower than without depreciation. But then it is easy to see that also the amount due for corporate tax will decrease. In other words: having fixed assets that are depreciated each year, **the tax system pays a part of that depreciation** by charging less corporate tax.

Imagine a privately owned company having depreciated an industrial building in 30 years from $ 600.000 to $ 0 It will have had an annual depreciation of $ 20.000. Depreciation lowers annual profits but also the amount of corporate tax! USA tax provides for 40% of that amount as a saving in tax payments annually.

This private businessperson may sell his property for well over $ 800.000 after those 30 years. From it's purchase price of $ 600.000 he experienced tax saving of 30 x (40% of $20.000) = 30 X $ 8.000 = $ 240.000. His net gain by selling it for $ 800.000 will be $ 800.000 less ($ 600.000 + $ 240.000) = $ 440.000! For many owners of a small private business this presents the only source to provide for their retirement income

4. **No cash flow is involved**

Let us se what happens to a car in time. It will lose value over time but will the owner physically notice that in his purse? No! Only at the time he would sell the used car to someone else.

The same applies to companies. Its **available cash was not affected at all by depreciating fixed assets**. Now we may understand better when a C.E.O. in a TV interview explained that his company did suffer a net financial loss in the past financial year, but that there was a **positive cash flow.** This company experienced large amounts of depreciation without any cash involved. And apparently this company's cash flow results were higher than the operating loss it suffered.

For the same reason he also may have expressed that the company did not have to borrow additional funds to pay for all of it's operating costs.

Current Assets

Are current assets less important or less exciting than fixed assets? Not at all. We explore.

A distinct difference with fixed assets is that there is, in principle, no annual depreciation. And the second difference can be found in the financing options.

1. Inventory raw materials and/or of products to be sold

    As said: for the financing of a commercial stock no bank will offer a mortgage. It may, however, offer a long term loan. 5 years to repay is standard in many countries. Almost always the condition will be that the inventory will contractually serve as a collateral. The interest rate is always higher than the rate for a mortgage. **Interest payments belong to the operating costs** of the company. The annual amounts for paying back are not a part of operational costs. They just ask for sufficiently available cash, which also is a current asset.

    Inventory shows in the balance sheet as a current asset. It also is a part of the company's **"working capital"** Some businesses, more specifically the large supermarkets, know to succeed in obtaining high volume sales with a minimum of inventory. This **inventory** is replenished more than one time per week throughout the year. **The lower the inventory without having to refuse an order from a client, the better a company's performance**.

    Look at the following example of a store selling TV sets. It's records show that monthly sales volume is 40 pieces. The store's purchase price is $ 700 and it's sales price is $ 990. The balance sheet on July 1, under current assets shows a stock to the amount of **160** pieces. The supplier guarantees deliveries within one week from receipt of an order. That means that an inventory of around 10 pieces would be sufficient. Over stock: 150! So, this store invested $ 105.000 in it's commercial stock where 10 pieces of $ 700 would have been sufficient to meet demand. If such stock would have required an excess of outside financing by more than $100.000 it would cost a lot of interest without good reason. The return on his capital employed suffered substantially also.

    Many companies know electronic warning systems to have an alert as soon as stock of any item is about to fall below a pre set limit. It helps them keep stocks to an optimal minimum.

    The lesson is that it is a challenge to make as much profit with a minimum of investments in current assets. However, we have to put this statement in the proper context. We have to realize that in selecting suppliers we find suppliers who maintain "ex factory" conditions, while others apply higher prices but maintain "free delivered" conditions. In both cases it is prudent to calculate the **landed cost price.** Distance by road transport plays an important role in this exercise. Ask any wine supplier in New York which wine will be more economical in terms of transportation costs, French wines or comparable Californian wines. Most of them will reply that it is more economical to have wine shipped from France than from California.

    So we are faced with a dilemma: large volumes per shipment combined with low costs of transportation per item and a low turn of inventory versus small volume per shipment and a high turn of inventory and relatively high costs of transportation.

In a table	Advantages	Disadvantages
Many Small Shipments	- high turn of inventory - no high financing - higher yield of capital	- high costs of transportation - lower profits
Few Large Shipments	- low costs per item of transportation higher profit	- low turn of inventory - high level of financing - lower yield on capital

2. **Debtors /accounts receivable**

   Usually and for the larger part these are clients to whom a term of payment was granted. In B.E. and on the balance sheet the term **Accounts Receivable** is used.

   Debtors also represent a pitfall for companies that are not alert enough to seek payments from their clients in time.

   Let us take a peek at such a company. The sales records of this company show sales to an amount of $ 1.800.000 on an annual basis. 50% of it's clients pay cash; the other 50% uses a term of payment of 1 month. On a monthly basis this translates into total monthly sales of $ 150.000 of which $ 75.000 is being paid in cash. Consequently, the balance sheet should show a figure for debtors of around $ 75.000. When, in fact, the company's balance sheet shows an amount of $ 125.000 it will be clear that this company is not alert enough. When we realize that all of a company's total assets will have to be financed by (share) capital plus outside financial sources showing the same total amount as the assets it will be clear that the return of this company suffers unnecessarily.

   Large companies do have a special department "accounts receivable", or **"cash management"** responsible to remind clients of their limited credit term. This is not a luxury but a useful tool to keep current assets as low as possible and the return on the investments as high as possible.

3. **Liquidity or Cash**

   This is the term collectively used for available money in the cash register and money on a bank account.

   Every sale generates a cash flow-in; every expense requires a cash flow-out. The more cash a company retains in the business, the less dependent on outside financing sources it will make itself. In chapter 5, liquidity format, we shall see how cash flows can vary from time to time which makes it essential to plan the periodic cash flows ahead as accurately as possible.

More about economical choices: Machinery capacity:

As we saw earlier **BE is about 80% in making the best economic choice** and about 20% in making a proper use of the available formats to always have an instant analysis of the company's status.

Here is a simple example of what is meant by making the best economical choice from a number of ice making equipment.

A large ice saloon called "the incredible penguin" needs a new machine that can mix all ingredients into a top-class ice cream.

Naturally, ice consumption varies from season to season. The calculated output in litres needed per quarter are as follows:

1st. quarter 1.000 litres, 2d. quarter 4.000 litres, 3d. quarter 8.400 litres, 4th. Quarter 2.000

The saloon decides on equipment that provides a capacity for these quantities plus an additional 20% capacity for extreme summer circumstances.

A choice can be made from the following machines:

	A	B	C
Annual capacity	36 000 litres	42 000 litres	48 000 litres
Purchase price	$ 8 000	$ 18 000	$ 16 000
Lifespan	5 years	5 years	5 years
Maintenance cost / year	$ 2 800	$ 5 700	$ 5 100

Which machine will provide the optimal economic choice?

It should be noted that the capacity needed is expressed per quarter and the offered capacity on an annual basis. What to do?

It would seem easy to add the 4 needed quantities and add 20% to the total: 18.480 litres. This would mean that machine A could easily do the job: 36.000: 4= 9.000 litres capacity per quarter. But look what happens in the 3d quarter: the basic need is 8.400 litres + 20% = 10.080 litres. Machine A cannot offer that capacity!

The right approach, therefore would be to make both the needed and the offered quantities comparable by adjusting the needed ones to annual volumes. **Not by just adding the 4 quarterly needs but taking the highest quarter and adjust that to 12 months**. The capacity needed can now be calculated as follows: (8.400 X 4) + 20% = 40.320 litres.

These rules out machine A. Would B now present the best option? That depends on the annual or **operating costs** comparison between B and C, both of which offer sufficient capacity.

So, let us look at the annual operating costs:

	B	C
Depreciation	$ 3 600	$ 3 200
Maintenance	$ 5 700	$ 5 100
Total operating costs	$ 9 300	$ 8 300

The conclusion can be no other than that C presents the best economic option. The fact that it offers more capacity than B does not change this. In B.E. this excess is called: **"rational excess capacity"**, meaning: a well considered choice any buyer would have made.

How to select a truck from two alternatives.

Before we follow Clark and his new business let us demonstrate one more time that **selecting the best option indeed is the heart of BE.** We can expect Clark to need a truck for his business. He found two alternatives

	Truck brand A	Truck brand B
Price	$ 160 000	$ 190 000
10 years depreciation	$ 16 000	$ 19 000
Maintenance costs per year	- 6 000	- 4000
Insurance	- 4 500	- 4 200
Fuel consumption in gallons of $ 1.50 each per 100 miles	8	4.2
Annual mileage	80 000	80 000

Like the farmer in the beginning Clark instinctively might prefer truck A because it is cheaper. We explore if his instinct is correct from the question which annual costs will be lowest, because a lower purchase price does not always guarantee the lowest annual operating costs. Annual costs for Clark can save operating costs by selecting truck B, although more expensive to buy. It will be obvious to all of us that finding options to choose from is a valuable B.E. –custom.

	A	B
Depreciation	$ 16 000	$ 19 000
Maintenance costs per year	6000	4000
Insurance	4500	4200
Fuel costs	800 X 8.0 X $ 1.50 9 600	800 X 4.2 X $ 1.50 5 040
TOTAL ANNUAL COSTS	$ 36 100	$ 32 240

Now that we know more about assets it is time to follow the previously announced intention of Clark to start his own company in TV-sets as a trading company. We saw that he owns $ 560.000 and that his bank accepts 65% of all of the assets being financed by outside sources. We calculated that the total assets should not exceed (560.000:35) X100= $1.600.000

Clark made a list of his needs to get started, **an investment budget**

Industrial building with 10.000 ft. of warehouse space and two offices, a workshop and a bathroom. He found two matching these needs:

	A $ 628 500	B $ 750 000
A rack system for storage. He found 2 vendors	C - 95 000	D - 120 000
Tooling for the workshop	- 8 500	- 8 500
A forklift truck for which he found 2 options	E - 80 000	F - 90 000
Two computers + software. He received 2 offers	G - 18 000	H - 22 000
Inventory 100 Philips TV's +150 Westinghouse	- 200 000	- 200 000
Both suppliers will grant 60 days for payment		
Finally, he needs 2 trucks for shipments totalling	J - 320 000	K - 380 000
Liquidity at the start	- 50 000	- 50 000
He totals both the lowest and the highest:	$ 1 400 000	$ 1 620 500

Since Clark would like also to have some liquidity at the start until sales promise to take care of that it is obvious that he cannot afford all of the highest options in view of the maximum amount for total assets of $ 1.600.000. The difference to the lowest option amounts to $ 220.500 He wonders what would happen if he decides to choose the lowest options except for the trucks.

This will mean that his investment will be $ 1 400 000 minus $ 320.000
$$= \$ 1.080.000 \text{ (2 trucks A)}$$
$$+ 380\ 000 \text{ (trucks B)}$$
$$\text{--------------------}$$
$$= \$ 1.460.000$$

It is obvious that this option is a viable one. There even is still room for extra investments to an amount of $ 1.600.000 - $ 1.460.000 = $140.000.

Clark now decides to start finalizing his investment budget, based on the choices he made.

Fixed Assets
- building $ 628 500
- rack system   - 95 000
- tooling workshop   - 8 500
- forklift truck   - 80 000
- computers + software   - 18 000
- 2 trucks   - 380 000

TOTAL FIXED ASSETS   **$ 1 210 000**

Current Assets

- inventory   - 200 000
- liquidity   - 50 000

TOTAL CURRENT ASSETS   **$ 250 000**

Clark's Total Investment   1 460 000

His $ 560.000 offers some space to survive, should his new operation fail or would take longer to succeed than he anticipated earlier. The **ratio capital: outside sources of finance** now is: ($ 560.000 : $ 1.460.000) X 100 = 38.35 % and, thus, liabilities will finance 61.65 %, which is lower than the 65% limit demanded by his bank. With this ratio of 38.35 – 61.65 banks will be very willing to extend any additional loan to Clark up to a maximum of $ 140.000 since the portion of outside sources of finance remains well below the agreed limit of 65% of all of the financing.

Clark now completed his investment budget. In Chapter 2 we will follow his exercise to find the best financing resources.

Exercises of Chapter 1
Investment Plan

1. Peter decides to start a business on his own. He counts his savings (account) and finds that he owns $ 220.000. The bank offers a mortgage for 100% of the value of the building he likes to buy, but demands that all assets must be financed by at least 40% of his own capital. Peter finds a building for sale at $ 300.000. Alternatively, he can lease a different building for an annual lease price of $ 7.000.   He needs: equipment to a total of $180.000, furniture at $ 90.000 and computers for $ 24.000.
Can Peter afford to buy the building?

    a. Yes, because...
    b. No, because…

2. Stan needs a commercial vehicle for his business and there are two options from which he wants to select as economically as possible

	vehicle A	vehicle B
Purchase price	$ 85 000	$ 105 000
Depreciation in years	5 years	5 years
Residual value after depreciation	$ 20 000	$ 15 000
Maintenance costs/year	- 8 000	- 5 000
Insurance premium/year	- 1 600	- 1 100
Mileage per year	70 000	70 000
Gasoline consumption per 100 miles	12 gallons	9 gallons
Gasoline price/gallon	- 1.30	- 1.30

Which of the two cars is the best choice, economically?
    a. Vehicle A, because . . .
    b. Vehicle B, because . . .

3. Making the best economic choice presents a daily challenge to companies. Here is one to solve. Derek needs equipment for a very critical production process. The options are to buy or to prefer operational lease with immediate technical assistance in case of defects.

Derek decides to prefer the lease option even if it will cost him more as long as the excess costs are limited to $ 10.000/ year. Here are his options:

	Equipment A	Equipment B
Purchase price	$ 120 000	lease price $ 26 400
Depreciation period	10 years	
Residual value after 10 years	0	
Cost of energy per year	6 000	3 600
Cost of maintenance per year	18 000	12 000

Which of the 2 options best fills Derek's needs?

a) Equipment A
b) Equipment B

4. Here is a list of items needed by a company. Place an X in the column indicating to which category each item belongs

item	fixed assets	current assets	operating costs
1) Architect's drawing table			
2) Waste containers			
3) 500 markers			
4) 200 packs of printing paper			
5) A container full of packing cartons			
6) Tooling in a workshop			
7) A forklift truck			
8) 10 computers			
9) Money in bank account			

5. Imagine that Tracy owns her own business by selling a hair growing stimulant lotion for $ 25/bottle which she purchases directly from the manufacturer for $ 10. After one year her success is expressed by volume sales of 5.000 bottles each month. The time of delivery to her store is 2 weeks. She receives an offer from the supplier to save 3% on her purchase price if she would buy 40.000 bottles in one shipment. All of her purchases are being financed by a credit limit in her current bank account which charges her 14% interest for each $ above $ 0 per year.

Should she accept the offer and save 3 %?

    a) of course, because ....!
    b) not at all, because ....!

6. Make the best economical choice from 2 machines for the production of 5.000 items per month. Depreciation time of both is 10 years, No residual value after that.

	MACHINE A	MACHINE A
Purchase price	$ 150 000	$ 250 000
Days of maintenance; no production	18 days	36 days
Cost of maintenance per day	$ 10 000	$ 3 500

    a. Calculate the cost of depreciation per manufactured item for each machine
    b. Calculate the cost of maintenance per manufactured item for each machine
    c. Calculate total of these operating costs per manufactured item for each machine
    d. Draw a conclusion: which of the machines presents the best economic alternative?

1) Machine A
2) Machine B

7. Bill developed a secret recipe for a windscreen spray that not only cleans a car's windscreen, but also effectively removes insects from the glass. Bill budgeted the following quarterly volumes of production: 1st. 6.000, 2d 10.00, 3d. 20.000, 4th. 4.000 litres.

Because of unpredictable weather conditions Bill demands a capacity of 20% in excess of his sales budget. He has a choice between:

	MACHINE A	MACHINE B	MACHINE C
Annual capacity	98 000 Litres	96 000 litres	94 000 litres
Purchase price	$ 28 000	$ 34 000	$ 42 000

Which of these machines presents Bill's best economic option?

    a) machine A
    b) machine B
    c) machine C

8. On the balance sheet of painting company "The rapid paintbrush" under current assets there appears a figure for accounts receivable of $ 120.000. A rule in it's general conditions demands clients to pay their invoice within 2 weeks. From the profit & loss statement it can be learned that annual sales were $ 480.000, equally divided over 12 months. Sales tax to be ignored.

Does this company show that it is alert on it's clients' payment attitude?

    a. Yes, it looks good
    b. No, they could do a lot better

9. The same "rapid paintbrush" company consumes 4.200 tins of paint annually, equally divided over 12 months. Purchase price per tin is $ 12 Their supplier can deliver within 24 hours from receipt of an order. What would be an economically sound balance figure for stock by the end of the year? Use 50 weeks to make up for a year.

    a) Approximately $ 1 200
    b) Approximately $ 1 000
    c) Approximately $ 500

10. A company buys new equipment for $ 240.000. Expected time of depreciation is 10 years. The company decides to write off $ 20.000 annually. What is the expected residual value now

    a) $ 20 000
    b) $ 40 000
    c) $ 0

Closing Assignment Chapter 1
The Investment Plan

Prepare a provisional investment budget for a new company, ELECTRONICS CORP. which activities will be to manufacture motorcar batteries, of which the budgeted volume for the 1st year is 150.000 pieces equally divided over the twelve months period. Sales price will be $ 35 each.

Expected annual growth in volume is 10% on top of each previous year. The founders of the company can invest their private savings of $ 550.000. Their bank is willing to extend a loan of 100% of the building based on a mortgage. And it will accept additional 5-year loans for equipment provided that all of the equipment serves as collateral and provided that outside financial sources do not exceed 60% of total assets. All of the equipment will have a time of depreciation of 10 years.

Here are the options from which to make the best economical choices

Fixed Assets

Industrial building can be bought for $ 355.000 or it can be leased for $ 50.000 per year

Equipment options:	Vendor A	Vendor B	Vendor C
Annual capacity	350 000 pieces	375 000 pieces	400 000 pieces
Purchase prices total	$ 265 000	$ 300 000	$ 270 000
Cost of maintenance/yr	$ 5 000	$ 7 000	$ 6 000
Depreciation time	10 years	10 years	10 years

Each vendor is willing to extend a 60 day's term of payment.
Office and warehouse furniture and fixtures $ 125.000 Computers $ 20.000
The respective suppliers demand that their invoice be paid within 30 days.

Current Assets

Raw materials: each battery requires synthetic carbon of 1 kilogram and 0.5 litres of battery fluid. A minimum stock for 3 months of production is needed.

There are 3 vendors	A	B	C
Price of carbon	$ 8.50/kg	$ 8.80/kg	$ 8.40/kg
Prices of battery fluid	- 6.00/litre	- 5.40	- 5.60
Delivery time	6 weeks	2 weeks	4 weeks
Rebate if both products are purchased	3 %	7 %	5 %
Costs for transport on top of net invoice	10 %	4 %	6 %

All of the vendors will grant a term of payment of 60 days.

Debtors: all of the clients will have a time of credit of 30 days. Every client will pay in time
Liquidity: for initial costs and payment of random installation costs the company needs $50.000 on its bank account.

Prepare the provisional investment budget in compliance with all of the above data and use the table below where a choice out of three must be made **per asset by selecting the correct letter**. When asked to write down a chosen source of finance choose from the following: equity, long term loan, current account loan, credit from supplier

FIXED ASSETS		**Insert Source (S) of Finance Per Asset. (More than one source allowed)**
1) Building	a) $ 0 b) $ 32 000 c) $ 429 000	
2) Equipment	a) $ 265 000 b) $ 290 000 c) $ 270 000	
3) furniture/computers and racks	a) $ 105 000 b) $ 145 000 c) $ 115 000	
CURRENT ASSETS		**Insert Source (S) of Finance Per Asset. (More than one source allowed)**
4) inventory	a) $ 335 864 b) $ 424 846 c) $ 417 000	
5) debtors	a) $ 437 500 b) $ 466 200 c) $ 428 700	
6) cash	a) $ 50 000 b) $ 102 500 c) $ 112 500	

Chapter 2
The Financial Plan at Start Up of a Company

Par. 2.1 Capital and Shareholders' equity

Anybody starting his own business has a choice: the founder either decides to stay just a private enterprise, like a small retail store, or he decides to become a **legal entity**. In that case there will be an official deed to found the business as a legal entity, like a **corporation or a limited liability company, which coincides with the emission of shares to the founders.** Larger businesses may opt for having the public buy shares through the **official stock exchange.**

The difference between a private company and an incorporated company is in the **liabilities to pay all debts.** If the privately owned company has insufficient means to pay for all of the debts the **private company and the private owner himself will be declared bankrupt.** In an incorporated enterprise the company itself, not the founders, will be declared bankrupt. A legal entity like a corporation is authorized to participate in the economic field, buy, sell, hire employees etc. The company is employer. The company, not the founders, can be brought to trial when there is a lawsuit brought against it. What all of these types of business have in common is the necessity to bring own money into the company before it can look for bank loans. This "own money" is called: **EQUITY.**

When a company is founded as an **incorporated there always will be share capital.** This is a sum of money made available first by the founders and possibly also by partners who make available larger sums of money in return of which they receive shares in the company. The offered shares are part of a **"share emission". Share capital or stock** is the primary source to shape the financing of all of the investments at start up. It is owned by the shareholders and it will remain their possession as long as they do not sell those shares to another party. Contrary to money to be paid to suppliers or to be paid back to a bank, this money received from participating parties never will have to be paid back.

From the first chapter we remember that any investment made by a company needs financing by one or another type of financial resource. Any company, be it at its start up or during its existence, will need equity if it also needs third parties for outside financing aid. No bank will extend a loan to a company if there is no, or hardly any, equity. But what do they require? Banks have their **standards for the relation between equity and outside financial resources.**

A bank is prepared to finance part of the investments of a company but will not be prepared to become exposed to the risks of the business. Banks translate this in what they demand to be the minimum of equity which should be a **buffer against financial risks.** They demand sufficient equity to finance a part of the total investments before granting loans, which will become a liability of the borrowing company. They set a standard for the **ratio equity: liabilities.**

One bank, in need of more clients may grant more concessions in terms of this ratio and will be satisfied as long as equity will finance 30% of all of the assets, while more conservative banks never will go below a ratio of 40 : 60 for equity : liabilities. It will be evident that also in the selection of a preferred bank economic options present themselves to select from. Let us look at a simple balance sheet at the start of a company.

Finally: every asset (debit side of the balance sheet) added after start-up raises the repeated question: how is it financed (credit side of the balance sheet)

Balance Sheet			
Fixed Assets	$ 400 000	Share capital / equity = 40% $ 240 000 = 40%	
Current Assets	- 200 000	**Long Term Liabilities** Mortgage loan 5%	$ 180 000
		Current Liabilities Current account credit Creditors	- 120 000 - 60 000
Total Assets	**$ 600 000**	**Total Capital**	**$ 600 000**

We see in this balance sheet that all of the possessions (assets) were financed by 40% equity and 60% liabilities. The ratio equity – liabilities is 40/60 or: 40: 60

Let us now start this chapter by retrieving Clark's investment plan

- building	$ 628 500
- rack system	- 95 000
- tooling workshop	- 8 500
- forklift truck	- 80 000
- computers + software	- 18 000
- inventory	- 200 000
- 2 trucks	- 380 000
- liquidity	- 50 000
CLARK'S TOTAL	**$ 1 460 000**

We also saw that Clark has $ 560.000 to invest in his new venture which accounts for 38,35% of total investment of $ 1.46 million. Every asset added to a balance sheet raises the question by which source it was financed. **(financial resources)** Both debit and credit side of the balance sheet always **must be "in balance"**

When setting up a financing plan it is wise always to follow a **sequence** in the financial resources **from cheap to expensive.** For Clark's business this may work out as follows, depending on his bank's cooperation and which payment term will be granted by suppliers.

We assume that his bank is prepared to grant a loan for the purchase of the building of 100% based on a mortgage and that the suppliers of his inventory will grant a term of payment of 60 days. We also assume that interest rates vary: a mortgage requires 5%, a 5-years' loan 8% and a **credit limit on his current account as allowed by his bank will cost 14% per year.**

Let us see how this would work out for Clark.

FIXED ASSETS		= TOTAL FINANCING NEED $ 1 460 000	
- building	$ 628 500	suppliers' payment term	- 200 000
- rack system	95 000		
- tooling workshop	8 500	still to be financed	$ 1 260 000
- forklift truck	80 000	private equity	- 560 000
- computers + software	18 000		
- 2 trucks	380 000	still to be financed	$ 700 000
		mortgage loan 5%	- 628 500
Total fixed assets	$1 210 000		
CURRENT ASSETS		still to be financed	$ 71 500
		5 years' bank loan 8%	- 71 500
- inventory	200 000		
- liquidity	50 000		$ 0
		From cheapest: suppliers to most	
Total current assets	$250 000	expensive: (8% bank loan)	
TOTAL ASSETS	$1 460 000		
Summary of Financial Resources:			
Clark's Total Need is		$ 1 460 000	
Stockholders' Equity		$ 560 000	
Long term liabilities		- 700 000*	
Current Liabilities		- 200 000*	
Total Financing		$ 1 460 000	

*see Par. 2 of this chapter 2.

We see that Clark's savings were high enough to remain at the safe side of the bank's demand that 35% of all of the assets should be financed by equity. He still has a borrowing capacity for additional investments of $ 140.000, bringing total assets at $1.600.000. Even then his $ 560.000 equity would represent 35% of total assets.

Now, let us have a look at private equity and how it will be affected by the company's activities. And in this book we will deal with middle sized incorporated companies only, since its activities and results are managed by the owner, or a small group of owners, only. Large corporations on the NYSE (New York Stock Exchange) are much more under the influence of investment corporations which would present more complications than useful for this elementary book on Business Economics.

Start up of a company always **requires private capital (equity)** to a sufficient level if it would qualify for bank loans. Again: a bank never is prepared to take over all of the risks inherent to doing business. This private capital starts by **an emission of shares, which are issued to the owner(s) against payment in cash.**

Once a company becomes successful by growing turnover figures the level of its inventory will grow as will the amount of accounts receivable. These two represent assets. And growth in assets always raises the question: **how will this growth be financed by equity and/or liabilities?** There is a saying: growing always costs money. And as long as the earnings will be higher than those costs of growth a company remains in healthy conditions.

Bank loans are less easily obtained by a private business compared to a private limited liability company or to a corporation, one reason among others being the vulnerability of a business depending on the health of its only owner.

A corporation, however, represents a legal entity, a subject of rights and obligations like human beings. The corporation, contrary to a private entrepreneur, cannot die. It can go bankrupt without hurting its owners privately. When a founder dies, he will be succeeded by an other managing director. So, anyone intending to start a business of his own would act wisely to start a private corporation based on **share capital**.

A corporation must file so called **Articles of Incorporation** which must contain several specific articles, e.g. how high the share capital will be at start up (= **Authorized Shares**) and which **nominal or par value** each of these shares will have ($ 10,00, $50,00, $100.00 or $ 1.000 each). Also it should be illustrated in the Articles of Incorporation if only common stock will be issued or also **preferred stock.**

Preferred stock may rend the owner stronger or exclusive voting rights on important issues or it may indicate that there is a stronger position in receiving dividends.

Once shares have been sold to the founders of the private corporation we will see a figure appearing on the credit side of its balance sheet, so on the right side of the T-vertical, under the name: (Stockholders') **Equity**. It heads all other sources of finance on the right side of the balance sheet. On the asset side the money received for the shares by the company is reported under "cash". Clark in our example may well have issued common stock to himself in the order of $560.000.

On the liability side (credit side) of a balance sheet we see two distinct financial sources for the financing of the assets: stockholders' equity and liabilities, the latter split up in two: **current liabilities and long term liabilities.** The most important difference between the two is that current assets must be paid back within one year. The long term liabilities are allowed from two to thirty years. The difference with equity is that **stockholders' equity will never have to be paid back** and remains at the disposal of the corporation indefinitely, whereas all of the liabilities will have to be paid back sooner or later.

BALANCE SHEET	
Fixed Assets	**Equity** Common Stock
Current Assets	**Liabilities** Long term liabilities Current Liabilities

The long-term liabilities may consist of a mortgage loan only, or also of loans granted for more than 2 years. The current liabilities mostly consist of money due to suppliers, but also of tax to be paid within one year, of repair jobs carried out and not yet paid, etc. Changes in the long-term liabilities mostly will show a regular pattern over the years because of paid back instalments of equal annual amounts. Current liabilities will show a much more dynamic pattern, coinciding with the flow of the business.

Now we would like to know what changes may occur in the stockholders' equity during the business life of a corporation.

In the first place the figure on the balance sheet under stockholders' equity may change when additional shares are issued to the existing shareholders or, with their consent, to outsiders.

In the second place the value on the balance sheet will rise as soon as **profits are retained** by the corporation. This is called **"retained earnings"**. It is obvious that shareholders having taken the risk to invest in a newly created corporation, will be entitled to these retained earnings since they are the exclusive owners of the corporation. Exception is made to that portion of the net earnings that **must be retained** by the company according to its Articles of Incorporation or to local legislation.

So, on the balance sheet we can distinguish two portions of equity belonging to the owners: **common stock plus retained earnings.** The figure on the balance sheet for common stock **shall not change unless there is a change in the number of shares issued.** So, every addition to equity other than newly issued shares, must be recorded under a different name.

Let us look at a simple example

Mike, having established his own private corporation has issued 1.000 shares of a nominal value of $ 100. On the balance sheet we will see:

Balance Sheet			
Current Assets		Equity	
Cash	$ 100 000	Stockholder' equity	$100 000

The corporation now shows a **cash figure as its only (current) asset,** financed by equity.

Mike purchases 50 laptops at a price of $ 400 each and pays them in cash. His balance sheet would now show the following:

Balance Sheet			
Current Assets		Equity	
Cash	80,000	Stockholder' equity	$100 000
Total Assets	$100 000	Total Equity	$100 000

Nothing changed in the equity. The **one current asset was used to buy another current asset.**
Mike sells 40 of the laptops at a sales price of $ 580 and receives payment in cash.

Balance Sheet			
Inventory	$4 000	Stockholder' equity	$ 100 000
Cash	$ 103 200	Retaining earnings	$ 7200
Total assets	$ 107 200	Total equity	$ 107 200

We note several changes and details

1. Stockholders' equity remained at its **original (nominal) value**, because no change took place in the number of shares issued.
2. The inventory level decreased at purchase price value for the 40 pieces sold. Inventory always appears on a balance sheet at purchase price or at it's variable costs (material cost), whichever is higher. (Cost prices: see chapters 8 and 9).
3. The generated total sales of $ 23.200 was added to the $ 80.000 available cash.
4. 4. A **profit** was made which **is the property of the owner.** Shareholder Mike booked under retained earnings 40 X ($ 580 - $ 400) = $ 7.200.
5. There now is an **equity value** per share which is higher than the nominal, or par, value of $ 100. This current value of $ 107, 20 is 7%+ compared to the **nominal value.**
6. The book value of the company increased from $ 100.000 to $ 107.200

Intermezzo

Retained earnings is a common term in B.E. for recording generated earnings. That raises the question: how to record if a corporation incurred a loss in its first year? Imagine Tom who started his business and who purchased an industrial building for $ 420.000 and put up $ 500.000 in equity. Before he can start operations, he is knocked down by a mean virus which keeps him in a hospital for

12 months. There was depreciation of the building in that first year of $ 420.000: 30 = $ 14.000. And since no turnover was generated nor other corporate expenses incurred there is an operating loss of that amount. How to record this?

On the balance sheet the best way to account for this loss is as follows:

Balance Sheet

Fixed Assets	$ 420 000	Stockholder' equity	$ 500 000
Depreciation	$ -14 000	Operating loss	- 14000
Total assets	$ 107 200		
Total fixed Assets	$ 406 000	Total equity	$ 486 000
Current Assets	80 000		
Tota Assets	$486 000	Total Capital	$486 000

Note that the depreciation did not lead to a payment; it only indicates a decrease in value. Hence, there was no cash flow involved. Instead of "retained earnings" we see a **negative reserve** under equity end of intermezzo

Let us go back to Mike's balance sheet showing a total of $ 107.200

What would have to be recorded if Mike would be in need of a second shareholder in order to strengthen the corporation's equity? Suppose his friend Carl would be interested to join forces. What would Carl have to pay for shares issued to him: $ 100 or $ 107,20?

It is obvious that the retained earnings increased the equity and it would be perfectly normal that Carl will have to pay $ 107,20 per share. Let us assume that Carl buys 200 shares at the price of $ 107,20. How will this transaction have to appear on the balance sheet?

In most countries and states law prescribes that the figure for common **stock on a balance sheet represents the nominal, or par, value of the shares.** In this case $100 each.

The excess amount paid will have to be booked under shareholders' equity but with a different name: **"additional paid-in capital" or "APIC"**. This way of phrasing may vary by country. In The Netherlands the term "Agio reserve" is used. Other countries may use the term "share (issue) premium, or paid-in surplus. Let us hope the global financial world will develop a uniform term everybody can understand for this purpose. In this book we will use the short term APIC.

In Derek's case the transaction will be booked the American way:

Balance Sheet

cash	+ $ 21 440	common stock	+ $ 20 000
		APIC	- 1 440
	--------------		---------------
increase assets	+ $ 21 440	increase equity total	+ $ 21 440

We now have seen how equity can comprise 1. share capital + 2. retained earnings + 3. APIC. The three terms and their amounts in dollars represent the ownership by the shareholders.

Is that all?

No. There is one more situation where equity can rise without any share being issued. Let us look at a business where the ratio equity – liabilities on the balance sheet is so delicate that no liability can be added without violation of its bank's condition of 35 :65 for the ratio equity: liabilities.

If this situation occurs, when no earnings can be reported yet, the business may find one more option to satisfy the bank: **the revaluation reserve**

It works as follows: on the balance sheet of the company the building, bought 5 years ago for $ 300.000 with a depreciation period of 30 years is reported for the amount of the depreciated value of $ 250.00. A registered appraiser requested by the business to reappraise the market value of the building certifies that market value is $ 425.000. There is a positive difference of $ 175.000. The business now can report on its balance sheet:

Balance Sheet

Assets		Equity	
Building	+ $ 175 000	Common stock	$ 210 000
Al other Assets	- 600 000	Revaluation reserve	**175 000**
		Shareholders' equity	$ 385 000
		Total liabilities	- 390 000
ASSETS TOTAL	$ 775 000	CAPITAL TOTAL	$ 775 000

The difference between book value and market value is **made visible on the balance sheet.** The original amount for assets of $ 600.000 grows by $ 175.000.

This reserve becomes the fourth possible part of shareholders' equity. The amount of $175.000 raises equity substantially and with that it changes the equity-liability ratio in a very positive way by which the bank will be very pleased. Equity now finances 49,68% of all of the assets which is distinctly higher than the required 35%.

What it does NOT do is that earnings or income will go up. There is no cash involved! Like no cash flow occurs at the moment of depreciation so is the case after a revaluation of a building. What it does: **it restores borrowing capacity**. We can draw conclusions:

1. The limit of liabilities was raised by the revaluation. Equity now is $ 385.000. Since this must be at least 35% of the total balance this total balance can grow to ($385.000: 35) X 100 = $ 1.100.000. The company can invest $ 325.000 in assets additionally and have all of these assets financed by liabilities without violating the 35-65 limits demanded by its bank: total assets would be $1.100.000 and equity represents ($ 385.000: $ 1.100.000) X 100 = 35%.
2. On the balance sheet we can also see that the original amount of equity of $210.000 financed 35% exactly of all of the assets at their starting value of $600.000
3. The increased shareholders' equity of $ 385.000 allows an increase in assets of $325000 up to a total of $ 1.100.000 and still equity will not come below the required 35% of the total assets: ($ 385.000: 35) X 100 = $ 1.100.000.
4. When so requested, the bank will be very willing to extend additional loans to this business.
5. After this reappraisal the business can opt to increase the annual depreciation figure for the very same building on the Profit & Loss Statement as an operating cost, thus lowering net earnings but also lowering its tax liability

In summary:

The credit side of a balance sheet contains all of the financial resources for the financing of all of the assets. The total of dollars of these sources is called CAPITAL. Those sources are divided in categories:

1. Shareholders equity =
    A. Common Stock at par value
    B. Retained earnings
    C. APIC (Additional Paid-In Capital
    D. Revaluation reserve

2. Liabilities

    a. Long term liabilities
    b. current liabilities.
    (see following paragraph 2.2)

For a successful corporation who reported solid net earnings for the past years it's success caused the total figure of equity to rise. That is very positive. There can be a disadvantage, however.

Let us look at the following balance sheet:

	Balance Sheet		
FIXED ASSETS	$ 600 000	Equity	
		Common stock	$ 250 000
CURRENT ASSETS	- 250 000	Retained Earnings	- 400 000
		TOTAL EQUITY	$ 650 000
		LIABILITIES	- 200 000
TOTAL ASSETS	$ 850 000	TOTAL CAPITAL	$ 850 000

We assume that par value of the shares is $ 1.000 per share. What is the **actual (=intrinsic) value per share now?** Total equity amounts to $ 650.000. This is $650.000:250 = $ 2.600 per share.

Suppose that shareholders received dividends of $ 200 per share during the past 4 years. That is a formidable return on their invested $ 1.000 of 20%!

Now, suppose that the corporation would have a rare opportunity to buy a competing company but could only accomplish this by attracting more share capital? If it requires an additional quantity of 400 newly issued shares from the **authorized capital**, what would new shareholders have to pay for one share?

Would these new shareholders be offered shares at $ 1.000? Or at $ 2.600? The latter amount would be much more likely. Existing shareholders who are the owners of total equity would not allow the board to issue shares to new shareholders at the same $1.000 price they paid at the start. First of all, these newcomers had not been exposed to all kinds of risks and should not be entitled to pay the lowest price. And, secondly,: once a new shareholder enters the existing group of shareholders this new shareholder becomes **co-owner of the total equity**, thus lowering the value of the proportionate part for the existing shareholders. But then the question is: would shareholder candidates hastily accept the offer at $ 2.600 for each share they like **to invest in** ?

Let us see how **their return** would look if dividend payments would, again, be $ 200. If they would pay $ 2.600 per share their return would be ($ 200 : $ 2.600) X 100 = 7.7% These candidates might find better investment opportunities easily. The corporation might not sell one share!

Most corporations are aware of this negative chance. They would not issue new shares before they would have brought down the equity value of the existing shares to a more attractive level. How can a corporation do that?

Given the fact that shareholders are proportionate owners of the amount of shares plus equity **the corporation may issue free shares = BONUS SHARES to the existing shareholders,** if these agree to the proposition during a general meeting of shareholders, required to decide on such an important proposition. The corporation might propose to issue 350 bonus shares to be given to the existing shareholders in proportion to their existing number of shares. If the general meeting agrees and the bonus shares will have been distributed the balance sheet would look as follows:

Balance Sheet

FIXED ASSETS	$ 600 000	Equity	
		Common stock	$250 000
		+Bonus shares	-350 000
CURRENT ASSETS	- 250 000	Retained earnings	-50 000
		TOTAL EQUITY	$650 000
		LIABILITIES	-200 000
BALANCE TOTAL	$ 850 000		$ 850 000

We can see that the balance total equals the earlier balance sheet above. But we also see that the number of shares now totals 600 and that the intrinsic value per share decreased to $ 650.000 : 600 = $ 1.083,33. At this price it would be much more likely that new shareholders can be convinced that the offer of $ 1.083,33 would promise them an attractive return when dividends are paid of $ 200 per share: ($ 200 : $ 1.083,33) X 100 = 18,46%

Summarizing: **all parts of the equity are eligible to be transformed into common (bonus) shares at any time**. It would be a logical step if the current value of the common stock is too high to tempt new shareholders to buy stock.

One last observation: a corporation considering to sell all of the outstanding shares to a new owner would act wisely to assess if there is any hidden reserve among its assets, e.g. increased market value of an industrial building, before extending a buy-out offer. Try to find the reason for this.

Exercises Of Chapter 2.1
Equity

10.1. Jack and his wife Anna each own 50 shares of $ 1.000 par value. They decide to increase the number of outstanding shares again after one year by purchasing 25 additional shares each against payment in cash. Report the consequent changes in the balance sheet by + or – per balance item.

    a. cash + $ 25.000 and equity + $ 25.000
    b. cash + $ 50.000 and mortgage loan + $ 50.000
    c. cash + $ 50.000 and common stock + $ 50.000

10.2. After three years Jack and Anna, together the owners of 150 shares at $ 1.000 par value decide to invite Jack's brother Hank to join them as a shareholder. But because of retained earnings accrued over the past years the total equity now amounts to $ 177.000. Hank is prepared to pay the book value per share and buys 20 shares, newly issued by the corporation.
Report the changes to the balance sheet by using + and -.

    a. Cash + $ 23.600, common share capital + $ 23.600
    b. Cash + $ 23.600, common share capital + $ 20.000, APIC $ 3.600
    c. Cash + $ 23.600, common share capital + $ 20.000, retained earnings $3.600.

11. Gordon founded his corporation in which he invested $ 240.000 for 240 shares. One month after his start-up he was hit by a tropical virus that kept him in hospital for a full year. The corporation had purchased an industrial building of $ 210.000 with the cash it received when Gordon paid for his shares. The building will be depreciated to $0 in 30 years.
Adjust the balance sheet after this first unlucky year by using + and – per item.

    a. Fixed assets - $ 7.000 and under equity: operating loss - $ 7.000
    b. Fixed assets - $ 7.000 and retained earnings - $ 7.000
    c. Fixed assets - $ 7.000 and revaluation reserve - $ 7.000

12. Gordon from exercise 2 recovered fully and is very satisfied with accrued net earnings after five years of operation. He now has the ambition to buy out a competing corporation and needs a long-term loan from the bank for that purpose. Before talking to his bank, he decides to correct the total value of fixed assets on the balance sheet by having the building reappraised. This building after five years of depreciation, proves to have a market value of exactly $ 300.000. What are the changes to be made in his balance sheet? Use + and – again per item to be changed.

a. fixed assets + $ 90.000, retained earnings + $ 90.000
b. fixed assets + $ 125.000, revaluation reserve + $ 125.000
c. fixed assets + $ 125.000, retained earnings + $ 125.000

13. The corporation Cyber Mate shows 60 common shares of $ 1.000 par value on its balance sheet. Under equity the balance sheet shows retained earnings of $120.000 and a reappraisal reserve of $ 60.000.

13.1.   What is the exact total equity of Cyber Mate?

   a. $ 200.000
   b. $ 220.000
   c. $ 240.000

4.2 What is the intrinsic value per share now?
   a. $ 1.000
   b. $ 4.000
   c. 3.000

5. Cyber Mate corp. has the ambition to buy out a large competitor. It decides to have the industrial building with a **book value** of $ 240.000 reappraised in order to sell and lease it back from the buyer. The market value after appraisal is $ 600.000 and the buyer pays that sum in cash. Report the consequential changes on the balance sheet by + and –

   a. fixed assets - $ 600.000, cash + $ 600.000
   b. fixed assets + $ 360.000, reappraisal reserve + 240.000; fixed assets - $ 600.000 and cash + $ 600.000
   c. fixed assets +$ 360.000, reappraisal reserve +$ 360.000; fixed assets - $600.000 and cash + $ 600.000

6. Geoffrey decides to start his own retail shop where he intends to sell i-pads and notebooks. He made a list of assets he will need: a store in Charleston of $350.000, store fixings of $ 85.000, storage racks of $ 10.000 and warehouse inventory $110.000. Suppliers, Samsung and Apple, grant a payment term of 60 days on their supplies, the bank will grant a mortgage loan of 100% of the building at 5% interest and a credit on current account up to an amount of 60% of total inventory at 15% interest.
Prepare Geoffrey's investment budget and financing plan. Show which amounts for fixed assets and which amount for current assets are involved. Record the financing resources in descending order of costs involved and show how much private capital Geoffrey will have to put in if the bank requires that private capital must finance 40% at least of all of the assets.

a. INVESTMENT BUDGET		FINANCING PLAN	
Fixed assets	$350 000	Credit by suppliers	$90 000
Current assets	205 000	Mortgage loan	350 000
Total assets	$555 000	Agreed financing	$440 000
		Equity Needed	115 000
			$555 000

b. INVESTMENT BUDGET		FINANCING PLAN	
Fixed assets	$ 445 000	Credit by suppliers	$ 110 000
Current assets -	110 000	Mortgage loan -	350 000
Total assets	$ 555 000	Agreed Financing	$ 440 000
		Equity needed -	95 000
		Total financing	$ 555 000

c. INVESTMENT BUDGET		FINANCING PLAN	
Fixed assets	$ 445 000	Financing need	$ 555 000
		Credit by suppliers	$ 110 000
Current assets -	110 000	Equity 40% -222 000	
		Available finance	$ 332 000
		Still needed finance	$ 223 000
		Mortgage loan	- 223 000
Total assets	$ 555 000	finance complete	$ 0

7. large corporation in medical equipment, Global Pharma, shows the following depreciations among its operating costs: building: -$ 15.000, warehouse equipment ---$10.000. Also, Global Pharma reports net earnings after tax of $80.000. Remember: depreciation does not create a cash outflow!

7.1 What was Global Pharma 's cash flow

   a. $ 110.000
   b. $ 105.000
   c. $ 90.000

7.2 Apply the changes from 7.1 by + and - to the balance sheet

   a. Retained earnings will increase by + $ 80.000, cash will increase by $ 80.000 - $25.000 = + $ 55.000
   b. Building will decrease by - $ 15.000, warehouse equipment by - $ 10.000 and retained earnings will increase by + $ 80.000 - $ 25.000 = + $ 55.000
   c. Cash will increase by net earnings + depreciations = + $ 105.000, building will decrease by - $ 15.000 and warehouse equipment by -$ 10.000, retained earnings will increase by + $ 80.000

8. Ex-barber Bing of 62 years intends to open up his own wholesale company in barbers' tools and lotions. He found a suitable warehouse of $ 180.000 where he needs storage racks to a total of $ 18.000. Office furniture will cost him $ 8.000 and two computers will cost $ 4.000 in total. He considers to start with an inventory of tools of $ 60.000 and of lotions of $ 25.000. His savings amount to $125.000. Consultation with his bank revealed that he can obtain a mortgage loan of 75% of the purchase price of the building against annual interest of 4.5% and a five-year loan of 60% of the purchase price of the other fixed assets against an interest rate of 7%. Finally, there is room for a credit on his current account to a maximum of $ 20.000 at an interest rate of 15%. The suppliers demand cash payment of their respective shipments of tools and lotions. The bank requires that equity will finance at least 40% of all of the assets. Bing accepts all of the conditions but firmly intends not to make use of the most costly credit. If necessary, he would rather reduce the purchase of tools and lotions proportionately.

Prepare Bing's investment plan and his financing plan and show how much less in proportion of the tools and the lotions he must purchase in order no to make use of the expensive credit

a. From the total investment in fixed assets of $ 210.000 he can count on mortgage of $135.000 and a 5-year loan of $ 18.000. He has room to spend $ 57.000 for inventory of tools and lotions which sum accounts for 76% of current assets. Tools maximum will be $45.600 and lotions $ 11.400

b. INVESTMENT PLAN		FINANCING RESOURCES	
Fixed assets building	$180 000	75% financed by mortgage	$135 000
		+ equity use	= $ 45 000
racks	$18 000		
+ furniture	$8 000		
and computers	$4 000	of which 60% financed by 5-year loan	= $ 18 000
		+ equity =	$12 000
		equity shows a balance of	$ 125 000
		less	– 57 000
Fixed assets:	$210 000	BALANCE =	$ 68 000

BALANCE=$ 68000 to be used for investing in current assets of tools and lotions = 80% of intended total of $ 85.000 > he can afford 80% of $ 60.000 for tools = $ 48.000 and 80% of $ 25.000 for the lotions = $ 20.000, totalling $ 68.000.

Tools	$ 48 000	Total investment	$ 278 000
lotions	- 20 000	financed by equity	$ 125 000
	-------------	mortgage loan	$ 135 000
Current assets	$ 68 000	long term loan	$ 18 000
	-------------		------------
Total assets	$ 278 000		$ 278 000

b. $ 125.000 accounts for 43.86% of the total investment. Consequently 56.14% will have to be financed by outside sources = $ 285.000. Mortgage will be $ 135.000 and the 5-year loan will be $ 19.500, totalling $ 154.500. Add his equity of $ 125.000 = $279.500. There is room for tools and lotions of $ 285.000 - $ 279.500 = $ 5.500 which is 7.33%. He can afford tools for $ 60.000 X 7.33% = $ 4.398 and lotions of $1.102

9. We see the following BALANCE SHEET

Building	$ 280 000	Common share capital	$ 150 000
Storage racks	- 95 000	Retained earnings	- 88 000
Office furniture	- 110 000		
Equipment	- 60 000		
FIXED ASSETS	**$ 545 000**	**EQUITY**	**$ 238 000**
Inventory	75 000	Mortgage loan 5%	$ 257 000
Accounts receive.	-35 0	long term loan 8%	- 120 000
Cash	-20 000	**LONG TERM LIABILITIES**	**$ 377 000**
		Creditors	- 60 000
CURRENT ASSETS	**$130 000**	**CURRENT LIABILITIES**	**$ 60 000**
TOTAL BALANCE	**$ 675 000**	**TOTAL BALANCE**	**$ 675 000**

This balance sheet represents the Thompson corp. The bank's demand is that equity must finance at least 40% of all of the assets at all times. Thompson is facing a dilemma. They could sell $ 60.000 from their inventory of electronic devices to a Taiwanese client in one shipment on which sale they can make a nice profit of 40% However, the client will only confirm their interest if Thompson accepts 6 months of payment for this special deal. Because of the strict demands by the bank and a too large increase in accounts receivable Thompson considers two options: enlarge the number of shares by attracting an outside shareholder or have the building **reappraised**, hoping there will be excess value. He prefers the latter. The official reappraisal report shows a market value of $ 430.000. Thompson makes the appropriate adjustments in his balance sheet based on a reappraisal

13.2 Make the proper adjustments in the balance sheet by + and/or –
   a. Assets: Building + $ 150.000, Equity: retained earnings + $ 150.000
   b. Assets: Building + $ 430.000. Equity: revaluation reserve + $ 430.000
   c. Assets: Building + $ 150.000, Equity: revaluation reserve + $ 150.000

13.3 What is the intrinsic value per share now if there are 150 shares

   a. Equity grows by $ 430.000 to $ 668.000: 150 = $ 4.453,33
   b. Equity was $ 238.000 and grows to $ 388.000 after the revaluation.
   c. Value per share is $ 388.000: 150 = $ 2.586,67
   d. Value per share will be $ 3.453,33

13.4 With which amount can assets and financing resources grow now in view of the bank's demand?

   a. Equity now amounts to $ 388.000 + $ 150.000 =$ 388.000. Assets grew to $675.000 + $ 150.000 = $ 825.000. Equity now is 47% of all assets. These now have a new limit of ($ 388.000: 40) X 100 = $ 970.000 leaving room of $ 145.000 for new investments.
   b. Equity of $ 668.000 allows additional borrowings of $ 430.000
   c. Equity of $ 388.000 allows $ 646.667 in assets. This is $ 408.667 higher

Chapter 2.2
Liabilities

Every starting company must prove to have sufficient private capital to invest if it wants to count on outside financial resources. We saw earlier that banks can demand that private equity finances 35% - 45% of all of the assets. And we also saw **that all of the liabilities must be paid back sooner or later.**

What types of liabilities do we see on most balance sheets?

1. Mortgage loan
2. Long term credit
3. Creditors
4. Credit on current account
5. sometimes: Bonds

It could look like this on a BALANCE SHEET

FIXED ASSETS	EQUITY
Building	Common Share capital
Equipment	Retained Earnings
Fixtures	Additional paid-in capital
Furniture	Revaluation reserve
CURRENT ASSETS	LONG TERM LIABILITIES
inventory of products	Mortgage loan 5%
accounts receivable	long-term loan 8%
cash	
	CURRENT LIABILITIES
	creditors
	current account credit line 15%

Let us explore the liabilities.

1. **Mortgage Loan**

    Mostly, such a loan is granted for a maximum of 30 years. Interest can either be fixed for that period or can be adjusted from time to time, depending on the contractual conditions. From all of the loans mortgage loans require the lowest of actual interest rates.

    The contract can stipulate periodic pay-back instalments or it waves pay back during the contract period. And, subject to agreement between bank and client, interest and pay back can be combined in one fixed instalment per year which comprises both interest and pay back. The proportion between the two changes over time: in the beginning the interest portion is high and pay back portion is low; in the course of the years this proportion changes such that the pay back portion will be higher and higher, so that the full amount of the loan will have been paid back at the end of the contract period.

Second and third mortgages can be granted on the same fixed asset, depending on the growing market value.

If the debtor discontinues his payment obligations the creditor will have the right of foreclosure, meaning that the creditor will have the right to have the fixed asset auctioned. In most countries this takes place by a notary public.

2. **Long term loan**

While a mortgage can be granted on built property or territory other fixed assets, such as equipment, office furniture and office machines qualify for financing by long term loans. Mostly the term is limited to five years and banks require pay back instalments on an annual basis. The reason behind this lies in the **decrease in value** over time of all of these assets.

The interest rate is always higher than the rate for a mortgage for the same reason. Sometimes the creditor requires the respective asset to be pledged by contract. It remains in use at the debtor as long as he fills his contractual obligations. Should he discontinue his payment obligations than the creditor can demand the asset to be removed from the debtor's premises in order to be sold at an auction. The right of the creditor remains strong even when the debtor goes bankrupt.

Many countries know **Personal Loans** especially for starters of a new business. It can be granted if the business plan was approved by the creditor. And in some countries the state warrants the pay back of the loan to a certain degree. This happens when a state decides to encourage individuals to start their own business. Mostly, long term loans are for a maximum of five years with annual pay back instalments.

3. **Creditors**

This term covers all of the parties entitled to payments by a company other than creditors having allowed long term loans. Mostly, payment terms are relatively short: 1-3 months.

Most of the times they are suppliers to a company, but also tax authorities can be listed under this term. And also, a bank entitled to periodic payments within a year, such as interest and instalments are considered creditors.

A creditor who is not yet familiar with a buying company can stipulate **to retain ownership** of the goods delivered until full payment will have taken place.

In a "buying market", where every supplier undergoes decreases in sales and in earnings the buyer has the opportunity to select the supplier with a) the longest payment term and b) the highest discounts. Every dollar saved this way is a dollar that the buyer does not have to borrow from his bank.

4. **Credit on current account**

This is a continuing credit limit allowed by a bank on the current account of the client. The client uses the account to make and to receive payments practically on a daily basis and can make use of the credit within the agreed limits.

Interest rates are very high: up to 15% - 18% on an annual basis. The credit is used mostly for the financing of current assets.

Also, under such a credit agreement a bank may require securities in the form of collateral of accounts receivable or of inventory of goods to be sold. As long as the debtor fills his payment obligations and remains within the allowed credit limit nothing will happen. Once he skips payments too frequently the bank can take ownership of receivables or can require the goods to be removed from debtor's premises in order to be sold at an auction.

5. **(Bearer)Bonds**

A bond is a paper, the bearer of which is entitled to what the bond pledges. In general, the bond states that it owes a certain amount of money to the bearer which the issuing organization promises to pay back in a specific calendar year and –month. Also, it pledges to pay interest to the bearer annually at a fixed rate, expressed in the bond. Most of the times this interest can be collected at a number of banks specified in the bond.

States and larger hospitals but also large international companies issue bonds to gather financing. Companies make bonds convertible occasionally: the bearer is granted the option to be either paid back in full or to convert the bond into shares of the issuing organization.

Starting companies would act very unwisely to issue bonds to the citizens. No one knows the company and neither deserves such company to be trusted in its starting phase.

Trade in bonds constitutes a very large market for investors, especially in times when dividends are low or even scarce. We will not deal with bonds in this book.

Looking at the liabilities we realize that all types of loans charge interest, which will appear on the Profit & Loss statement (also: financial statement) after the operating result. (see chapter 4). **Even and may be foremost the fastest growing companies are subject of growing interest costs. The reason is that growing may generate earnings, but it also forces levels of inventory and of accounts receivable upward. This happens in those companies where lack of sufficient cash forces them to increase loans or their credit in current account.**

Conservative leaders retain as much of the earnings in the company, especially in the growing stages.

Let us pick up the information of Clark again and see how the financing worked out.

We know that his bank was prepared to grant a loan for the purchase of the building of 100% based on a mortgage and that the suppliers of his inventory granted a term of payment of 60 days. Finally, we saw which interest rates applied in Clark's case: his mortgage requires 5%, and the 5-years' loan 8% and a credit limit on his current account as allowed by his bank would cost him 14% per year for every $ 1 borrowed. Notice that **the financing sources best be ranked from "cheap" to "high interest costs".**

This was Clark's financing plan:

FIXED ASSETS TOTAL		FINANCING NEED	$ 1 460 000
- building	$ 628 500	suppliers' payment term	- 200 000
- rack system	- 95 000		----------------
- tooling workshop	- 8 500	still to be financed	$1 260 000
- forklift truck	- 80 000	private equity	-560 000
- computers + software	- 18 000		----------------
- 2 trucks	- 380 000	still to be financed	$700 000
	-------------	mortgage loan 5%	-628 500 -
Total fixed assets	$ 1 210 000		----------------
		still to be financed	$71 500
		5 years' bank loan 8%	-71 500

			$0
CURRENT ASSETS			
- inventory	- 200 000		
- liquidity	- 50 000		

Total current assets	$ 250 000	CLARK'S **TOTAL CAPITAL** IS $ 1 460 000	

SUMMARY OF FINANCIAL RESOURCES

STOCKHOLDERS' EQUITY	$560 000	
LONG TERM LIABILITIES*	-700 000	* = mortgage and long-term loan
CURRENT LIABILITIES*	-200 000	* = suppliers and current account credit
	-----------------	
TOTAL FINANCING	$1 460 000	

As we saw in chapter 1 the bank demands that 35% of all assets are financed by equity. In Clark's case his equity represents 38,356% of all of the assets. He may have made a wise choice not to stretch his liabilities too far. His equity allows a limit to a total level of assets of ($ 560.000 : 35) X 100 = $ 1.600.000. Clark still would have room for additional investments of $ 1.600.000 - $ 1.460.000 = $ 140.000 and then, still would meet the bank's demand that 35% of all of the assets be financed by equity: $ 560.000 is exactly 35% of $ 1.600.000.

The good news for Clark is that this additional space allows for an increase of inventory and accounts receivable in his growing phase. This is not unimportant to note. Overstretching of borrowing capacity right from the start might have brought Clark's business under pressure from the side of his bank.

For this reason, quite a number of starters of a new business may afford to buy an industrial building but prefer to start leasing this until there are sufficient retained earnings which will then serve them as a buffer.

The **credit on current account represents a Trojan horse** for many companies where inventory and accounts receivable increase constantly. We know: every growth in assets, booked on the balance sheet, leads to the question how this growth was financed. There may be revenues, but as long as these insufficiently help equity to grow proportionally a bank may take drastic steps. One of these might be to terminate the credit in current account instantly. Every bank reserves the right to put an immediate end to this type of financing. It takes place by a summon from the bank to bring back the balance of this credit to the agreed maximum level within two weeks. If that does not happen it means the end of the company. Bankruptcy will follow shortly thereafter.

The **two financing resources which do not generate operating costs are equity and creditors**. Obtaining longer payment terms from suppliers is a common effort by many companies for exactly this reason. Also Clark succeeded in obtaining payment terms of 60 days which allows sales to get started and to generate a growing income and growing retained earnings before he has to pay the bills of his suppliers.

Suppliers on their part also look for advantages and security. They cannot control what is happening to their clients. One of the instruments they use frequently is to offer a cash discount if the client pays in cash for a shipment. The other instrument they use is **retention of ownership** which can be found in the general conditions of sale most of the times. The advantage for these suppliers is that, if they prove that the retention clause applies, they can retrieve the goods delivered as their property even in bankruptcy situations.

Exercises of Chapter 2.2

Liabilities

1. Starter Vincent is preparing to start his own business in medical supplies. He saved $225.000 and is not sure yet if this will be sufficient to meet the bank's demand that 40% of the assets be financed by equity. His investment plan shows a warehouse building with two offices and a warehouse for the price of $ 300.000. There also is a warehouse for rent at an annual lease price of $ 38.000. He also needs packing and assembly equipment for $240.000. Racking and furniture plus printers and computers will cost $ 40.000. At start up he wants to have inventory of goods to be assembled for $ 30.000 and he wants available cash of $ 10.000. His bank agrees to a mortgage loan of 90% of the purchase price of the building at 5% interest, a long-term loan for five years of $ 220.000 at 8.5% and a credit on current account with a limit of $ 25.000 at 14%. Suppliers are prepared to grant payment terms of 60 days during his first year.

1.1 Prepare Vincent's investment plan and indicate the sources of finance with the proper amount in dollars per asset. Draw the conclusion if Vincent can afford the purchase of the building

a.
Assets		Financing sources			
Fixed assets					
Building	$ 300 000	mortgage loan	$165 000	equity	$155 000
Equipment	-240 000	5-year loan	210 000	equity -	20 000
furniture etc	-40 000			equity -	40 000
inventory	-30 000			suppliers -	30 000
cash	-10 000			equity -	10 000
	------------		------------		---------------
	$620 000		= $375 000		+$255 000

b.
Assets		Financing sources			
Building	300 000	mortgage loan $ 270 000		equity	$30 000
equipment -	240 000	5-year loan - 95 000		equity	-145 000
furniture etc -	40 000			equity	-40 000
inventory -	30 000			suppliers	-30 000
cash -	10 000			equity	-10 000
	--------------				--------------
Investment total $ 620 000		liabilities $ 365 000		+ equity	$ 225 000

$ 225.000 is 36% of all assets against the bank's demand.

c. With ownership of a building all of the assets would amount to $ 620.000 and equity represents 36.35% in that case. So, Vincent should lease the building:

Assets			financing sources			
Building $	0				equity	$175 000
equipment -	240 000		5-year loan $ 65 000		equity	-40 000
furniture etc. -	40 000				suppliers	-30 000
inventory -	30 000				equity	-10 000
cash -	10 000					
Assets	$ 320 000		$ 65 000			$255 000

Sound financing: equity $ 225.000, suppliers $ 30.000 and long-term loan $ 65.000

1.2 How much too low is equity in view of the bank's condition of 40% when building is purchased?

  a. 40% of $ 620.000 is $ 248.000. Equity falls short by $ 23.000
  b. Vincent's equity should be $ 240.000. He needs an additional $ 15.000
  c. Investment is $ 610.000. 40% is $ 244.000. A shortage of $ 19.000

2. Vincent negotiates with another bank before picking one of two options: either a bank is found who agrees to a lower portion of equity or Vincent will have to lease a building. He finds a new bank who agrees to a minimum of 35% equity, a mortgage of 100% of the price of the building at only 4% and a full long-term loan at 7.5%.

2.1 How does his financing plan look now?

a. Vincent needs $ 620.000 in assets. He must take the mortgage of $ 300.000 and $ 120.000 of the long-term loan His equity is sufficient to finance half of his equipment and all of the furniture = $ 160.000. He pays all of the inventory and still will have $ 35.000 as starting cash balance.

b. The best choice is to take the mortgage of $ 300.000 and the payment term of the suppliers of $ 30.000 and invest $ 100.000 of his equity in equipment and $ 40.000 in his furniture. The best way to assure sufficient cash of $ 85.000

c.
Assets		financing sources			
Fixed assets					
Building	$ 300 000	mortgage loan $ 300 000		equity -	175 000
Equipment -	240 000	5-year loan -	65 000	equity -	40 000
furniture etc -	40 000				
inventory -	30 000	suppliers	30 000		
cash -	10 000			equity -	10 000
	$ 620 000	=	$395 000	+	$225 000

The best economical choice is to use as much equity for equipment to save the higher interest rates of a long-term loan.

2.2 What will be the ratio of equity: liabilities after the best economical choice

a. Equity versus liabilities will be 35: 65
b. Equity finances 36,29 of the assets, liabilities 63,71%. Ratio = 36,3: 63,7 .
c. Equity: liabilities ratio will be 33: 67

2.3 How much interest will Vincent have to pay in his first year without any pay back?

a. 4% of $ 300.000 and 7.5% of $ 240.000 = $ 12.000 + $18.000 = $ 30.000
b. 4% of $ 300.000 and 7.5% of $ 120.000 = $ 12.000 + $ 9.000 = $ 21.000
c. provided Vincent uses a large portion of his equity ($ 175.000) for equipment his mortgage will cost 4% of $ 300.000 = $ 12.000 and long-term loan 7.5% of $ 65.000 = $ 4.875. Total interest first year: $ 16.875.

3. Michael operates a franchise store of "Pets animal feed". On his year end balance sheet inventory of animals feed packs is shown at purchase price value of $ 30.000. His annual sales were reported to have been $ 120.000 at a purchase value of $ 90.000. His annual sales are equally divided over the 12 months' period = **50 weeks**. His supplier can deliver within one week. two weeks of inventory would be a good choice. All of his clients order by phone and their order is delivered the same day. They have to pay their bill within half a month. On the balance sheet accounts receivable are $ 40.000.

Both his inventory and his accounts receivable are financed by a credit on current account at an annual interest rate of 16%

3.1 For how many months of sale will Pets inventory last

a. 7.5 months
b. 4 months
c. 6 months

3.2 What was the payment term used by his clients

a. 4.0 months
b. 4.5 months
c. 5.0 months

3.3 Apparently, Pets must pay too much interest for the credit on current account. How much excess interest in dollars on an annual basis?

a. Needed inventory is $ 120.000: 50 = $ 2.400. Excess is $ 27.600. Accounts payable should be $ 120.000: 100 = $ 1.200. Excess is 38.800. Total: $ 66.400. Excess interest is 16% of $ 66.400 = $ 10.624
b. Needed inventory is $ 90.000: 25 = $ 3.600. Excess is $ 26.400. Accounts receivable allowed was $ 120.000: 50 = $ 2.400. Excess is $ 37.600. Total = $ 64.000 Excess interest is 16% of $ 64.000 = $ 10.240
c. Based on purchases of $ 90.000 two weeks would require $ 3.600. Excess is $30.000 - $ 3.600 = $ 26.400. Sales were $ 120.000. Divide by 25 = $ 4.800 which tells the amount of allowed accounts receivable. Excess is $ 40.000 - $ 4.800 = $ 35.200. Total excess: $ 61.600. Interest could be 16% of ($ 3.600 + $ 4.800) = $ 1.344. Actual interest costs 16% of ($ 30.000 + $ 40.000) = $11.200. Excess: $ 9.856.

4. If a starting businessman owns $ 300.000 in equity and his bank demands that 40% of the assets to be chosen will be financed by equity how much in liabilities can this starter afford

   a. $ 480.000
   b. $ 450.000
   a. $ 430.000

5. When a company owns shares in another corporation they have to be treated as

   a. current assets
   b. fixed assets

Closing Assignments of Chapter 2

Fred intends to start his own Butcher's store where he also plans to sell meat from exotic places like Argentina for steaks and Iceland for seal meat. His savings which he can invest in his new business are $ 270.000. He will need a store building in a lively district which will cost him $ 300.000, a cold room for $ 180.000, a cool counter of $ 50.000 and furniture and tooling for $ 12.000. He decided on a starting product inventory of $ 15.000 which amount is to be paid within 60 days. He also wants $ 20.000 in cash for his first expenses. Finally, he needs a cool van which will cost $ 80.000.

His bank, after having approved his business plan with a focus at the high end of the market, is prepared to grant a mortgage loan for 80% of the price of the building at 5% interest and a five year loan up till 50% of the price of both cold room and cool counter at 8.5% interest. Finally, Fred can count on a credit on current account with a maximum tolerance of $ 40.000 at 15%. The bank demands that 40% of all the assets will be financed by equity.

1. Prepare Fred's investment plan and split this plan in fixed and current assets.

solution:	a	b	c
fixed assets	$812 000	$622 000	$610 000
current assets	-127 000	-35 000	- 37 000
total investment	$939 000	$657 000	$ 647 000

2. Prepare Fred's financing plan and show the percentage by which equity will finance the assets.

	A	B	C
Total investment	$ 622 000	$ 637 000	$ 657 000
Equity in %	- 270 000	-270 000	-270 000
	=43.4%	= 42.4%	= 41.1%
liabilities needed	$ 352 000	$ 367 000	$ 387 000
mortgage loan	- 240 000	- 220 000	- 240 000
long term loan	- 105 000	- 112 000	- 115 000
creditors	- 2 000	- 35 000	- 15 000
available so far	$347 000	$367 000	$370 000
still needed credit on current account	$5 000	0	-17 000
Liabilities total	$352 000	$ 367 000	$ 387 000

Which amount of interest will Fred have to pay based on the correct financing plan?

- a. $ 24.325
- b. $ 23.325
- c. $ 24.070

Chapter 3
Opening Balance Sheet at start-up of a company

3.1 The Opening Balance Sheet

At the start of a business an opening balance sheet is prepared where all of the assets from the investment plan and all of the financing resources from the financing plan are recorded in a logical manner. Assets on the debit side are split in FIXED and CURRENT assets. The financing resources on the credit side are split into two main groups: EQUITY and LIABILITIES. And, finally, the liabilities are split into two groups: LONG TERM liabilities and CURRENT liabilities.

A balance sheet is also prepared after the **Profit & Loss Statement** (also: financial statement) has been completed. This P & L statement (see chapter 4) records turnover, less cost prices, less operating costs, less financial costs (interest) leading to a net profit. Among the operating costs we find **depreciation. This item and the net profit are always transferred to the closing balance sheet directly.**

Back to the balance sheet and how it works

	BALANCE SHEET	
debit side		**credit side**
FIXED ASSETS		EQUITY
CURRENT ASSETS		LIABILITIES: - LONG TERM - CURRENT

It is important to note at this point that a balance sheet

  a. can be prepared independently from a Profit & Loss Statement
  b. is always made at the start of a company
  c. is prepared periodically during a business year from 1 to 12 times per year
  d. the P & L Statement (also: financial statement) feeds the balance sheet with three data only:

1. **costs of depreciation** directly influencing the fixed assets on the balance sheet
2. the **net earnings after tax** or the net loss which in- or decreases the figure of equity
3. **provisions.** (see chapter 4). Example: if the company believes that not all of the accounts receivable will be received it is allowed to take that amount as a cost on its P & L statement, which lowers profit and, thus, taxes and which same amount must appear on the balance sheet under liabilities.

e. **any investment and all payments of debts** during an operating period are booked first in a so-called **general ledger**. From this all of these data are transferred to the balance sheet at the moment this is prepared at the end of an operating period.

Remember: the balance sheet can be used only for recording properties (assets) and all of the sources of finance.

Further, for all people not familiar with a balance sheet yet, a balance sheet is like a pair of scales with one dominant characteristic: the scales on the left side (assets) are always in balance with the scales on the right side (sources of finance) and every business decision having an impact on either assets or on sources of finance will have to take into account how to balance the consequences of this decision on the balance sheet. This will be demonstrated in this chapter.

Let us first experience point "b" here above by resuming the financing plan of starter Clark and prepare his opening balance sheet

This was Clark's financing plan:

FIXED ASSETS		TOTAL FINANCING NEED	$1 460 000
- building	$628 500	suppliers' payment term -	200 000 -
- rack system	-95 000		------------
- tooling workshop	-8 500	still to be financed	$1 260 000
- forklift truck	-80 000	private equity -	560 000 -
- computers + software	- 18 000		------------
- 2 trucks	- 380 000	still to be financed	$700 000
	------------	mortgage loan 5% -	628 500 -
Total fixed assets	**$ 1 210 000**		------------
		still to be financed	$71 500
		5 years' bank loan 8%	- 71 500

			$ 0
CURRENT ASSETS		SUMMARY OF FINANCIAL RESOURCES	
- inventory	- 200 000	STOCKHOLDERS' EQUITY	$560 000
- liquidity	-50 000	LONG TERM LIABILITIES*	-700 000
Total current assets	**$ 250 000**	CURRENT LIABILITIES*	-200 000
CLARK'S TOTAL INVESTMENT	**$ 1 460 000**	**TOTAL FINANCING**	**$1 460 000**

From the model above we now can prepare Clark's opening balance sheet:

OPENING BALANCE SHEET

FIXED ASSETS		EQUITY	
- building	$628 500	Ordinary share capital	$560 000
- rack system	-95 000	**LONG TERM LIABILITIES**	
- tooling workshop	-8 500	mortgage loan 5%	-628 500
- forklift truck	-80 000	5 years' bank loan 8%	-71 500
- computers total	-18 000		--------------
- 2 trucks	-380 000	Total long-term liabilities	$700 000

Total fixed assets	$1 210 000	**CURRENT LIABILITIES**	
CURRENT ASSETS		Creditors	$200 000
- inventory	-200 000		----------------
- liquidity	-50 000	**Total liabilities**	$900 000

Total current assets	$250 000		
	----------------		----------------
investment total	$1 460 000	**Financing sources total**	$ 1 460 000

From this balance sheet we already can deduct some of Clark's operating costs during his first operating year: depreciation costs from his fixed assets. And we can see what at least his financial expenses will consist of: interest from both the mortgage loan and the long-term loan.

We know already that depreciation does not cause any outflow of cash! We will see this confirmed later.

We also know that a building may lose value on paper and still may increase in market value which a company can put to good use to increase its borrowing capacity

It would not be wise, economically, not to depreciate the value of the building owned by a company even when it's market value would increase. The company would miss the fiscal advantage from depreciation: depreciation is a cost; a cost lowers net profit; lower net profit saves fiscal charges.

Another misunderstanding would be to think that equity on the credit side of the balance can be used time and again to finance investments in new assets. Once equity will have been realized it just is one of the financing sources initially used to finance the current asset "cash" from where all kinds of different amounts of money were used to finance all types of assets. So, if we look at the figure of share capital on a balance sheet it only tells us which amount was made available to the company historically and permanently and also the ratio between equity and the liabilities can be compared.

Equity consists of **A. Share capital**, recording the total of dollars the company received in return of shares issued at **nominal value** to shareholders and

B. three types of reserves:

1. **APIC**
2. **Retained earnings**
3. **Revaluation reserve**

Share capital rarely, if at all, changes under rare circumstances only: **only issued and paid for shares are booked under "capital" or under "ordinary share capital"** So, only a change in the number of shares issued creates a change in this ordinary share capital.

Additional paid-in capital (APIC), retained earnings and revaluation reserve all are part of the balance item "equity" as well. We will get acquainted more intimately later with these terms.

A company's first question when in need of more assets is not to look at its equity, but to look at its available cash reservoir. If the new assets cannot be financed by available cash, then the company will look for financing sources at the credit side of its balance sheet. First question would be: is there a payment term from the supplier? If yes, it found its source of finance. If not, it may want to raise the use of its credit on current account without violating the agreed limit to such credit. If it is a fixed asset it wants to add then a long-term mortgage loan may be the right source. And only if the company stretched the use of liabilities to their maximum financing portion agreed to with its bank, it will be forced to see how equity could be increased.

Sequence from cheap to expensive of finding sources to add new assets:

1. Credit term from suppliers (= **creditors**)
2. Available cash
3. Add equity by issuing new shares from the authorized capital, or try to create a revaluation reserve on the building.
4. A mortgage loan in case of a building
5. Long term loan
6. Available limit of credit on current account

From point 2 above we can see that total balance between debit side and credit side can be maintained also when an asset on the debit side is financed by cash on the same debit side. **One current asset is exchanged for another asset.**

But in case one position on the balance sheet changes an other position will have to change simultaneously, be it **on the same side of the balance or on the opposite side.**

Changes on the credit side without simultaneous changes on the debit side can take place also: if there is a position **"retained earnings"** under equity, the combined shareholders have the full right to issue free shares from that position. The amount by which retained earnings decrease is used to increase share capital by issuing **BONUS SHARES.** (free of charge) Naturally, the total amount of the share capital involved must be a multiple of the par, or nominal, value per share. Retained earnings is nothing else but the portion of the net profit which is **not** made available to shareholders as a dividend.

3.2 The Balance Sheet and How to Apply Changes

Let us now start with a simple balance sheet and then take subsequent actions which cause all kinds of changes to that balance sheet. And the reader will discover how easy this exercise is in fact.

Burt inherited $ 75.000 and decides to start his own corporation active in the import and sale of mp3-players. He deposits all of his inherited dollars into the bank account of his corporation in return of which he receives 75 shares at their par value of $ 1.000. Then he buys 400 mp3-players at $ 10 and sells them at $ 15 a piece.

Step 1 establishing a corporation based on common share capital

	BALANCE SHEET	
Cash $75 000		Equity $75 000

Step 2 Buy inventory of 4.000 mp-3 players at $ 10 each for $ 40.000 and pay in cash

	BALANCE SHEET	
Inventory $40 000		Equity $75 000
Cash -35 000		
------------		-------------
total assets $75 000		total capital $75 000

We see an example where changes occurred on the debit side only! We also see how equity is put to use in more than one asset now and, thus, cannot be considered as a reservoir of dollars.

Step 3 Sell 1.000 pieces of MP-3 players at $ 15, 00 cash, = $ 15.000

		BALANCE SHEET		
Inventory	$40 000 (at cost price)		Equity	
Less	-10 000		-Ordinary share capital	$75 000
	------------		+Retained earnings	-5 000
Inventory	$30 000			
Cash	$35 000			
+sales	-15 000			

Cash	$50 000			
	-------------			---------------
TOTAL	$80 000		TOTAL BALANCE	$80 000

We see how the **net profit made found a position on the balance sheet under equity** in terms of **retained earnings**. Like the share capital the retained earnings are property of the shareholders.

We also saw how inventory, always at cost price or purchase price on the balance sheet decreased by the quantity sold X $ 10,=

Step 4 Burt buys additional 200 pieces of mp-3 players; the supplier grants 60 days payment term

BALANCE SHEET

Inventory	$30 000	Equity	
Purchased	**-2 000**	+ordinary share capital	$75 000
	--------------	retained earnings -	5 000
inventory	$32 000		------------
		total equity	$80 000
		current liabilities:	
Cash	-50 000	creditors	**-2 000**
	-------------		-------------
TOTAL	$82 000	TOTAL BALANCE	$82 000

We see that nothing changed in the amount of cash, because payment is deferred by 60 days. Inventory now found a second financing source after cash: **creditors**, a current liability.

Step 5 Burt buys a small warehouse for $ 25.000 based on a mortgage loan for that amount.

BALANCE SHEET

FIXED ASSETS		EQUITY	
Warehouse building	**$25 000**	Ordinary share capital	$75 000
		Retained earnings	-5 000
CURRENT ASSETS			-------------
Inventory	$32 000	total equity	$80 000
Cash	-50 000	LONG TERM LIABILITIES	
	---------------	Mortgage loan	**$25 000**
Total current assets	$82 000		
		CURRENT LIABILITIES	
		Creditors	-2 000
	----------------		----------------
TOTAL BALANCE	$107 000	TOTAL BALANCE	$107 000

This 5th step may have taken plays in two stages: the bank pays the mortgage loan to Burt who reports this payment under currents assets "cash". After having done that Burt buys the warehouse and pays in cash. We now see an asset where depreciation will take place on an annual basis: the warehouse. We also see that assets increased to over $100.000 and so did the financing sources among which the mortgage is new.

Step 6 Burt redeems $ 5.000 of the mortgage loan

BALANCE SHEET

FIXED ASSETS		EQUITY	
Warehouse building	$25 000	Total equity	$80 000
CURRENT ASSETS		LONG TERM LIABILITIES	
Inventory	-32 000	Mortgage	-20 000
Cash	-45 000		
	----------	CURRENT LIABILITIES	
Total current assets	$77 000	Creditors	-2 000
	----------		----------
TOTAL BALANCE	$102 000	TOTAL BALANCE	$102 000

We see a cash outflow and an equal decrease of a liability. Equity is not involved at all. So, **pay back of a loan is NOT an expense or an operating** cost and, therefore, does not influence equity in any way, nor does it belong on a P&L statement, since it is not a cost of operations.

Step 7 Burt reports a $ 2.000 depreciation on his fixed assets. No income, nor other expenses to be reported.

BALANCE SHEET

FIXED ASSETS		EQUITY	
Warehouse building	$25 000	Ordinary share capital	$75 000
less depreciation	**-2 000**	Retained earnings	$5 000
	----------	less net loss of	**-2 000**
Warehouse	$23 000	retained earnings	-3 000

CURRENT ASSETS		total equity	$78 000
Inventory	-32 000	LONG TERM LIABILITIES	
Cash	-45 000	Mortgage loan	-20 000

Total current assets	$77 000	CURRENT LIABILITIES	
		Creditors	-2 000
	----------		----------
TOTAL BALANCE	$100 000	TOTAL BALANCE	$100 000

We see that a net result, be it **net profit or a net loss, directly influences equity**. This means that the net result at the end of a Profit & Loss statement is booked **directly** under equity.

The decrease in equity in this case equals the amount of depreciation of the warehouse since there were no other operating costs or earnings.

Finally, we see confirmation that depreciation does not cause any outflow of money: The amount of cash after step 6 still is unchanged after this step 7.

Step 8 Burt made net earnings in his second year of $ 12.000, after depreciation of $2.000

BALANCE SHEET

FIXED ASSETS		EQUITY	
Warehouse	$23 000	Ordinary share capital	$75 000
Depreciation	-2 000	-Retained earnings	$3 000
	----------	+annual profit	**-12 000**
	$21 000		----------
		Total equity	$90 000
CURRENT ASSETS		LONG TERM LIABILITIES	
Inventory	$32 000	Mortgage loan	$20 000
Cash	$45 000		
+ net **profit**	**$12 000**	CURRENT LIABILITIES	
+ depreciation	**$2 000**	Creditors	$2 000
	----------		----------
TOTAL BALANCE	$112 000	TOTAL BALANCE	$112 000

When we look at the bold figures it is not difficult to see that these are in perfect balance. The net earnings of $ 12.000 are added on the credit side of the balance sheet directly under retained earning. Nothing else changes on the credit side.

On the debit side we see that profit + depreciation represent the **net cash flow**. Clients paid such a price that also the costs of depreciation were paid by his clients (= cash flow in) but that no "cash flow out" occurred by the depreciation. Therefore, that amount of depreciation remained in Burt's cash.

Step 9 To secure growth Burt invited his father to join him by buying 50 shares at the intrinsic value. His father agrees and pays 50% in cash and 50% 6 months later.

BALANCE SHEET

FIXED ASSETS		EQUITY	
Warehouse	$21 000	Ordinary share capital	$75 000
		+ 50 newly issued shares	**-50 000**
CURRENT ASSETS		**Additional paid-in capital**	**-10 000**
Inventory	$32 000	Retained earnings	-15 000
Cash	$59 000	LONG TERM LIABILITIES	
+ 50% of $60.000	**-30 000**	Mortgage loan	-20 000
Accounts receivable	**-30 000**	CURRENT LIABILITIES	
		Creditors	-2 000
	----------		----------
TOTAL BALANCE	$172 000	TOTAL BALANCE	$172 000

Also, in this step 9 we clearly can see what exactly happened: share capital increased by its **par value** of 50 shares X $ 1.000. But in step 8 the $ 90.000 of equity meant a higher value per share of ($ 90.000 : 75 shares) = $ 1.200 intrinsic value per share. Burt's father agreed to pay more than the nominal value. The **"additional paid-in capital"** (APIC), therefore is 50 X $ 200 = $ 10.000. By having the positions of retained earnings and the additional paid-in capital it is clear very quickly what the book value or intrinsic value per share is now: $ 150.000: 125 = $ 1.200.

Step 10 Burt had the building reappraised by an expert. Market value reported is $ 36.000.

BALANCE SHEET

FIXED ASSETS		EQUITY	
Warehouse	$21 000	Ordinary share capital	$125 000
added value	**-15 000**	additional paid-in capital	-10 000
	$36 000	retained earnings	-15 000
		revaluation reserve	**-15 000**
CURRENT ASSETS		TOTAL EQUITY	$165 000
Inventory	$32 000	LONG TERM LIABILITIES	
Cash	-89 000	mortgage loan	-20 000
Accounts receivable	-30 000	CURRENT LIABILITIES	
		Creditors	-2 000
TOTAL BALANCE	$187 000	TOTAL BALANCE	$187 000

Why would a company have its building reappraised? Can it earn money in the bank? No. There are two situations for a company to do this: 1. The company intends to sell all of the issued shares to a third party. It would be **foolish not to take advantage** of a possible higher value of the building than its book value. The price for the shares will increase by the excess value of the building. 2. The company stretched its liabilities to such an extent that there is no room left to borrow extra money or to add additional liabilities such as creditors The only option then is to strengthen equity. This can be done in either of two ways:

a. issue additional shares (see step 9) or

b. add a reserve to equity in order to improve the ratio between equity and liabilities.

Conclusion: like depreciation, the opposite, reappraisal, does not generate any cash to flow. But what it does effectively is to **extend its borrowing capacity**

Step 11 To allow for further expansion Burt and his co-shareholder, his dad, consider to invite a strong company to become a new shareholder in their company.

In view of a very high intrinsic value per share and, thereby, a possibly too high a price per share for a new shareholder to generate favourable return percentages for a new shareholder on his first dividend they first decide to eliminate all of the extras under equity by **issuing free of charge shares, bonus shares**, to the both of them before offering shares to a new shareholder. This works out as follows

BALANCE SHEET

FIXED ASSETS		EQUITY	
Warehouse	$36 000	Ordinary share capital	$125 000
		+ 40 bonus shares	-40 000
CURRENT ASSETS		LONG TERM LIABILITIES	
Inventory	-32 000	Mortgage loan	-20 000
Cash	-89 000	CURRENT LIABILITIES	
Accounts receivable	-30 000	Creditors	-2 000
TOTAL BALANCE	$187 000	TOTAL BALANCE	$187 000

We note that the total figures of the balance sheet of steps 10 and 11 do not differ. Nothing was added on either side of the balance sheet. One type of equity was transformed into the main type of equity. The intrinsic value per share in step 10 was $1.320 and after having issued 40 new shares intrinsic and nominal value are equal. As a consequence, a buyer of shares who may receive a dividend of $ 120 per share would not have a slim return of $ 120: $ 13,20 = 9.09% but a more attractive return of 12%, ($120: 1% of $ 1.000 par value per share).

So far, our exercise in steps. They were meant to prove that changes in a balance sheet are not very hard to apply. In every decision or action of a company having a financial consequence it always is smart first to **ask the question: are these earnings or costs**? If the latter is the case then the balance sheet will not be involved. As soon as it has to do with: an **investment, or a pay back on a loan, or an action regarding equity, a purchase against credit, a receipt from a client then the balance sheet should or could be changed.**

As said earlier, the facts here above are recorded in the **general ledger** where each of these subjects has its own place. At the end of a period all the accrued payments received from customers are totalized and deducted from the amount of accounts receivable on the balance sheet last made. And all of the sales to clients with a payment term are recorded in the general ledger as well. Also, these are totalized at the end of an operating period and added to the amount of accounts receivable on the balance sheet last made. Similarly, pay back of a loan, payment to a creditor are NOT recorded in the P&L statement, but are recorded in the general ledger to be transferred to the balance sheet

The balance sheet has everything to do with INVESTMENTS in ASSETS and with PAYMENTS AND RECEIPTS in relation to these investments, be it investments in fixed or in current assets.

Fixed assets are financed best by **LONG TERM EMPLOYED** financing = equity and long-term liabilities. Current assets are financed mostly by equity plus current liabilities.

However, there is one part of the current assets which would be financed better by long term employed financing: inventory. The reason can be explained best by the following. If a company is going downhill rapidly and cannot be saved, then foreclosure and seizure will take place. Before this happens, the company may have tried desperately to sell parts of its assets. Equipment can be sold to help paying back a long-term loan. The building can be sold to be leased back to repay a mortgage debt etc. In the field of current assets, it is less obvious.

A general statement is: : as long as current assets are higher than current liabilities a company can repay its debts. But is that true? Do all current assets bring revenues as high as their book value?

An account receivable is not very hard to sell at a 90% price to a factoring company. Of all of the current asset's inventory is the toughest to sell quickly. It is unthinkable that there would be a strong buyer who happened to notice that inventory is for sale who would be willing to pay the book value of inventory and take it all. 40% is a more common offer received by the selling company. For that reason, many companies prefer to finance their inventory with long financing sources. This may sound conservatively and maybe it is. At the same time, it pictures such company as a solid and trustworthy party. **If a company succeeds to have inventory financed by long term financing, then the "GOLDEN BALANCE RULE" applies to it**. Such company finances its fixed assets plus its inventory with equity plus long-term liabilities. In chapter 7 we will elaborate further.

Here are two examples:

1st BALANCE SHEET

FIXED ASSETS			EQUITY	
Building	$330 000	**A**	**C** Ordinary share capital	$130 000
CURRENT ASSETS			**C** Retained earnings	-50 000
inventory	-110 000	**A**	LONG-TERM LIABILITIES	
accounts receivable	-50 000	**B**	**C** Mortgage loan	-100 000
cash	-10 000	**B**	**C** long term loan	-30 000
			CURRENT LIABILITIES	
			D Creditors	-150 000
			D Credit on current account	-40 000
TOTAL BALANCE	$500 000		TOTAL BALANCE	$500 000

This first example shows a balance sheet where we can see that equity finances 36% of all of the assets. That is positive. Further, we see that current assets of $ 170.000 are less than current liabilities of $ 190.000. So, if we could sell all of the current assets at book value, which is virtually impossible for inventory, then current liabilities still could not have been paid. Not a healthy situation.

As for the GOLDEN BALANCE RULE we shall find out if Fixed Assets + Inventory were financed by long term financing = equity + long term liabilities. Because that would be a very healthy situation. In fact total equity plus long term liabilities are $ 310.000 and fixed assets plus inventory are $ 440.000. So, this company is not very fortunate in this respect.

If the Golden Balance Rule would have applied then C-total (=long term finance) on the credit side should be bigger than A on the debit side. In that case B would always be bigger than D.

It can never happen on a balance sheet that C is bigger than A and D is bigger than B.

A company with the above balance sheet faces big challenges to redress the financial situation

The second balance sheet

2nd BALANCE SHEET

FIXED ASSETS			EQUITY	
Building	$330 000	**A**	**C** Ordinary share capital	$130 000
CURRENT ASSETS			**C** Retained earnings	-120 000
Inventory	-80 000	**A**	LONG-TERM LIABILITIES	
Accounts receivable	-50 000	**B**	**C** Mortgage loan	-100 000
Cash	-40 000	**B**	**C** Long term loan	-90 000
			CURRENT LIABILITIES	
			D Creditors	-50 000
			D Credit on current account	-10 000
TOTAL BALANCE	$500 000		TOTAL BALANCE	$500 000

What do we see? The balance totals do not differ from the previous balance sheet. However, in this case the respective company lowered inventory by $ 30.000 but increased cash by the same amount. It lowered creditors by $ 100.000 and credit on current account by $ 30.000 by keeping more earnings in the company of + $ 70.000 and increasing its long-term loan by $ 60.000. These steps cannot be taken overnight. It requires a stricter policy in terms of strengthening the long-term financing and better controlling its current assets.

The result is that **current assets are far more than current liabilities** and also that **THE GOLDEN BALANCE RULE is working** now: C definitely is larger than A. Very healthy! A company which succeeds in keeping this ratio will not be in financial trouble easily. If, like in this balance sheet, C is a higher value than A, then D can NEVER be a higher value than B. So, short term liabilities can be paid easily.

Exercises of Chapter 3

Opening Balance Sheet

When working on an exercise use + and – together with the relevant balance sheet item

1. Henry's investment plan looked as follows: warehouse building $ 280.000, storage racking $ 110.000, furniture and equipment $ 80.000, inventory $ 75.000, cash $35.000. He put all of his savings of $ 220.000 into the company's equity, agreed on a mortgage loan of $ 250.000 at 5% and a long term loan of $ 35.000 at 8% and his inventory had to be paid in sixty days. Prepare Henry's opening balance sheet and answer the questions

1.1 How high equity in a percentage of total assets?

   a. 38,6 %
   b. 37.9 %
   c. 36,4 %

1.2 What is the total of interest Henry will have to pay on an annual basis

   a. $ 15.300
   b. $ 15.240
   c. $ 15.180

1.3 What is the total amount of long term liabilities

   a. $ 360.000
   b. $ 250.000
   c. $ 285.000

2. In a corporation the ordinary share capital at the opening balance sheet shows an amount of $ 100.000. In its first year the corporation suffered a loss of $20.000. What should be the correct specification of equity on the balance sheet now?

   a. Ordinary shares $ 80.000
   b. Ordinary shares $ 100.000 and retained earnings $ 20.000
   b. Ordinary shares $ 100.000 and retained earnings -$ 20.000

3. After having made an investment plan Rudy also prepared a provisional P & L statement which shows an annual sale of 7.800 pieces of i-pads at $ 220 each. He buys an i-pad from the importing corporation at $ 130. Delivery time always two weeks. His opening balance sheet shows an inventory of $ 87.100. Comment on this amount and correct it.

a. the amount is correct. Each company should have sufficient inventory
   b. An inventory of $ 87.100: $ 130 means 670 pieces in the warehouse. Annual sales of 7.800 pieces converted into two weeks of inventory results in 7.800 : 24 = 325 pieces X $130 = $ 42.250 This will cover the two weeks' delivery time. Inventory shows 670 pieces. Irrational excess inventory: $ 87.100 - $ 42.250 = $ 44.850. Or: 670 – 325 X $130= $ 44.850.
   c. The $ 87.100 for inventory is too high. It should be (7.800 : 12) X $ 130 =$84.500

4. The Smith company buys 5 high-tech computers for a total of $ 25.000. 40% must be paid in cash; 60% must be paid in 2 weeks. There is only $ 10.000 in cash available. Smiths agrees with its bank on a long-term loan for $ 15.000. Apply the changes to the balance sheet of Smith. This may be done in two steps

   a. current assets + $ 25.000, cash - $ 10.000, long term loan + $ 15.000
   b. fixed assets + $ 25.000, current assets, cash - $ 10.000, creditors + $ 15.000
   c. cash + $ 15.000 and long-term loan +$ 15.000. Fixed assets + $ 25.000, cash - $10.000 and creditors + $ 15.000

5. An industrial building with a book value of $ 280.000 was reappraised. Its market value reported is $ 340.000. What are the changes on the balance sheet if the owning company decides to make the real commercial value visible on its balance sheet.

   a. fixed assets + $ 60.000, mortgage loan - $ 60.000
   b. fixed assets + $ 60.000, revaluation reserve + $ 60.000
   b. fixed assets + $ 60.000, retained earnings + $ 60.000

6. A company suffered a net loss of $ 25.000. Its costs of depreciation were $ 45.000. The balance sheet shows ordinary share capital of $ 100.000 but does not show other equity. What should be the changes?

   a. Fixed assets - $ 45.000, cash + $ 20.000. Retained earnings - $ 25.000
   b. Cash - $ 15.000, fixed assets - $ 10.000, retained earnings - $ 25.000
   c. Cash - $ 25.000, retained earnings - $ 25.000

7. A company sells 10 computers for $ 750 each in the last week of the operating year. The cost price per computer is $ 510. Clients must pay 50% in cash and must pay the other 50% before the end of January. Make the correct changes in the balance sheet

   a. Inventory - $ 5.100, cash + 7.500 and retained earnings + $ 2.400
   b. Cash + $ 7.500, retained earnings + $ 7.500
   c. Under current assets inventory decreases by 10 X $ 510 = - $ 5.100. Cash increases by (10 X $ 750) : 2 = + $ 3.750 and accounts receivable increase by + $ 3.750. Retained earnings increase by + $ 2.400.

8. On a balance sheet we see that 125 shares of a nominal value each of $ 1.000 were issued initially. The retained earnings are $ 45.000 and there also is a revaluation reserve of $ 95.000.

8.1 What is the intrinsic value per share now?

  a. Intrinsic value per share is $ 1.000
  b. Intrinsic value is $ 170.000: 125 = $ 1.360
  c. Total equity is $ 265.000. Divide by 125 shares = $ 2.120 intrinsic value

8.2 The company now wants to issue another 50 shares at intrinsic value = price. It succeeds in selling 10 shares at that price only. Buyers pay in cash. Apply the changes in the balance sheet.

  a. Cash is + $ 21.200. Share capital is + $ 10.000. Additional paid in capital is + $11.200
  b. Cash is + $ 21.200. Share capital is + $ 10.000. Retained earnings + $ 11.200
  c. Cash is + 10.000, share capital is + $ 10.000

8.3 The company is desperate. It follows advice from the controller and issues as much shares to the existing shareholders as the total amount of equity less share capital. What has to be changed now? How are the shares to be issued called.

  a. The company issues 45 new shares called "free of charge shares"
  b. Equity less share capital is ($ 135.000 + $ 45.000 + $ 95.000) - $ 135.000 = $140.000. The company issues 140 bonus shares to eliminate the retained earnings and the revaluation reserve.
  c. The company issues 95 new shares called bonus shares

9. A company reported annual sales of $ 2.064.000. These were divided proportionally over the 12 months. Half of the sales took place in cash. The other half was paid by clients after 30 days. Its closing balance sheet reports a figure of $ 154.000 for accounts receivable. Specify the difference to the figure it should have been

  a. $ 68.000
  b. $ 18.000
  b. $ 26.000

We see the following BALANCE SHEET

FIXED ASSETS		EQUITY	
Building	$480 000	Ordinary share capital	$360 000
Machinery	-362 000	Retained earnings	-120 000
Tooling	-85 000		

		LONG TERM LIABILITIES	
Total fixed assets	$927 000	Mortgage loan 5.5%	-440 000
		Long term loan 8.5%	-265 000

CURRENT ASSETS			
Inventory	$253 000	CURRENT LIABILITIES	
Accounts receivable	-140 000	Creditors	-190 000
Cash	-180 000	Credit current account at 15%	-125 000
Total current assets	$573 000		
TOTAL BALANCE	$ 1 500 000	TOTAL BALANCE	$1 500 000

9.1 Explain if the balance sheet conforms to the golden balance rule

  a. No, fixed assets + inventory are higher than long term financing
  b. Yes, because fixed assets + inventory are financed by long term financing
  c. No, there is a shortage in long term financing of $ 5.000

9.2 If no changes will take place in the three loans during a full year, then, which will be the amount of interest to be paid in that year

  a. $ 63.475
  b. $ 63.275
  b. $ 65.475

Closing Assignment of Chapter 3

The Balance Sheet

1. We see the following BALANCE SHEET

FIXED ASSETS		EQUITY	
Building	$ 400 000	ordinary share capital	$200 000
Machinery	120 000	retained earnings	160 000
Tooling	80 000		
Total fixed assets	$600 000	Total equity	$ 360 000
CURRENT ASSETS		LONG TERM LIABILITIES	
Inventory	$100 000	Mortgage loan 6%	$300 000
Accounts receivable	90 000	Long term loan 8%	100 000
Cash	110 000		
		Total long-term liabilities	$400 000
Total current assets	$300 000		
		CURRENT LIABILITIES	
		Creditors	$10 000
		Credit on current account at 18.5%	130 000
		Total current liabilities	$140 000
TOTAL BALANCE	$900 000	TOTAL BALANCE	$900 000

1.1 A reappraisal of the building indicates a true market value of $ 700.000. Apply the changes to the relevant balance items by using + and/or –

   a. building + $ 300.000, retained earnings + $ 300.000
   b. building + $ 300.000, revaluation reserve + $ 300.000
   b. building + $ 300.0000, additional paid-in capital + $ 300.0000

1.2 The total of issued shares is 200. What is the intrinsic value per share as per the balance.

   a. $ 1.800
   b. $ 1.000
   c. $ 1.600

1.3 The corporation issues 40 new shares and investors are happy to pay $2.500 per share in cash. Make the changes in the balance sheet

   a. cash + $ 100.000, share capital + $ 100.0000
   b. cash + $ 100.000, share capital + $ 40.0000, retained earnings + $ 60.0000
   c. cash + $ 100.000, share capital + $ 40.000, additional paid-in capital + $ 60.000

1.4 Depreciation costs during the closed operating year were as follows: building - $40.000, equipment - $ 12.000, and furniture - $ 10.000. The net profit after tax was $70.000. How should the balance be adjusted?

   a. Building - $ 40000, equipment - $ 12000, furniture - $ 10000, revaluation reserve - $ 62000
   b. Building - $ 40.000, equipment - $ 12.000, furniture - $ 10.000, cash + $ 132000 and retained earnings + $ 70000
   b. Building - $ 40.000, equipment - $ 12.000, furniture - $ 100.000, share capital $62000

1.5 During the past year the corporation reported sales of $ 465.000 equally spread over the twelve months. The cost price was 68%. For how many months the inventory on the balance sheet above will last if sales remain at the same level. (use max. of 2 decimals)

   a. 3.28 months
   a. 3.44 months
   b. 3.79 months

1.6 How high will the financing costs be next year if no changes occur in the loans

   a. $ 49400
   b. $ 50050
   c. $ 48800

1.7 Does this balance sheet meets the GOLDEN BALANCE rule?

   a. no, because . . . .
   b. yes, because . . . .

Chapter 4
The Financial Statement Or: Profit & Loss Account

The generating of sales, or turnover, is the purpose of any and all companies, small and large. The objective long term is to secure **continuity**. And to reach that objective sales must generate adequate annual earnings to survive.

First, a company invested in assets. Now it will have to make operating costs to generate sufficient sales results. It is a critical phase for starting companies in particular. Some investments cause immediate costs: electricity, depreciation, transportation etc. On top of this the starting company faces the challenge to build a customer base for which purpose commercial communication costs will have to be sacrificed.

As we saw earlier a company faces many options to choose from when investing and when selecting sources of financing. It is not different when a company starts its real operations: which products shall we offer to the market? At which particular markets are we aiming? At what sales prices do we have a good chance to gain our customers' sympathy? What is the strength and the weakness of the competition and how best can we make use of these?

And in all of these considerations there are instruments that help to give the company guidance in making the right decisions. No company can do without them: the investment plan, the financing plan, the balance sheet and, now the (provisional) P & L statement.

A model of a P & L statement can look like the following

SALES/TURNOVER $	= 100%
COSTS OF SALES	- % which is the material costs total
	------------------- -
PROFIT MARGIN $	= % A
OPERATING COSTS	
Costs Of Personnel	= %
Housing Expenses	= %
Marketing Costs	= %
Office Expense	= %
Costs Of Transport	= %
Costs Of Depreciation	= %
--	
TOTAL COSTS OF OPERATION $	% B
OPERATING RESULT$	= % = A - B
FINANCIAL EXPENSES	=%
--	
GROSS PROFIT$	=%

```
        PROVISIONS                      =%
        ------------------------------------
        NET PROFIT BEFORE TAX$          =%
        CORPORATE TAX                   =%
        ------------------------------------
        NET PROFIT AFTER TAX$           =%
```

This is a general example. In practice companies are free to eliminate or add items to such a P & L statement.

What do we see? First of all, every item ends with a percentage, derived from the **turnover** percentage which always is 100%. The reason is simple: rather than compare raw dollar figures the percentages give a quick and effective over view to the company from where it can see quickly where an increase and where a decrease is needed.

We also see that not all of the items lead to the "operating result". That is done for a reason: when a mortgage loan exists then the costs of interest are not part of the ordinary operations. Therefore they are separated from the operating costs. We also can phrase it in an other way: **operating costs are those costs which have a direct relation to the operations and most of which can be influenced, controlled, by management**. The latter does not apply to interest. In particular this is important for larger corporations with a number of general managers. Should a fine result be reported and should that result have been caused because the parent company (the holding) paid back a large portion of a mortgage with consequent large savings in financing costs then this result should not be claimed by the general manager as a result of his hard work. Depreciation of e.g. a truck stands in direct relation to the operations. They are controllable since management could use the lease option instead.

To make things more tangible we will take a look at Clark's provisional P&L statement which he prepared at the start of his operations and before he placed his purchasing orders at the domestic and foreign suppliers. He had already decided to not only buy and sell television sets but, based on his market research he also added note books and i-pads to his assortment as well as fixed and mobile antennas.

Clark realized that competition is strong and that he will have to invest relatively heavily in costs of marketing, part of which will consist of costs of advertising and of participation at regional trade shows. He looks at the longer term and accepts a very low profit or even a loss during his first year of operations.

He intends to discuss his provisional statement with a financial friend before deciding what he really wants to do. So, an evaluation will be called for before he really will make his start!

But let us first see how **turnover, cost price and profit margin are linked.**

Example 1		Example 2	
Sales price=	$10.00=100%	Sales price=	$18=100%
Cost price=	7.00=70%	Cost price=	?
	---------------		-----------
Profit margin=	$3.00=30%	profit margin=?	40%=$7.20

We can see that cost price and profit margin in dollars can be derived from the sales price, which always is 100% In example 2 the sales price is $ 18 (= 100%) and the profit margin is 40%. Now, if the profit margin is known in a percentage, then we can calculate the cost price: 40% of $ 18 = $ 7.20. Then cost price must be $ 18 - $ 7.20 = $ 10.80 and this cost price must be 100 – 40 = 60%. Or: 60% of $ 18 = $ 10.80. One more example: if a profit margin is $ 15 and it's % is 5, then sales price can be calculated: $ 15 = 5% ; 100% = (15: 5) X 100 = 3 X 100 = $ 300 = sales price. $ 300 - 15 = $285 = cost price and this must be 100% - 5% = 95% of $ 300 = $ 285. Or: (15:5)X95 =$285

```
Sales price is $300      =100%
Cost price is  $285      =95%
               ----------  ----------
Margin is      $15       =5%
```

We can conclude that as long as **2 data *** out of the 6 in this calculation are known the 4 others can be extrapolated rather easily: sales price $???   =100%

```
                    Cost price   =$48*    =  ??%
                                 ----------  ----------
                    profit margin  $??    = 20%*
```

We only know the cost price in dollars and we know that the profit margin is 20%. How to fill the open spots with question marks?

If the margin is 20%, then the **cost price must be 100 - 20 = 80%.** We know that the cost price is $ 48. Now we can calculate the sales price: (48:80)X 100= 0.6 X 100 = $ 60. That means that the profit margin is $ 60 - $ 48 = $ 12 and that is exactly 20% of $ 60 and 48% of $ 60 is $ 48. This type of **calculation is used when a sales price must be calculated with a given cost price and a targeted profit margin**: if the cost price is $48 and management demands a margin of 20% then the sales manager can easily calculate at which price he must sell: (48:80*)X100 = $ 60. The * stands for cost price %.

Here is Clark's provisional P & L statement specified as follows:
PROJECTED P & L STATEMENT

TURNOVER
Sales volume of German TV's	600 X $800=$480.000
Sales volume of Japanese TV's	725 X $ 920 =-667.000
Sales volume of notebooks	450 X $ 420=-189.000
Sales volume of i-pads	800 X $ 289=-231.200
Sales volume of antennas	300 X $ 150=-45.000
TOTAL TURNOVER 1 ST YEAR	$1.612.200=100%

COSTS OF SALE with the cost price in $$ and in % of the sales price
German TV's 600 X $600	$360.000=75%
Japanese TV's 725 X $782	566.950=85%
notebooks 450 X $330	148.500=78,6 %
i-pads 800 X $175	140.000= 60.5%
antennas 300 X $90	27.000=60%
TOTAL COSTS OF SALE	$1,242.450=77,065 %

PROFIT MARGIN OF SALES	$369.750=22,935 %

OPERATING COSTS

Costs of personnel	$62.000=3,846 %
Costs of housing	-18.000=1,116 %
Marketing expenses	-225.000=13,956 %
Costs of transportation	-45.000=2,791 %
Costs of depreciation	-12.000=0,744 %

TOTAL OPERATING COSTS	$362.000=22,453 %
OPERATING RESULT	-7.750=0,481 %
Costs of finance	-17.500=1 .085 %

LOSS	$9.750=-0,604 %

Sitting on his veranda with Jake, his friend, he shows the provisional P & L statement for him to comment on. A long silence follows. Finally Jake looks at Mark and says: "you cannot be happy with this plan". Look at the Japanese TV sets: they cost you 85% of their sales price and your profit margin of only 15% is too slim. Mark nods and asks "what should I do?"

Jake comments further on the operating result which is far too small in view of several costs and the burden of inventory to finance. Starting at the bottom he suggests that a net profit after tax of at least 8% should be aimed at. And also that profit margins on products selling at relatively small quantities should be very high. He indicates the policy of most supermarkets: sell millions of pieces of one single product and ultra short delivery time and a small margin of 10% will do. And that is because with a very small stock of products this stock is sold many, many, times a year. In supermarkets its stock turns 40 times easily.

Jake strongly suggests that Mark should not start with any product unless each product generates a profit margin of at least 30% because of the relatively high inventory to be kept at all times. If that is not Mark's idea then the only option left for him would be to keep operating costs at an absolute minimum.

We look at the above plan like Jake did with focus on two angles:

1. the profit margin per item and
2. the operating costs.

1) The smallest profit margin is made on Japanese TV sets. Cost price is 85%, so the profit margin is 15% only. Mark considers not to take on the Japanese TV : sales would decrease to $ 945.000 = 100

purchases would decrease to   675.500   = 71,48
                                                                    ----

profit margin would decrease in dollars to $ 269.500 = 28,52

Contrary to the original plan this profit margin is coming closer to the 30% limit already.

The second smallest margin projected is on the notebooks: 21.4%. Also here a challenge is waiting.

We suppose Mark did some more buyers' research and found a good alternative for both the Japanese TV sets and the note books. He checked the reputation of LG-TV's and concluded a deal with the Chinese exporter for direct importation. He can buy a set at an average price of $ 625 and discovers that he can sell them at $ 859

And for the notebooks he found a good alternative in Singapore from where he can count on regular shipments, paying $ 290 only. The sales price of $ 420 will be accepted by the market.

We can set up the revised sales- and cost price figures now

PROVISIONAL P&L STATEMENT
TURNOVER

Sales volume of German TV's 600 X $ 800	=$480.000
Sales volume of Chinese LG TV 725 X $ 859	=622.775
Sales volume of notebooks 450 X $ 420	=189.000
Sales volume of i-pads 800 X $ 289	=231.200
Sales volume of antennas 300 X $ 150	=45.000

TOTAL TURNOVER 1 ST YEAR $1.567.975 = 100%

COSTS OF SALE

German TV's 600 X $ 600 $ 360.000 = 75%
Chinese LG TV 725 X $ 625 - 453.125 = 72,76%
notebooks 450 X $ 290   - 130.500 = 68.8 %
i-pads 800 X $ 175   - 140.000 = 60.5%
antennas 300 X $ 90   - 27.000 = 60%

TOTAL COSTS OF SALE $1.110.625 = 70,8%

Profit margin on sales	$457.350 = 29,2%
Operating costs	362.000 = 23,1%
Operating result	$95.350 = 6.1%
Costs of finance	17,500 = 1.1%
Profit before tax	$77.850 = 5 %

This is a significantly better result for Mark and he decides to put the plan into action. In the second year he already intends to cut down on the marketing expenses in order to improve his net profit even more.

2) As to **the operating costs** the pressure to economize has dropped significantly with the strong improvement of profit margins. If at all, Mark may have a second look at the projected marketing expenses. A decrease of $ 50.000 would bring the net profit before tax to over 8%.

What we see in the above exercise we did not see earlier in this book: predicting the future as best as one can. Both in terms of sales results and in operating costs. As for the latter we have to distinguish between **CONTROLLABLE AND UNCONTROLLABLE costs.** Marketing expenses are based on a management decision and, therefore, are controllable. But interest costs for a loan are dictated by the bank and are by definition uncontrollable. Working with these factors is **one of the essentials of business economics.**

The investment plan at least gave concrete matter to select from as did the financial plan. And the opening balance sheet is the result of conscious decisions made by a company about which assets to buy and which types of financing would be solid to make a start.

But a provisional P & L statement, which also is a plan not only is affected by the investments made. It mostly is affected by the projected sales, costs of sale and the operating costs. Here a company faces the challenge not to get carried away on a super optimistic cloud, but to conservatively and carefully project it's turnover and it's operating costs.

The format of a provisional financial statement/P & L statement is not a famous magic stick which can make the future a reality. It is more like a mirror reflecting the vision and the projections of the maker. That does not disqualify the value as we saw here above where Mark changed directions to improve the projected results. That still does not mean a guarantee. Many factors and circumstances decide on the outcome as much as do the initiatives and choices of the businessman.

It is undeniable that preparing a provisional P & L statement is a "must" to confront the businessman with his ideas and to provoke **better economic choices.**

We also saw the value of all the percentages: those in the costs of sale by item gave clear ideas where profit margins by far would be too low to survive.

Let us now look at the details: we see sale = volume X sales price = turnover (be it one piece or a million pieces) = 100%; turnover less cost price = profit margin; profit margin less operating costs = operating result

When a business man is not satisfied with his results here are the options for him from which to get new directions:

1. **increase sales volume without changing sales prices;**
2. **or: increase sales price per piece**
3. **or: lower the cost price; and if none of these works there is one last option:**
4. **lower operating costs**

Markets change more rapidly than ever. No business can afford to lean back. So, numerous questions must be answered frequently: what would happen if we raise sales price of an item: will we lose more than we will gain? Which options can we find to lower our cost prices? Like a provisional P & L statement a company makes a final P & L statement where the reality is reported. This can be done once a year. But better is to have clear insight in results very frequently. Making a P & L statement on a monthly basis is a general policy today worldwide.

In setting up the P & L statement and filling it with historic data we have to be clear if a transaction belongs on this statement: buying a machine has nothing to do with sales, or cost price, or operating costs but everything with assets and therefore with a balance sheet only .

Payments due neither belong on a P & L statement, but on a balance sheet or in a **general ledger**. A sale concluded in May belongs on the P & L statement of May even when payment from the client is due in 60 days.

It is good to realize that costs do not always coincide with expenditure and that revenues not always coincide with income. We can put this in a frame work:

EXPENDITURES BUT NOT COSTS	COSTS BUT NOT EXPENDITURES
An asset is bought and paid in cash	depreciation to fixed assets
Part of a loan from the bank is paid back	a provision for future maintenance costs
invoice from supplier is paid	repair costs incurred to be paid later
a state warrant is purchased and paid for	

The same can be done for revenues:

REVENUE BUT NOT INCOME	INCOME BUT NOT REVENUE
a sale is made; client pays in thirty days	a client pays us for our invoice
	a shareholder pays for his shares

Using the percentages per line in a P & L statement has several distinct advantages. They quickly tell us where the score is too low to be left alone. But more than this can be done:

if a commercial company operates several departments, each with a manager on top it gives the opportunity to set percentage limits for some of their operating costs. Example: a company had three departments, each with 15-20 employees. Each department made its own P & L statement. When the managing director of the company noted strong variations in costs of personnel in percentages of sales he sat together with the managers to create more grip on trends in figures. The decision was reached to have at least 2 temporary employees per department, to be hired from the same agency. For every $20.000 of sales per month one employee was allowed to be on the payroll. As soon as a manager suspected to go below this standard he had to send one person home. As a result this company kept the costs of personnel under control much more effectively. This company **standardized its costs of personnel**

The same can be done with marketing expenses. There is nothing wrong with relating the expenses allowed to the results obtained. Mostly this is done by a percentage limit of turnover, e.g. 4% of realized turnover is the limit to marketing expenses It is the responsibility of the manager to control and to adjust the expense level to remain within the allowed limits.

We already saw that most of the **operating costs are "controllable"** It suggests that when sales show a decreasing trend the operating result can be kept at its level if the operating costs are adjusted in time. Les us look at a number of operating costs. Those in bold letters are indeed 100% controllable: costs of personnel and marketing expenses. Not, or **much less, controllable** are transportation costs, depreciation costs, housing costs, office expenses.

Let us have a look at what happens to a company and the difference it would make if both costs of personnel and of marketing would have been **standardized** when sales go down. Suppose that the standard for marketing and for personnel are 9.1% and 14% of sales respectively.

SITUATION >	ORIGINAL PLAN	NOT STANDARDIZED	STANDARDIZED
Sales	$ 250 000 100%	$180 000 100%	$180 000 100%
Cost price	$175 000 70%	$126,000 70%	$126 000 70 %
Profit margin	$75 000 30%	$54 000 30%	$54 000 30%
Costs of personnel	$22 750 9.1%	**$22 750 12.64%**	$16 380 9.1%
Housing expenses	$6 250 2.5%	$6 250 3.47%	$6 250 3,47%
Office expense	$2 000 0.8%	$2 000 1.11%	$2 000 1.11%
Marketing expenses	$35 000 14 %	**$35 000 19.44%**	$25 200 14 %
Depreciation	$4 000 1.6%	$4 000 2.22%	$4 000 2.22%
Operating costs	$70 000 28 %	$70 000 38.89%	$53.830 29.9 %
Operating result	$5 000 2 %	$-16 000 8.89%	$170 = 0.1 %

The less controllable costs remain the same in this overview.

We see what a great difference standardization would make: a substantial loss (-8.89%) is suffered by the company who carries on as usual and does not know how to adjust versus the company which standardized two important parts of the operating costs.

It is not difficult to work out some standard for really controllable costs and it might mean the difference between survival and bankruptcy!

Business economics for 80% is to make the best economical choices and for 20% to make use of the formats we saw earlier to help making those best possible choices. Later on we will see other formats and formulas which can help a company to experience the consequences of choices made and to help further in going in the right direction.

In the financial statements we have worked with in this chapter there are two additional items which we did not discuss yet: 1) **extraordinary profits and losses and**
2) **provisions.**

1. **Extraordinary profits & losses**

These must be reported in a P & L statement if there is an unexpected earning. Example: on equipment of $ 200.000 a normal time of depreciation would be 10 years. In the last year the depreciation leads to a book value of $ 0,00. But if such equipment is sold to an interested party who is willing to pay $ 25.000 for it in year 10, this $25.000 is to be handled as an extraordinary profit, thus increasing net earnings and the amount of corporate tax to be paid. This is logical because during those ten years taxes were saved by the annual costs of depreciation.

An unexpected loss may occur if a part of the inventory does not find any interested buyer any longer and has to be destroyed. The book value of that portion represents an extraordinary loss.

2. Provisions.

If a company fears that not all of its accounts receivable will be received it is authorized to take up a "provision for doubtful debts" at the end of its P & L statement. The company anticipates to suffer a future loss on its accounts receivable. This item is reported also at the end of the P & L statement, because it does not belong to the operating costs. I

It lowers net earnings and thereby it lowers tax liability.

This same item must be reported **on the balance sheet also under liabilities**, specifying clearly which purpose this provision will have to serve.

If and when it becomes clear that the respective accounts receivable will never be received, the item may disappear from the balance sheet. However, should a portion of the respective accounts receivable, though very late, were received, that income will have to be reported in the P & L statement and from there it will be taxed.

There are provisions where it is certain that these were reported correctly without any chance that they would have to be reversed. A company closing an agreement with a contractor to do major maintenance work or reconstruction work to its building three years from the date of the agreement and the contracting sum is e.g. $ 30.000 the company is authorized to take up a **"maintenance and repair provision"** in its P & L statement of $ 10.000 annually in each of the three years. It will save taxes annually to equal amounts. For quite many companies this is more attractive than to deduct the total amount of $30.000 in year 3. Also this provision must appear on the balance sheet under liabilities specifying the purpose: maintenance and repair. In summary: **provisions on a balance sheet must be labelled under "liabilities" in order to be recognized by official tax inspectors so that they can track if and to what extent the provisions fit reality.**

Let us look at how recording takes place.

P & L STATEMENT and the relation to the BALANCE SHEET

Turnover	$665.000	
Cost price	-400.000	

Profit margin	$265.000	
Operating costs	-70.000	
depreciation	**-60.000**	**direct effect** to balance sheet; booked
	---------------	directly as a minus to fixed assets
OPERATING RESULT	$135.000	
Provision for		
Maintenance	**-30.000**	**direct effect** to balance sheet by adding the
Costs of financing	-5.000	relative position under liabilities
	---------------	
Net profit before tax	$100.000	
Corporate tax 40%	$40.000	

Net profit after tax	**$60.000**	**direct effect** to balance sheet
		by adding it to equity (retained earnings)

Now these data are transferred to the balance sheet:

ASSETS		EQUITY	
FIXED ASSETS		Share capital	$150 000
-depreciation=	- $60 000	Retained earnings	60 000

Cash	+ $150 000*	Total equity	$210 000

* Depreciation and a provision never affect liquidity: there simply is no cash outflow!
So: net profit + depreciation + the provision are added to the balance of cash.

		LIABILITIES	
		Provision for maintenance	-30 000
	---------------		---------------
net change:	+ $90 000	+ net change	+ $90 000

Provisions should be treated exactly like depreciation. Think ten seconds why that is so. While in depreciation the value of a fixed assets goes down without any dollar disappearing out of the cash or the bank account depreciation takes place without human interference. A provision, however, is booked as a direct result of a human decision.

Like in depreciation costs there is no movement of cash when taking up a provision in the P & L statement. This means that from the example above **cash on the balance sheet grows with net profit + depreciation + provision = + $ 150.000.** Fixed assets decrease by the amount of depreciation of $ 60.000. So, debit side of the balance grows by $ 150.000 - $ 60.000 = + $ 90.000. The credit side must grow with the same amount: Retained earnings grow by $ 60.000 and the Provision under liabilities is recorded with $30.000 = + $ 90.000

Exercises Chapter 4
Profit & Loss Statement

1. The company TV-galore sells 15.000 flat screens per year at $ 840 each. Its manager believes that a price increase of 5% would lead to a decrease of sales of 4 % only Should the company decide to increase prices then, indeed, its yield would

   a. decrease
   b. increase

2. Video Gaming Paradise sells 75.000 games at an average price of $ 42. Its cost price is $ 28,56. The salesmen tried to convince the manager that a price decrease of 5% would lead to a spectacular growth in sales volume of 10%. The manager declined because he believes that his profit margin would suffer from this move. This manager

   a. was right
   b. was wrong

3. If a company buys a product for $ 42 and makes a profit margin of $ 8 then its purchase price in percentage of sales prices is

   a. 19%
   b. 84%
   b. 92%

4. The cost price of a product is $ 15 and the profit margin is 25% What is the sales price, what is the profit margin, both in dollars and what is the cost price in percentage?

   a. sales price $ 20, profit margin $ 5 and cost price 75%
   b. sales price $ 60, profit margin $ 15, and cost price 80%
   c. sales price $ 24, profit margin $ 6, and cost price 75%

5. When depreciating a building in 30 years

   a. cash will decrease
   b. mortgage will decrease
   c. equity will decrease

6. Controllable costs in a company are

   a. costs of marketing and interest

b. costs of personnel, of marketing and sales
b. costs of personnel and depreciation

7. A company manufactures bicycles and employs 60 people. Average annual wage per employee is $ 32.000. In the past years production volumes were: 2006: 90.000, 2007: 84.000, 2008: 54.000. The historic, family owned, company is unsure why net earnings have been falling constantly. How many people seem to be in excess? Which number really is needed and how much of personnel costs could be saved if the excess of people is fired.

   a. Half of the people is redundant. The company could save $ 960.000
   b. 20 people are redundant. The company could save $ 640.000
   c. When 60 people could reach a volume of 90.000 then 1 person can make 1.500 bicycles per year. In 2008 54.000: 1.500 = 36 people could have done the job. So, 24 people could be sent home. A saving of $ 768.000 per year

8. A company operates 6 large trucks it purchased at $ 320.000 each. The depreciation period was set at 5 years. Each truck drives 60.000 kilometres per year and fuel consumption for each truck was 8 litres per 100 kilometres 1 litre costs $ 1,20. Maintenance costs per year for each of the trucks are $ 8.000 and insurance costs $ 1.500 per year. What are the total costs of the trucks per year and what should be reported in the P & L statement

   a. Under transportation costs fuel, maintenance and insurance should be reported =(6 X 60.000) : 100 = 3.600 X 8 X $ 1.20 = $ 34.560 + 6 X $ 9.500 = $ 57.000. Total transportation costs $ 34.560 + $ 57.000 = $ 91.560. The depreciation should be reported under fixed assets: (6 X $ 320.000): 5 = $ 384.000
   b. The costs should be split: depreciation costs are $ 192.000. All the other costs fit under transportation costs: 5 X 60.000 X 0.08 X $ 1.20 = $ 28.800 + $ 40.000 for maintenance and $ 7.500 for insurance = $ 76.300
   c. To be reported under transportation costs is 300.000 miles $ 28.800 plus $ 48.000 plus $ 9.000 = $ 85.800. Under depreciation $ 380.000.

9. An architects firm purchases 2 copying machines of $ 18.000 each in November and it intends to use them for the next five years. And early January it buys 2 special cameras of $ 12.000 each, to be used over a period of ten years. In every quarter of the new year it purchases 10 capsules of toner of $ 42 each and 25 packs of architect paper of $ 24,50 each. One of the items on the P & L statements is office costs. What will this firm show in its P & L statement by the end of that new year.

   a. It will record $ 60.000 as depreciation and $ 4.130 as office costs
   b. It will record $ 420 plus $ 612,50 per quarter = $ 4.130 under office costs plus (2 X $ 18.000) : 5 and (2 X $ 12.000) : 10 as depreciation = $ 9.600
   c. It will record $ 36.000 + $ 24.000 + 4X($ 420 + 612,50) under office costs = $64.130

10. A P & L statement shows:

sales	140.000 X $72 =	$10.080.000	=100%
Cost of sales	140.000 X $49 =	6.860.000	=68,05%

profit margin	$3.220.000	=31.95%
Housing costs	$42.000	
Costs of personnel	-1.600.000	
Office costs	-84.000	
Marketing costs	-744.000	
Costs of transport	-60.000	
depreciation	-120.000	
TOTAL OPERATING COSTS	$2.650.000	=26,30%
OPERATING RESULT	$570.000	=5,65 %
Costs of finance	-90.000	=0,89 %
Net profit before tax	$480.000	=4,76%

The management is not satisfied with these results and decides to cut both costs of personnel and of marketing by equal percentages to attain a profit of 8 %

By which percentage will personnel and marketing costs have to be cut?

a. Personnel is the largest figure 2.15 X that of marketing (2.15: 3.15) X the required improvement of $ 340.400 = $ 232.336,65 and marketing with the balance of $108.063,35. Both cuts are 14,52%
b. Personnel and marketing must decrease by $ 493.200 each
c. 8% of sales is $ 806.400. Add financing costs = $ 896.400 which is the required operating result. This is higher than the actual results by $ 326.400. That amount must come from personnel and marketing by the same ratio. Personnel and marketing costs total $ 1.600.000 plus $ 744.000 = $ 2.344.00. Economizing on both costs means a cut of ($ 326.400 : $ 2.344.000) X 100 = 13,925 % from each of the two.

Closing Assignment of Chapter 4

The P & L Statement

The Meat Giant corporation buys cattle locally and imports meat from South America to service the whole of the East coast. They had a large factory built in 1998 for $ 3.600.000 which is depreciated in 30 years' time. Costs of energy are $ 60.000 per year. They also have cold rooms and freezing rooms for $ 2.100.000, with a depreciation period of also 30 years.

Maintenance costs are $ 50.000 per year. They operate 20 new automatic machines for preparing their packaged products since 2009. Each machine was purchased at $ 90.000 and their depreciation time is ten years. Costs of energy $ 6.000 per machine and maintenance costs for all these machines are $ 150.000.

There are 6 cooling trucks purchased for $ 280.000 each in 2010 and to be used for 5 years.

Each truck drives 72.000 kilometres per year and use 12 litres per 100 kilometres of gasoline at $ 1,40 per litre. Insurance per truck is $ 7.500 and maintenance is $ 15.000 per truck.

The Meat Giant employs 180 employees with an average wage of $ 1.800 per month, which includes a holiday bonus. Social charges are 18% and are paid monthly to social Security.

Their annual advertising on television costs $ 900.000 and their participation at shows costs $ 280.000. Advertising in leading trade magazines costs $ 10.000 per month.

In their office there are five copying machines, purchased in 2009 at $ 84.000 each and to be used for 5 years . Annual consumption of toners and printing paper costs $ 28.000 per machine per year.

There is a mortgage loan of $ 1.900.000 at an interest rate of 5.5%. Also, there is a long-term loan of $ 620.000 at an interest rate of 8%. Their credit on current account is $220.000 and the interest rate is 16%.

In 2011 their turnover reached the amount of $ 45.000.000 and cost of raw materials was $ 34.255.284.

Prepare their P & L Statement for the year 2011 in the table here below. Consider costs of energy and maintenance related to the building as housing costs. Consider insurance, maintenance and fuel consumption of the truck as cost of transportation.

Item	Dollars	percentage
turnover		
costs of raw material		
profit margin on sales		
costs of personnel		
costs of housing		
marketing costs		

office costs	
costs of transportation	
depreciation	
TOTAL OF OPERATING COSTS	
OPERATING RESULT	
costs of financing	
NET PROFIT BEFORE TAX	

4D.1 This is a P & L statement where a number of data is missing. Fill in all the spots indicated by a?

Turnover?	=100
Cost prices of sales?	=65

Profit margin $182 000	=?

Operating costs

Costs of personnel -?	=15
Housing -13 000	=?
Depreciation -?	= 4

Total operating costs $?	= ?

Operating result $?	= ?
Costs of financing -?	= 8

Net profit before tax $?	= ?

4D.2 The International Cheese Corporation buys assorted cheese locally and imports special cheeses from Switzerland and from France to service the many hotels and restaurants on the East coast. They had a large factory built in 1998 for $ 4.800.000 which is depreciated in 30 years' time. Costs of energy are $ 72.000 per year. They also have cold rooms and freezing rooms for $ 3.900.000, with a depreciation period of also 30 years.

Maintenance costs are $ 65.000 per year. They operate 15 new automatic machines for preparing their packaged products since 2009. Each machine was purchased at $ 110.000 and their depreciation time is ten years. Costs of energy $ 8.500 per machine per year and maintenance costs for all these machines are $ 184.000 per year.

There are 8 cooling trucks purchased for $ 320.000 each in 2010 and to be used for 5 years.

Each truck drives 94.000 kilometres per year and uses 14 litres per 100 kilometres of gasoline at $ 1,60 per litre. Insurance per truck is $ 9.600 and maintenance is $ 19.000 per truck, both per year.

The Cheese corporation employs 220 employees with an average wage of $ 2.400 per month, excluding a holiday bonus of 8%. Social charges on wage plus holiday bonus are 22% and are paid monthly to social Security.

Their annual advertising on television costs $ 1.000.500 and their participation at shows costs $ 340.000. Advertising in leading trade magazines costs $ 18.000 per month.

In their office there are 8 copying machines, purchased in 2009 at $ 98.000 each and to be used for 5 years. Annual consumption of toners and printing paper costs $ 37.000 per machine.

There is a mortgage loan of $ 2.600.000 at an interest rate of 5%. Also, there is a long term loan of $ 940.000 at an interest rate of 8,5%. Their credit on current account is $310.000 and the interest rate is 15%.

In 2011 their turnover reached the amount of $ 52.000.000 and cost of raw materials was $ 36.900.000.

4D.2.1 Prepare their P & L Statement for the year **2011** in the table here below. Consider costs of energy and maintenance related to the building as housing costs. Consider insurance, maintenance and fuel consumption of the trucks as costs of transportation.

Use percentages per item, starting with 100 for turnover and use 2 decimals.

Item	Dollars	percentage
turnover		
costs of raw material		
profit margin on sales		
costs of personnel		
costs of housing		
marketing costs		
office costs		
costs of transportation		
depreciation		
TOTAL OF OPERATING COSTS		
OPERATING RESULT		
costs of financing		
NET PROFIT BEFORE TAX		

4D.2.2 Which figures are transferred to the closing balance sheet now if tax on profit is 35%?

4D.3 Gomez Sportswear reported on December 31 a net loss of $ 140.000. The costs of depreciation were $ 260.000. Is Gomez capable of paying wages to its 25 employees in January if they earn $ 4.000 each?

4D.4 In the survey below several actions are listed. Fill in **both** columns Y(es) and/or N(o)

TRANSACTION	EARNING	INCOME
A client pays his bill of two-month-old		
A client buys and is allowed 60 days of payment term		
The company receives a tax refund		
A client purchases products and pays in cash		
The company issues share to a new shareholder in cash		
The company sells a truck for $ 10.000 although it had been written of to $ 0		

4D.5 In the survey below several transactions in the area of costs are listed. Fill in **both** columns Y(es) and/or N(o)

TRANSACTION	OPERATING COST	CASH OUT FLOW
A company has its building repaired and painted and can pay 60 days from the date of invoice		
A company pays the invoice of 60 days ago to its supplier		
A new truck is purchased. The invoice to be paid after 30 days		
The company pays holiday bonuses to its employees		
The company buys inventory and pays in cash		
The company takes on a provision for doubtful debts of $10.000 in its P & L statement		

Chapter 5
Liquidity

Hardly no frustration for a businessman is as big as to find that in a relatively profitable situation bills cannot be paid in time because of a lack of sufficient cash.

Many companies will recognize such unfortunate developments. The questions that are in place to ask are: can you blame a business for a lack of cash? Can the business man avoid to get into liquidity shortages? Let us find out.

Unexpected shortage of cash

Imagine what can happen to a car dealer of a certain brand: a sudden publication in the press that "technical break downs were reported of that brand because of manufacturing shortcomings". From the twenty reported incidents two ended in a crash where, fortunately, no fatal injuries occurred."

This car dealer can only passively undergo a steep drop in sales of the respective vehicle. Let us see how such a situation can lead to a serious problem.

Dealer Tom used to sell twenty cars per month of that brand for $ 35.000 each and cashed 20% in earnings on those sales = $ 7.000. On a monthly basis he earned $140.000. If his monthly operating costs were $ 100.000, he could report net earnings of $40.000 per month. If he used to take $ 10.000 for the private costs of himself and his family, he left $ 30.000 per month in the cash of the company. Suppose his sales drop by 50% since the negative publications. Then we see the following:

normal situation		after the publications	
monthly sales 20 cars		10 cars	
turnover= volume X price	$700 000		$350 000
Cost price is 80%	- $560 000		- $280 000
	----------------		----------------
Profit margin is 20%	$140 000		$70 000
Operating costs/month	-100 000		-100 000
	----------------		----------------
net result	$40 000		- $30 000

This car dealer will survive only if the historic period of retaining his earnings in the company was long enough to bridge a period of monthly losses. If it would take ten months to let the storm die and to resume normal levels of monthly sales again than the retained earnings should have been $ 300.000 to overcome that period.

What could pose a serious problem to this car dealer is the timely payment of his bills. He will have to cut heavily in his operating costs and he will have to use distinctly less dollars for private consumption.

It would be good for any business to project situations tentatively like the above and to plan how high the periodic retained earnings should be to avoid cash problems in the future.

Seasonal influences on liquidity

It is not difficult to suppose that a business in ice cream for the public will feel the great differences per quarterly sales and earnings. These businesses realize that they can survive the low seasons only if they retain sufficient earnings during the high seasons if they are eager to avoid the problems of the car dealer above.

This type of businesses no doubt will employ people from employment agencies so that they can be sent home on a daily basis in order to keep a firm control over the fixed costs.

What more may cause liquidity shortages ?

Is it a weakness when a business runs into such shortage? Sometimes it is. Especially when two facts concur:

1. too much funds were used for investing in fixed assets and the borrowing capacity suffers as a result of this. Such a business will feel that no creditor will sympathize with his situation and they firmly will hold a business to it's payment obligations.

A business man with a very low borrowing capacity and finding no additional means to add a new loan from the bank phrased it like this: "a bank is an institution lending you an umbrella during sunshine and requiring its return when it starts to rain"

2. Those businesses which, especially during their first 5 years, did not retain sufficient net earnings in the company, will be much more vulnerable than those who did.

Position of creditors in times of liquidity shortages. A bank exposed to the risk that a business no longer fills his pay back duties will observe the progress of such business very closely. It will require to have a copy of the monthly P & L statement and sometimes will execute its right to have a copy of the quarterly balance sheet. If a bank does not take these precautions it may be taken by surprise later.

And after a bank's analysis of the documents it will be able to predict the short term financial future of its business client. And if it finds that the risks of not collecting bills has come above a certain limit it will put an immediate stop to its existing financing of that business. The most common way to do this is to make use of its right to cancel the **credit facility in current account** by demanding that the balance of this account will have been brought back into the black within two weeks. If that does not happen it will exercise all of its rights reserved for a quick execution: mortgage and pledges of inventory will be recalled and in effect it means the end of the business. The building will suffer foreclosure. The inventory and the accounts receivable which had been pledged by the business will come under the control of the bank.

Taking care of sufficient liquidity is more than a magic trick

Many business books treat liquidity and how to control the flows of cash as an accounting formula using a liquidity format **while it should be treated as an indispensable part of the business policy as well.**

Every business should make permanent monitoring of liquidity an integrated part of its daily policy by anticipating the level of expenses and of income.

This is much more than just looking at growth percentages and resulting profit scenarios. A company which is neglecting this runs the risk of unpleasant surprises. Creditors will have no sympathy for losers. They want their money and they demand timely payments.

It is not more complicated than a family with a holiday budget during a period of two or three weeks. This family will weigh possibilities and risks of spending too much in too short a time constantly.

How to prevent liquidity shortages

As we saw in the example of the car dealer liquidity problems cannot be avoided always. However, a business which retained earnings to a very good extent will not go under as easily as a business which did not take those precautions. Sound policy would be to continue to retain the larger portion of the earnings until equity reaches 55%-60% of the book value of all of the assets.

Right at the start of a business it would be a solid policy to project two scenarios for its policy. A positive one and a less positive one. Nobody can predict the future. But everybody can take precautions not to be caught by surprise.

It would be good to manage the borrowing capacity very carefully from the start by opting for the lease of equipment rather than to borrow funds for the purchase of it. And also the lease of a building sometimes is better and nothing is wrong with a choice to postpone the substantial investment needed for a purchase of it so that a good buffer of borrowing capacity will be left.

Those two elements: retained earnings and **borrowing capacity** are the keys of the starting business to create a kind of security should an unexpected shortage of liquidity occur. This may sound conservative, but in the end it mostly is the conservative businessman who survives a crisis.

Another, simple, method is to monitor inventory levels closely and constantly. Inventory needs to be financed. Too high levels create unnecessarily high levels of finance. Many companies work with so called "blanket orders": one portion is to be delivered immediately, the other portion shall not be delivered until after having been called by the buying company.

Suppliers do not like this type of orders but in a buyers market they mostly have no choice.

"Cash management"

Large companies employ a "cash manager" in their financial department. The key responsibility of this manager is to monitor all flows of cash closely and constantly and to make recommendations to management to take appropriate steps that must avoid a shortage of cash. Such a task must be fulfilled by the business man himself when he is operating a small private business.

The cash manager makes sure that accounts receivable will be collected timely and that creditors should not be paid before the end of the term of credit allowed.

There are systems for accounts receivable which generate letters automatically to remind clients who did not pay within the term allowed.

The same applies to inventory of products. Intelligent systems exist which generate purchase orders as soon as the pre-set minimum level of inventory per item has been reached. Both systems together will help extremely well to avoid that funds will be tied too long to finance these two current assets. The simple wisdom here is that each dollar invested in current assets cannot be used for more important investments.

If the systems mentioned do not create the security of sufficient liquidity then it will be time to change to an other vehicle: cut operating costs.

Make operating **costs of personnel "flexible" by "standardizing"**.

Many companies apply a policy to lay off employees timely when sales tend to drop. This is not easy in every country. Many countries protect workers against dismissals by complicated and time consuming formal procedures.

But in every country around the world a company has the option to hire temporary workers through specialized agencies. These workers may be laid off instantly when circumstances require this.

Think about companies with large variations in sales per season like ice cream vendors. Such companies could not survive at all if they were not allowed to adjust the number of employees instantly when needed.

In practice it happened that a company with three sales groups spread geographically gave each of the groups the instruction of a standard sales figure per employee of $10.000 per month. The moment a drop in sales was anticipated one or more had to be sent home. Hiring back was allowed only when sales were at the standard level again. Thus, the company succeeded to bring the operating costs of personnel back from a variation between 12 % to 18 % of sales to a narrowed limit of 10 % to 11 %.

Standardization of this type of costs proves to be an enormous help in controlling expenses and, therefore, its liquidity.

An other example involves a large chain of technical products. In each store there was a repair department with large variations in demand. One of these chains analysed the costs versus the number of repairs and found that with six technicians there were 240 hours weekly for repair jobs. They also found out that the average time per repair job was two hours. That means 120 repair jobs capacity per week. **A standard** of 120 repair jobs per week was set. Instruction was given to send one or more technicians home the moment a lower number of repairs was anticipated for a next week.

A last example: in a large international corporation the marketing costs showed a rather constant level of $ 272.000 each year. This amount of expenses also was paid in a year with distinctly lower sales than last year's. The corporation standardized the marketing expense to 6% of total sales. The marketing president was made responsible to adjust expenses timely when a drop in sales was anticipated.

Anticipation and planning for change are essential tools.

Everybody knows companies which show a relatively strong growth in sales. This growth will demand higher inventories of products and will create higher amounts in accounts receivable and in debts to be paid to suppliers.

The first two are current assets. **Growth in assets always requires financing** in one way or the other. Paying debts requires sufficient levels of cash. It is not difficult to understand that it is essential to monitor the cash position, the long term debts and the short term debts in relation to equity constantly and closely. As soon as the amount of equity versus the debts on the balance sheet may become lower than the ratio demanded by its bank a company can end up in serious financial trouble if appropriate adjustments are not made in time.

Good policy in a pioneering phase is to prepare a balance sheet on a monthly basis in order to be able to make such adjustments in time. Once a company has reached maturity and shows rather constant sales figures and costs levels the frequency of preparing a balance sheet may be adjusted downward.

In larger companies this is an ongoing process of communication between all departments and all levels culminating in top level decisions as to the required steps. In a phase of growth the number of employees must be increased rather frequently. Knowing that it will cost between two and three months to have the right person for a vacancy it will be clear that anticipation is a key factor for success.

All of these considerations and decisions ultimately will find their way to the treasury department where figures are adjusted and then feed back is communicated to all of the departments for their considerations and adjustments. The future flows of cash in this process take a dominant position to be observed by all of the managers who are accountable for their actions.

How to make a liquidity plan

To prepare a liquidity plan there are two important elements required:

1. Flows of cash must be reasonably predictable
2. In order not to ignore any movement of cash a special format is recommended.

Such a format can be prepared for weekly planning, or monthly, quarterly etc. All depends on the sensitivity of cash flows under individual circumstances. Also, a format must enable to include estimated **unexpected expenditures** and must also indicate at each end of a period what the amount of dollars should be at the beginning of the next period.

The value of such liquidity planning is to anticipate on possible cash shortages during the next periods so that consultation with the bank can be planned in time. For a bank such a professional approach works much more effectively than the business which, caught by surprise, sends an urgent message to the bank to discuss additional financial aid.

A liquidity plan may look as follows:

LIQUIDITY PLANNING PER QUARTER (q)

	1st q.	2d q	3d q	4th q
INCOME				
Cash balance at begin of period				
payments received from clients				
value added tax received				
other income				
	--------	--------	--------	--------
Total income				
EXPENDITURES				
payments to suppliers				
net payments of salaries/wages				
payment of holiday bonus				
payment of taxes on salaries				
pension premiums				
value added tax paid				
corporate tax paid				
interest payments				
maintenance and repair costs				
marketing expenses				
office appliances				
cash investments in assets				
unforeseen expenditures				
	--------	--------	--------	--------
Total expenditures				
BALANCE + OR –				
Needed cash next period				
	--------	--------	--------	--------

Surplus/Shortage

This format is rather general. It can be adjusted to the needs and circumstances of the individual company.

Sometimes such formats show two columns per quarter: one for the planning, the second for the real figures at the end of a period. It helps adjusting future preparations of the liquidity plan.

This is how it could work in practice.

A wholesale company distributing electronic games starts the year with $ 90.000 in cash. It expects cash sales during the first three months as follows: January: $ 280.000, February: $ 130.000 and March $ 390.000. The purchases which are paid within one week after receipt of shipments are planned as follows: January $196.000, February $ 110.000, March $ 180.000. At the end of every month $ 110.000 is paid in salaries and also the sales tax of 6% over that month are paid. Every month interest of $ 2.000 on a bank loan is paid. It is expected that a tax refund will be received of $ 105.600 in March. For office costs $ 3.800 will be paid every month. And for energy and maintenance an amount of $1.600 is expected to be paid per month. We now can prepare a liquidity plan

Receipts	January	February	March
Starting balance beginning of the month	$ 90 000	$ 39 800	$ - 65 400
Income from sales	$ 280 000	$ 130 000	$ 390 000
Other income			$ 105 600
Total cash	$ 370 000	$ 169 800	$ 430 200
Expenditures			
Purchases	$ 196 000	$ 110 000	$ 180 000
Salaries	$ 110 000	$ 110 000	$ 110 000
Sales tax month	$ 16 800	$ 7 800	$ 15 600
Interest bank loan	$ 2 000	$ 2 000	$ 2 000
Office costs	$ 3 800	$ 3 800	$ 3 800
Energy and maintenance	$ 1 600	$ 1 600	$1 600
Total expenditures	$ 330 200	$ 235 200	$ 313 000
Cash balance for next month	$ 39 800	$ - 65 400	$ 117 200

In February a shortage of cash is expected. So, either the company shall have to turn some of it's possessions into cash, like some of it's current assets, or it will have to talk to the bank for an extension of it's credit on current account for a short period. Again: planning for liquidity requires best estimates about market development in the short run and about expenses. And if such is the only alternative to bridge a short period of shortage of cash the company may have to lay off employees since other expenses do not seem to contribute to fill the financial gap.

Exercises of Chapter 5
Liquidity

1. Put an X under Balance Sheet or P & L Statement, depending on the relative action in the first column. Place a V in one or more of the columns 1 to 4 reporting the meaning of the actions.

ACTION	Balance sheet	P & L statement	1 revenue	2 costs	3 receipt	4 expenditure
Example: client pays his bill	X				V	
payment of $ 4 000 in wages						
client buys for $ 100 and may pay after 30 days						
a printer is purchased for the office and paid in cash						
a client purchases a product and pays cash						
A contractor repairs the roof; payment in 30 days						
equipment is purchased; payment in 60 days						
10 Christmas presents are bought for employees and paid in cash						
Depreciation of building of $ 30 000						
20 new shares are issued; buyers pay in cash						
interest on mortgage is paid						
the bill of a supplier is paid						
an employee borrows $1 000 from the company to buy a computer privately						

> Long term loan is increased by $ 50 000; money received one day later
>
> credit in current account is lowered buy paying back $ 10 000 to the bank

2. A company can always plan the following expenditures in a liquidity plan
   a. payment to suppliers, tax payments, interest payments
   b. payment of depreciation, wages and repairs
   c. payments for paying back a long-term loan two years from now and of next year's sales costs

3. The most important advantage of preparing a liquidity plan is

   a. that a company can predict its annual profit
   b. that all possible invoices can be paid in time
   b. to see if a need of more financing in the course of a year may rise.

4. It is very important to plan income and expenditure well ahead because, if not:

   a. the company cannot make the P & L statement
   b. a million-dollar company can get into financial trouble
   c. the bank can use its rights resulting from the mortgage

5. A company reaches a monthly turnover of $ 125.000 in March. Clients are allowed a term of payment of thirty days. $ 60.000 of maintenance costs for equipment were incurred in January, to be paid in April. In March additional inventory was purchased to an amount of $ 75.000, to be paid by the end of April. If all the payments are made in time then what is the balance of the cash flow by the end of April

   a. - $ 10.000
   b. - $ 5.000
   c. - $ 20.000

6. The financial planning of Peterson corp. shows that sales in June will be $ 70.000 in cash. In July it will be $ 22.000 in cash only. Balance of Cash was $ 15.000 on the last day of May. Wages and lease to be paid in June amount to $ 70.000. What is the maximum amount Peterson can use to make purchases of inventory in June when the respective invoices must have been paid before the end of July and assuming that no other income or expenditure will occur?

   a. $ 32.000
   b. $ 35.000
   b. $ 37.000

7. The Italian Giovanni's Ice Parlour expects a very good July. He sells 40 tastes of ice cream which all are displayed in his cooled counter in 5 litre stainless steel containers. Of the 40 tastes he expects in 10 of these to sell 30 containers, in 10 other tastes 20 containers and in the remaining 20 tastes he expects to sell 10 containers. One such a container yields sales of $ 300. In July he will have to pay income tax from last year of $ 10.000. Giovanni expects to purchase $ 25.000 in raw materials in cash. He employs two regular employees of $ 2.000 each per month. At the end of the month he wants to have a cash balance of $ 150.000. How many part time employees can he afford in July if these will cost him $ 50 a day and the Ice parlour is open 31 days?

   a. 13.5 employees
   b. 13.0 employees
   c. 12.5 employees

8. Johnson Controls requests the treasury department to prepare a liquidity plan for the second and third quarter by consulting all responsible heads of departments. There is an unlimited borrowing capacity on the current account. Register all of the data in the format here below. Only full $-amounts should be registered.

The balance of cash on the 1st of April is $ 100.000. At the end of each quarter the interest on the mortgage loan is paid. Mortgage is $ 1.200.000 and the interest is 6%. In each even month (2,4,6 etc) office appliances are purchased in cash for $ 2.000. The turnover for the year is planned at $ 1.920.000 excluding value added tax of 19% and monthly sales are identical in dollars. All clients pay promptly after 30 days.

Advertising takes place monthly for $ 9.500 to be paid before the end of the same month. Purchases on an annual basis are $ 1.344.000 including value added tax of 19%. The monthly amounts of purchases are identical. Payment term allowed by all of their suppliers is 60 days. The value added tax balance is paid monthly = the difference between tax received from clients and tax paid to suppliers. (Use full dollar amounts only and ignore decimals).

Salaries and wages are $ 240.000/year to be paid equally divided over the twelve months. 70% of these wages are paid to employees; 30% is pay-roll tax also to be paid every month. Johnson prepared a pension fund for its employees and pays 20% of gross salaries and wages by way of a premium. In May 8% of annual gross wages excluding tax and pension premium is paid as a holiday bonus to every employee. 60% is paid to employees and Pay-roll tax is 40% and is paid in June.

In June a new copying machine will be purchased for $ 58.000 to be paid in July. In April additional storage racks will be purchased for $ 15.000, to be paid in June. After July 1 a major maintenance job will take place which will cost $ 10.000, to be paid in September. Last year a net profit before tax was achieved of $ 450.000. Corporate tax of 25% on this amount must be paid in 4 instalments, starting May 1. A tax restitution of $ 120.000 is expected in August.

8.1 Fill the format here below

ACTION	2d QUARTER	3d QUARTER
Cash balance begin of period		
payments received from clients		
other payments received		
TOTAL PAYMENTS RECEIVED		
To be paid to suppliers		
Salaries and wages paid (=70%)		
Holiday bonus paid		
pay-roll tax to be paid		
pension premiums to be paid		
balance of value added tax to be paid		
corporate tax to be paid		
interest to be paid		
marketing expenses to be paid		
purchased assets to be paid		
maintenance costs to be paid		
office appliances		
TOTAL EXPENDITURES		
Surplus or shortage of CASH		

8.2 What is Johnson's cash surplus or shortage at the end of the 3d quarter

   a. + $ 167.956
   b. + $ 157.596
   b. + $ 177.596

9. Giovanni's sells the following quarterly quantities of ice cream: first quarter 1.500 litres second quarter 4.600 litres, third quarter 11.000 litres and last quarter 3.000 litres. Sales price per litre is $ 30 and his raw materials per litre cost $ 12. His fixed costs are $ 27.400 per month. In which quarter(s) will Giovanni face a shortage of cash

a. in quarter 2 and quarter 4
b. in quarter 1 and quarter 2
c. in quarter 1 and quarter 4

Closing Assignment of Chapter 5
Liquidity Plan

1.1 Prepare the projected liquidity plan for 6 months based on the following information

BALANCE SHEET DECEMBER 31			
Building	$620 000	Share Capital	$400 000
Equipment	-460 000	Retained earnings	-110 000
Office furniture	-120 000		
		Mortgage loan 0.5%/month	-400 000
		Long term loan 0.75%/month	-250 000
Inventory of products	-160 000		
Accounts receivable	-140 000	Creditors	-260 000
Cash	-100 000	Credit current account 1.5%/month	-180 000
TOTAL	$1 600 000	TOTAL	$1 600 000

The following is to be expected in the next six months. Turnover will be $ 600.000 per month. Clients all pay exactly at 30 days. Depreciation on the building is $ 20.000 per year, on equipment $ 18.000 and on office furniture $ 10.000.

Purchases of inventory will be $ 400.000 per month to be paid after 60 days. The figure of creditors on the balance sheet stands for purchases in November and in December 50/50. Salaries and wages cost $ 150.000 each month. In May 8% of annual salaries and wages is paid as a holiday bonus.

A tax restitution of $ 80.000 is expected in March. A new machine will be purchased for $150.000 in June. Payment after 60 days. Maintenance work executed in December for $250.000 must be paid in March. All sales managers will participate in a week's seminar in February. Costs of $ 120.000 to be paid in cash in the same month.

Interest for the balance of the credit on current account at the end of one month is to be paid in the next month. Positive monthly net income lowers the credit account figure. The interest payments thereafter should be adjusted accordingly. Every cash shortage at the end of any month, which brings the balance of the current account to over $ 180.000 leads to a one time penalty interest of 6% of the excess amount used and must be paid in the next month. Here is a method of recording the monthly balance of the current account and the interest due:

CURRENT ACCOUNT PROGRESS

Balance at start of month nr. ...	Net flow of cash end of month nr ...	balance current account end of month nr	Interest due in ensuing month nr....
1	1	1	2
2	2	2	3
3	3	3	4

Interest for the long-term loan will be paid every **even** month (Feb., April etc). And interest for the mortgage loan will be paid each month. Monthly costs for office supplies are $ 8.000. Two computers will be purchased for $ 750 each in April and will be paid in cash. Advertising costs are $ 1.600 per month. Participation at a trade show will take place in June for $90.000 to be paid before the end of June.

Office space will be painted again in February for $ 15.000 to be paid in the same month. In May an obsolete machine will be sold for $ 120.000 against cash payment and there will be a second tax restitution of $ 100.000 in the same month.

Prepare the liquidity plan using the format her below. Ignore decimals and use full dollar figures.

ACTION	January	February	March	April	May	June
Balance of cash						
sales income						
other income						
TOTAL INCOME						
purchases inventory						
salaries and wages						
office costs						
purchase of assets						
interest						
marketing costs						
costs of maintenance						
other expenditures						
TOTAL EXPENDITURES						
BALANCE						

1.2 In which of the six months was the total income above $ 100.000

    a. in February and June
    b. in March and May

    b. in February and May

1.3 How much interest will have been paid in total during the six months

    a. $ 38.492
    b. $ 34.762
    c. $ 37.248

1.4 In which of the six months was the cash balance negative

    a. in January, and April
    b. in January and June
    b. in January and March

Chapter 6
The Closing Balance Sheet

In the previous chapters we saw how the opening balance sheet was made before the company undertook any sales or purchase activity. It means that to prepare a balance sheet a P & L statement is not required. But the joint purpose of all of the formats which we have seen before is to present insight to the business man leading a company. The phase in which the company is dictates the frequency of the preparation of these formats.

Remember: the formats do not present a goal in themselves. They were designed to support the business making the best possible economical decisions.

The P & L statement presented an active picture of the commercial activities of a company during a certain period. Costs and earnings; profit and cash flow. Prepared on a monthly basis it enables the company to make smaller or major adjustments in its course during the remainder of the year.

By the end of the year a balance sheet is prepared. This is a legal instruction in most countries around the world and these instructions are meant to inform tax authorities of the taxes received and the taxes due. It is a mechanism of control.

For the company **a balance sheet is kind of a "snapshot" on a certain day.** Very different from the character of the P & L statement. Does that make the meaning of a balance sheet less important? On the contrary! The one source of information is completed by the other source. One alone has little meaning.

What elements build the closing balance sheet from the first day of the year? We already learnt about changes in equity, in fixed assets because of the depreciation. But there is more.

The elements that build the closing balance sheet come from two sources, one of which is the P & L statement, the other is the **general ledger**. Bearing in mind that the balance sheet records possessions (= assets) and sources of finance (equity on the one hand, liabilities on the other) the question is which elements from the P & L statement have a close link to assets and to liabilities and are, therefore, essential to prepare the closing balance sheet.

Let us take the following P & L statement to answer that question.

Turnover $	=100%
Cost price	=-%

Profit margin $	=%
OPERATING COSTS	
Housing	=%
Personnel	=%
marketing costs	=%
office costs	=%
depreciation	straight to balance sheet % lowering fixed assets = A

99

```
           TOTAL OPERATING COSTS $      =%
                                        ----------------------------
           operating result $            =%
              financial costs $          =%
           provision for future maintenance    straight to balance sheet under liabilities = B
                                        ----------------------------
           net profit before tax $       =%
           tax$
                                        ----------------------------
           net profit after tax $        =% straight to balance to equity =C
```

A + B + C =CASHFLOW > INCREASE liquidity/cash> straight to the balance sheet

Looking at this P & L statement we can ignore all of the operating costs except depreciation costs. This is the only operating cost that has a direct link to the balance sheet: fixed assets are decreased by the figure of the depreciation.

The second figure which can be recorded directly to the balance sheet are "**provisions**" As we saw earlier every company is entitled after the operating result to record a provision for e.g. doubtful accounts receivable, or for future maintenance which figure can be clear in an early stage.

The figure for future maintenance is taken up in the P&L statement under provisions **for equal amounts per year until the planned date of maintenance will have arrived.** (Example: $ 120.000 is the contractual sum for a major maintenance job 3 years from now. The company can record $ 40.000 under provision for maintenance in its P & L statement in every of the next three years). These provisions lower the net profit and also the corporate tax due. From a fiscal point of view a tax auditor needs to understand which provision it is which he finds on a balance sheet. The company therefore must record **provisions by name under liabilities.** (e.g. "provision for maintenance expenditures")

The provision for doubtful accounts receivable is a one-time recording, contrary to the provision for maintenance. It can occur year after year, but it is determined every year's end.

Provisions on a P & L statement have one thing in common with depreciation: there is NO cash out flow, no expenditure involved in the year the provisions were recorded. So, also **provisions on a P & L statement contribute to cash flow in the same way depreciation does.**

The third element on the P & L statement which has a direct link with the balance sheet is net profit after tax. It is the reward for a period of hard work and of taking risks. After having transferred the net profit figure to equity **(retained earnings)** officially the owner or owners of the company are entitled to decide what to do with this net profit: pay dividends to shareholders or transform this reserve into (bonus)shares, the choice depending on what the Articles of Incorporation demand in terms of which percentage of net profit must be retained.

And, finally, there is one more figure to be transferred from the P & L statement to the balance sheet: **the cash flow.** Clients who caused a profit for the company logically also paid for depreciation and, as the case may be, for provisions. But these did not cause expenditures!

So: net profit after tax + depreciation costs + provisions = cash flow. That figure increases the figure of CASH on the balance sheet.

Let us make this visible by the following P&L statement and the closing balance sheet.

P&L Statement				BALANCE SHEET	
Turnover	$ 900 000	Building	$300 000	Share capital	$500 000
		Depreciation	$-30 000 A		
			$270 000		
Cost price	$ 400 000	Equipment	$200 000	Retained earnings	$120 000
		Depreciation $	20 000 A	+ net profit	$110 000C
			$180 000		$230 000
Profit margin	$ 500 000	Trucks	$250 000	Total equity	$620 000
		Depreciation	$25 000 A	+ net profit =	$730 000
			$225 000		
Depreciations A	**$ 75 000**				
Operating costs	$ 200 000	Inventory	$140 000	Mortgage	$ 250 000
Operating result	225 000	Accounts rec.	$80 000	Long term loan	$ 100 000
Financial costs	$ 40 000	Cash	$120 000	**Provision**	
		+ net profit	$110 000C	**maintenance**	**$ 25 000 B**
		+ depreciation	$75 000A		
		+ provisions	$45 000B		
		total cash	$350 000		
Provisions:					
Maintenance	**$ 25 000 B**				
Doubtful accounts B	**$ 20 000**				
Profit before tax	$ 140 000			**Provision doubtful**	
				accounts	**$ 20 000 B**
Tax	$ 30 000			Creditors	$ 120 000
Net profit after tax C	**$ 110 000**	Total balance	$ 1 245 000	Total balance	$ 1 245 000

First, we examine the net changes to the original balance sheet caused by the figures from the P&L statement:

------------------------------- BALANCE SHEET ---			
depreciations	- $75 000	equity	+ $110 000
cash	+ $230 000	provisions	+ $45 000
	----------------		------------------
	+ $155 000		+ $155 000

We see how depreciation arrived on the balance sheet under fixed assets; how the net profit was transferred to equity, how the provisions found their place under liabilities and how cash was increased by net profit + depreciation + provision. (= cash flow).

While a P & L statement is prepared frequently throughout the operating year, the balance sheet is prepared rarely: one or two times a year. That raises the question where changes in assets can be derived from if there were new investments during the year. They will not appear on the P & L statement because they did not form earnings, nor operating costs.

Or which vehicle tells the company which instalments to which loans were made during the year and have a changing influence on the liabilities on the balance sheet. Instalments were expenditures, but not costs.

The answer to all this is: **all of the actions that do not belong in a P & L statement but which do have an influence to positions on a balance sheet are kept in a so called GENERAL LEDGER** during the operating year. It is a supporting reservoir, carefully updated very frequently and from which all kinds of adjustments to the balance sheet can be made without the necessity of changing that balance sheet after every relevant action. **So, issue of new shares, investments in assets, instalments to or increase of loans all are recorded in the general ledger.** Toward the end of an operating year this general ledger will be emptied by transferring all of its data to the balance sheet.

To close the list of sources of information for correctly adjusting the balance sheet there are some other **supporting ledgers: for inventory, for accounts receivable, for creditors.** And the liquidity report serves as a control mechanism for the final balance of cash: its total must equal the cash flow as defined above.

Summarizing: the closing balance sheet is adjusted: A from relevant recordings in the P & L statement and B from the general ledger which records all those changes to assets, equity and liabilities which cannot be found back on the P & L statement.

One action which we did not discuss earlier in relation to a balance sheet is: suppose company A buys shares in company B. How to record such a transaction? In chapter 3 we saw that shares can have two values:

1. their nominal value per share attributed by the founders of the company
2. their **intrinsic value**, or book value to be derived from the company's share capital plus retained earnings plus additional paid in capital plus revaluation reserve on its balance sheet

A general rule is that shares of company B acquired by company A are recorded by the latter at their INTRINSIC value at the time of purchase, regardless the price paid. Was this price higher than the intrinsic value than the excess is recorded by A as GOODWILL. It is a so called "immaterial asset" contrary to inventory which forms a "material asset".

Also, the **purchased shares** are to be booked by A under **FIXED financial assets.** And to distinguish this possession from tangible assets, like equipment on the balance sheet the purchased shares are recorded under **INTANGIBLE ASSETS.**

Let us look at an example.

	BALANCE SHEET COMPANY B		
Fixed assets	$300 000	Share capital 200 X $ 1 000 =	$200 000
Current assets	200 000	Retained earnings	80 000
		Revaluation reserve	120 000
		Total equity	$400 000
		Liabilities	$100 000
Total Balance	$500 000	Total Balance	$500 000

The intrinsic value of one share in company B is clear: $ 400.000: 200 shares = $ 2.000.

Suppose company A agreed to buy 50 shares in company B at a price of $ 150.000.

A now will record this on its own balance sheet as follows

BALANCE SHEET OF COMPANY A

Intangible fixed assets

50 shares company B $ 100 000 (50 x $ 2 000)

GOODWILL 50 000

Total intangible assets $150 000

We can imagine that the intrinsic value of the shares on the balance sheet of company B will undergo a lot of changes. Still, these do not influence the value of the shares in the possession of company A as recorded on its balance sheet. In most countries depreciation on such shares is not allowed. What is allowed, though, is to **depreciate the goodwill** over a period of time. That depreciation figure will appear on the P & L statement of company A in the same way it does for buildings and other fixed assets.

When preparing the closing balance sheet **no economical choices are made.** These were made in the operating period preceding the date of the balance sheet. The balance sheet is to give financial information to the company, to the shareholders, to the tax authorities and, often, to the money lending bank. From that balance sheet the management can derive the relation between equity and liabilities; the cash available etc. In chapter 7 we will work on analysing a balance sheet to test the health of a company.

When facing the preparation of a closing balance sheet it is, again, important to realize that there can be costs which cause expenditures (cash decreases on the balance sheet) and other costs which do not cause expenditures, or not at the time of preparing the balance sheet. These are booked under liabilities: creditors.

We know already that costs of depreciation belong to the P & L statement and they affect the value of fixed assets on the closing balance sheet. And they affect the balance of cash on that balance sheet positively. The same applies to provisions.

But costs which have been made in December of the operating year can lead to expenditures in the next year. They affect the P & L statement of the operating year and they lead to record the same figure under "creditors" on the closing balance sheet if they are to be paid in the next year.

We also saw that expenditures not always relate to costs: when a computer is purchased in December no costs were made, so the P & L statement does not have to be adjusted. But the balance sheet will: it concerned an investment increasing the assets figure on the balance sheet. Also, a pay back of a part of a loan is an expenditure but it will affect the balance sheet only. Not the P & L statement, because **repayment never means a cost**.

The same applies to revenues. These can lead to income, but not always simultaneously. A sale which was concluded in December for which the buyer is allowed a term of payment of thirty days affects the P & L statement of the operating year positively by increasing the turnover figure and the net profit figure at the moment of the sale. It affects the balance sheet by recording the amount of the sale under "accounts receivable". When the buyer pays for the invoice in the next year only the balance sheet is involved. Not the P & L statement.

It may be good to repeat the two frames for income and expenditures here below.

Costs and expenditures

COSTS BUT NO EXPENDITURE	EXPENDITURE BUT NO COST
Provision for future maintenance costs (P&L)	Pay back of a portion of a loan (balance sheet)
Depreciation costs (P & L)	Payment of invoice of a supplier (balance sheet)
A repair job to be paid after sixty days (P & L for the costs and balance sheet: creditors)	Asset purchased and paid in cash (balance sheet)

Revenue and income

REVENUE BUT NO INCOME	INCOME BUT NO REVENUE
A client purchases and will pay 30 days later (P & L statement and balance sheet: accounts receivable)	Payment from a client is received (balance sheet only)
Appraisal of building higher than book value (balance sheet only)	Shareholder pays for shares issued to him (balance sheet and liquidity report)

When the operating year ends and the net profit earned is known there always is a group of interested parties desiring to know what will happen with the profit: the shareholders.

It stands to reason that shareholders expect a reward for having risked their money when they **invested** in shares in the company. **This reward is called DIVIDENDS**. Articles of incorporation (or: of association) being the internal rules for a corporation and all of its organs (the board of directors, the shareholders and supervisory board) must provide for the destination of the net profit. **In many cases 60% of this net profit will remain in the company's treasury as "retained earnings".** So 40% will be available to divide among the shareholders proportionately to their number of shares owned.

The percentages mentioned may vary from company to company and from country to country. There is one common basis for having the rule which part of the profit should (or must) be retained by the company: **security for creditors to get their invoices paid and supporting the continuity of a company.**

Mostly dividends are paid in cash. Sometimes this is not possible. If a company was profitable but its strategy leads them to acquire (part)ownership of another company's shares this company will prefer not to use too much of the available cash for paying dividends. In such a case the board may propose not to pay the dividends in cash but in the form of new shares to be issued in proportion to the shareholders' number of shares. It saves the company's funds for acquiring part ownership in another company. If the general meeting of shareholders agrees to the proposition, then the dividends will be paid by issuing new shares. **Such dividend is called STOCK DIVIDEND**

Exercises Of Chapter 6
The Closing Balance Sheet

1. We see the following opening balance sheet at the beginning of an operating year

BALANCE SHEET

Factory building	$450 000	Ordinary share capital	$310 000
Equipment	200 000	Retained earnings	200 000
Furniture	150 000		
		Mortgage loan 5%	400 000
Inventory	250 000	Long term loan 8%	240 000
Accounts receivable	320 000		
Cash	90 000	Creditors	220 000
		Current account credit 14%	90 000
TOTAL	$1 460 000	TOTAL	$1 460 000

The P & L statement shows the following.
Depreciation of the building was $ 15.000, of equipment $ 20.000 and of furniture and fixtures $ 25.000. Interest costs were $ 20.000 for the mortgage, $ 19.000 for the long-term loan and $ 12.000 for the current account credit. Net profit after tax was $ 180.000.

From the general ledger is derived that equipment was purchased in April for $ 50.000. At the same time the long-term loan was increased by $ 40.000 to finance this equipment. The equipment was paid in June.

New printing machines were purchased in November for $ 60.000, to be paid by February 1 next year. During the operating year $ 20.000 was paid back on the mortgage loan.

1.1 Give the changes for the closing balance by + or – per item and answer the questions below.
1.2 What will the figure for cash be on the closing balance sheet

   a. $ 150.000
   b. $ 300.000
   b. $ 260.000

1.3 What will the figures for mortgage and long-term loan be on the closing balance

   a. mortgage will be $ 360.000, long term loan will be $ 220.000
   b. mortgage will be $ 400.000, long term loan will be $ 300.000
   c. mortgage will be $ 380.000, long term loan will be $ 280.000

2. We see the following opening balance sheet

BALANCE SHEET

Factory building	$350 000	Ordinary share capital	$260 000
Equipment	120 000	Retained earnings	80 000
Furniture	90 000	Mortgage loan 5%	170 000
Inventory	120 000	Long term loan 8%	130 000
Accounts receivable	140 000		
Cash	90 000	Creditors	80 000
		Current account credit 14%	190 000
TOTAL	$910 000	TOTAL	$910 000

The P & L statement offers the following information.

Depreciation was $ 25.000 for the building, $ 30.000 for equipment and $ 9.000 for furniture.

From the general ledger the following facts are derived. In May additional furniture was purchased for $ 15.000 and paid for in cash. In December additional equipment was purchased for $ 60.000 which will have to be paid in February next year.

In view of expected maintenance in two years from the closing balance sheet which work is estimated at an amount of $ 40.000 it was decided to take up a provision of $ 20.000 on the P & L statement. The net profit after tax for the operating year was $ 120.000. Rather than pay dividends to the shareholders it is decided mutually that the retained earnings amount on the opening balance sheet will be used to pay shareholders a stock dividend. There are 260 shares in the hands of a total of four shareholders.

2.1 Prepare the closing balance sheet.
2.2 How is the figure of the cash flow composed

 a. Cash flow is $ 120.000 + $ 64.000 + $ 20.000 less $ 15.000 = $ 189.000
 b. Cash is $ 90.000 + $ 120.000 + $ 20.000 + $ 64.000 less $ 15.000 = $ 279.000
 c. Cash flow is $ 120.000 + $ 64.000 + $ 20.0000 = $ 204.000

3. On an opening balance sheet, we see the following figures

BALANCE SHEET

Inventory of products	$80 000	retained earnings	$0
Cash	$40 000	current account credit	$120 000

During the year the inventory was sold and payments were received. The profit margin on sales is 36%. Excluding the starting inventory turnover for the year was $1.620.000. The inventory needed was purchased throughout the year. It is a policy of the company to have an inventory of products enough for three months of sale. Financing of stock takes place only by the available current account credit.

Calculate the figures of Cash and of the current account credit for the closing balance sheet

 a. Cash $ 1.745.000, Current Account Credit $ 1.007.400
 b. Cash $ 1.620.000, Current Account Credit $ 2.044.200
 c. Cash $ 1.785.000, Current Account Credit $ 1.416.000

4. In company the annual depreciation costs were as follows: building $90.000, equipment $ 74.000, furniture and office equipment $ 48.000. The net loss was - $40.000.

4.1 What are the changes to the closing balance sheet (use + and – per item)

a. Building - $ 90.000, equipment - $ 74.000, furniture and office equipment -$ 48.000 Cash + 212.000, retained earnings -$ 40.000

b. Building -$ 90.000, Equipment -$ 74.000, Furniture and office equipment -$ 48.000, Cash + $ 172.000, Retained earnings -$ 40.000. Net change debit and credit side is -$40.000

c. Building -$ 90.0000, Equipment - $ 74.000, Furniture and office equipment -$48.000 Retained earnings - $ 40.000

4.2 What was the annual Cash Flow

a. $ 40.000 -

b. $ 132.000

c. $ 172.000

5. On a closing balance sheet the amount of accounts receivable is $ 55.000 and the figure for inventory is $ 42.000. Delivery time by suppliers is 3-4 weeks. The turnover for the year was $ 480.000 and all of the clients pay exactly after 30 days. The profit margin on sales was 32%. Calculate the excess of accounts receivable and of inventory compared to what would have been sound practice economically.

a. Accounts receivable were too high by $ 15.000, inventory by $ 14.800

b. Accounts receivable were too high by $ 12.000, inventory by $ 11.400

c. Accounts receivable were too high by $ 14.000, inventory by $ 14.200

6. Which items from the P & L statement can be transferred to the closing balance sheet directly

a. Depreciations, investments and repayments of loans

b Net profit and depreciations

c Depreciations, net profit, and provisions

7. If during an operating year depreciation costs of fixed assets totalled $ 102.000 and there was no profit nor a loss, then what would be the changes to be recorded in the closing balance sheet?

a. Fixed assets and cash decrease by $ 102.000

b. Fixed assets and retained earnings decrease by $ 102.000

c. Fixed assets decreased by $ 102.000, Cash increased by the same amount. No changes in retained earnings since there was no result to record

Closing Assignment of Chapter 6

The Closing Balance Sheet

1. This is the opening balance sheet of year 2012 and the P & L statement of 2012.

Opening Balance	Sheet	P &L	Statement	%
Building $400 000	Share capital $ 500 000	Turnover	$ 1 500 000	100
Equipment 460 000	Ret. earnings 120 000	Cost price	900 000	60
Furniture 240 000		Profit margin	600 000	40
	Mortgage 5% 340 000	**Operating Costs**		
Inventory 120 000	Long t.loan 8% 300 000	Personnel	100 000	6.7
Acc.receiv. 80 000		Housing	50 000	3.3
Cash 200 000	Creditors 100 000	sales costs	82 000	5.5
	Curr. account 140 000	office costs	30 000	2
		freight costs	24 000	1.6
TOTAL $ 1 500 000	TOTAL $ 1 500 000	depreciations:		
		- building	14 000	0.9

- equipment	46 000	3.1	
- furniture	48 000	3.2	
TOTAL COSTS	$ 394 000	26.3	
OPERATING INCOME	206 000	13.7	
Interest costs	57 800	3.9	
Provision for maintenance	60 000	4	
Net profit before tax	88 200	5.8	
Corporate tax	22 050	1.47	
Net profit after tax	$ 66 150	4.33	

The general ledger shows that in the course of the operating year furniture was purchased for $ 40.000 and paid in cash. On the mortgage $ 20.000 was paid back. Equipment was purchased for $ 120.000 of which $ 20.000 was paid in cash and the difference came from an extension of the long term loan. $ 80.000 of the retained earnings was turned into newly issued shares of $ 1.000 each.

1.1 Prepare the closing balance sheet and answer the subsequent questions
1.2 What were the figures for share capital and for retained earnings on the closing balance sheet

  a. Share capital $ 580.000, retained earnings $ 226.150
  b. b Share capital $ 500.000, retained earnings $ 66.150
  c. Share capital $ 580.000, retained earnings $ 106.150

1.3 What is the figure for cash on the closing balance sheet and how is it composed

  a. Cash is $ 354.150. Opening balance $ 200.000 + cash flow of $ 174.150 ($ 66.150 profit plus depreciations of $ 108.000) plus provision for maintenance of $60.000 (it lowered net profit, but, still, clients paid also this amount while no outflow of cash occurred!) – part payment of $ 20.000 for equipment - $ 40.000 for cash payment for furniture and - $20.000 for repayment of the mortgage loan = $ 354.150
  b. Cash is $ 186.150. It started with $ 120.000 and to be added is the profit of $66.150. To deduct: payment for furniture of $ 40.000, repayment of mortgage of $20.000 and part payment for equipment $ 20.000
  c. Cash is $ 148.000. To the starting figure is added a cash flow of $ 108.000 and to be deducted are the payments for equipment, furniture and mortgage of $ 80.000

1.4 What is the intrinsic value per share based on the closing balance sheet

  a. Intrinsic value per share is $ 1.194
  b. Intrinsic value per share is $ 1.178
  b. Intrinsic value per share is $ 1.183

Chapter 7
Ratio Analysis of a Company

7.1 Liquidity and Solvency

So far, we have seen companies getting started with their investments and their financing. We saw results from operations and how liquidity works. And, finally, we saw all of these efforts resulting in a closing balance sheet. Now it is time to use the close-up picture, which a balance represents by its nature, to analyse how the company has been doing.

There is a lot we can see from a balance sheet for analysing the health and wealth of a company. Let us start by analysing its **potential to pay its debts,** both the long term liabilities and the current liabilities.

Before we enter into the analytical process the following question is justified: who may have an interest to see the results of such an analysis? We list them as follows.

1. **Shareholders** are interested because they shared the risk of the company by investing their money in it. They stand the risk of losing all of such investment for which they will have had other options: savings account, government bonds etc. Their interest is focussed on the question what the revenues from their investment were after the closing of an operating year. They also are interested in knowing if the book value of their shares exceed the price they paid for them initially. And, finally, they are interested to estimate the future of the company in order to decide whether or not to hold on to their shares. If shareholders become very nervous about all of these points of interest they may decide to sell off their shares in order to find more promising investment opportunities

2. The **board of directors** continuously bears the responsibility to use the equity of the company in such a way that they can satisfy the shareholders by making a profit from which it can pay an attractive dividend. It also must keep their bank satisfied by not overstretching the borrowing capacity of the company and by paying interest and instalments in time always. Also, the board looks in the mirror and asks itself the question whether it succeeded in **safeguarding the continuity of the company for the long term** and if the stakeholders of the company still have confidence in its strategy.

It is the responsibility of the board to watch the borrowing capacity of the company very closely. And if this seems to be dangerously low it must consider to move a resolution to issue additional shares in order to restore the agreed balance between equity and liabilities.

One of the foremost responsibilities of a board is to change the strategy or the mission of the company when it finds itself operating in a stagnating market. Going for more viable product/market directions is a crucial decision to make after having received permission from the owners of the company. One of the more interesting examples of this can be found in the pharmaceutical industry. For a long time the products of this industry were protected by patents. But many of these matured and protection was discontinued. Competitors jumped at the opportunity to duplicate products and to offer them at lower prices worldwide. In light of the massively high costs of Research & Development in this type of industry many larger companies have been looking to be acquired by others. The total number of pharmaceutical companies will keep decreasing for quite some time for that reason. And, in the coffee industry we saw the ending of Nespresso's patent on coffee capsules recently. At least four newcomers jumped in and offer similar capsules fitting in Nespresso machines but at 44% lower prices per capsule.

A number of this type of companies anticipated this situation already long time ago and adopted a fundamentally different strategy: diversification. They acquired majority participations in chemical companies, food companies and paint companies just to try to survive. Nespresso acquired shares in coffee plantations.

It underlines that, contrary to public organisations, private companies must be very alert all the time and must consider new opportunities seriously. It seems, though, that this is most difficult for family owned businesses, where traditions from generation to generation are respected beyond a reasonable expiration date.

3. Financial money lenders

Banks and larger creditors keep a close look at their client company. Not out of human interest but to monitor the ongoing business in their own interest.

There are many companies which are late in paying their interest, their instalments and their invoices. They are observed constantly and visited frequently in order to acquire some security as to the future. There are long standing relations between a single company and its bank with relatively high risks at stake. Such a bank sometimes appoints one of its managers as the guardian of that company with the responsibility to monitor developments very closely.

As long as perspectives are positive, realistically, such a bank even declares itself prepared to extend the borrowing capacity of the company.

4. Employees

In times of difficulties in finding a new job employees demonstrate a keen interest in the developments of the employing company. There is one crucial question in everybody's head: will I have a job two or three months from now? Their interest is described best by the word: **continuity.**

5. Large accounts

For products made to specification, especially in the automobile world, it is a prominent interest of the motor company that the supply line for the components never stops. Not for a minute. These large companies study the closing balance sheets of their suppliers and compare these to earlier ones. The moment they smell that risks of stagnation increase they invite others to make their bids for the same product To a large extent such companies have a lot of manufacturers of parts, like dashboards, exhaust piping etc. Should a supplier from this category go down it will create significant delay in the assembly operations of the motorcar brand.

What To Analyse

One of the foremost items a board of directors is keen to study is the company's
1. potential to repay all of its **short-term debts** in time. These debts consist mainly of creditors who most of the times are the suppliers of the raw materials and repair companies. They also consist of their banks which count on timely payments of interest and instalments and of tax authorities awaiting tax payments by a company. That is their short-term interest concerning current liabilities. The second item to be studied is the company's
2. long term potential to repay all of its debts. And the third is

3. the return which is made by the company and by other parties related to the company like a bank and shareholders on their respective financial stakes in the company.

To conduct a proper analysis let us have a look at the cross links on a balance sheet first:
balance sheet items which have an important relation to:

EQUITY Share capital:	fixed assets
Retained earnings	have a relation to cash
LONG TERM LIABILITIES	have a relation to fixed assets
Mortgage loan has one relation:	to buildings only (fixed assets)
Long term loan has a relation	to other fixed assets
CURRENT LIABILITIES have a relation to	CURRENT ASSETS
Creditors have a foremost relation	to inventory
current account credit shows a strong relation	to accounts receivable

From this summary we can easily see that fixed assets which will be in the company's possession for many years mostly and predominantly are financed by **equity plus long-term liabilities.**

Current Assets that change constantly mostly are financed by current liabilities. Exception is made for **the inventory of products** (finished products or raw materials). From the three current assets this item **will take longest to turn into cash**, when needed in a short period of time. Receivables mostly have a limited payment term. Cash is available immediately. But inventory is a very different matter.

Suppose a company has a large inventory of scrap rubber it transfers into sidewalk tiles etc. They sometimes have an inventory of 300.000 tons or more of it. In time of crisis where deadlines for paying current liabilities are imminent, who in the world would be interested to buy this scrap material? The total quantity of it? At the book value of its inventory? Nobody!

In Business Economics such inventory, therefore, is treated as a fixed asset in similar circumstances, meaning that financing preferably takes place by long term financing sources.

We now start our analysis of the potential of a company to pay its current and long-term liabilities in time.

There are four tests to analyse the potential to pay the short-term liabilities:
1. current ratio; 2 quick ratios; 3 **working capital** and 4 **the golden balance rule.**

1. CURRENT RATIO and WORKING CAPITAL

The liquidity ratio tells us about a company's potential to pay its current liabilities in time. And since current liabilities' most intimate relationship is with current assets the two groups are compared. We show the relevant portion of a random balance sheet

BALANCE SHEET

Inventory	$180 000	Creditors	$400 000
Accounts receivable	160 000	Current account credit	120 000
Cash	250 000		
	---------------		---------------
Current assets	$590 000	Current liabilities	$520 000

The current ratio divides the amount of the current assets by the amount of the current liabilities. When the outcome is higher than 1 the company is considered liquid enough to pay the $ 520.000. It is as if all of these assets would be sold at once at their balance value or book value to pay the current liabilities

So: current assets $ 590.000
$$\frac{\text{current assets } \$ 590.000}{\text{current liabilities } \$ 520.000} = 1.13 \text{ is} > 1: \text{liquid enough.}$$

Would it have been < 1: payment problems are imminent

So, is the outcome smaller than 1 the company will face payment problems shortly even if all of the current assets can be sold in one day for their book value. Banks for the interest due, which is a current liability, and creditors are highly interested to see what the current ratio is.

And if a bank fears that their will be payment problems ahead, it has the possibility to cancel the current account credit facility at an ultra short period of, mostly, 1 to 2 weeks. In many cases this practically is the beginning of the end for the company. Bankruptcy is creeping near.

Even companies which are very profitable can land in such a pitfall especially in the case where most of its financial resources had been used to finance fixed assets. One fatal fact can put an end to even these companies. Think about the motorcar dealer who faces very negative technical publicity about the brand he is selling.

Even when the outcome of this ratio is > 1 then, still, there is no guarantee that all of the current liabilities will be paid in time. An interested buyer facing a company which is desperately trying to sell all of its inventory never will pay its book value. He wants a bargain and if there is no bargain there will be no deal. In practice parties offer 35% - 40% of book value.

A similar ratio to test a company's ability to pay its current liabilities in time is "working capital.

2. WORKING CAPITAL

Working capital shows us the difference in dollars between current assets and current liabilities. If the current assets are much higher than the current liabilities then this company can be trusted to pay its current liabilities in time. The formula is easy. We take the same figures from the above portion of a balance sheet:

current assets - current liabilities = working capital
 $ 590.000   - $ 520.000   = $ 70.000

So, working capital is the positive difference between current assets and current liabilities. It would mean trouble for a company when working capital is a negative: more current liabilities than current assets means the incapability to pay it's short term debts.

From this simple deduction it is not difficult to see that a margin of $ 70.000 on more than half a million dollars in current assets does not offer a maximum of security. Especially since we understand that selling off all of the current assets will not result in the receipt of their book value. If we think about the company processing scrap rubber it will not be difficult to understand that even with a margin of $ 70.000 the respective company can still end up in great difficulty. We also understand that no company can ever sell its inventory at book value.

Suppose in the above example the company faces a large claim and parties reach a settlement of $ 100.000. Suddenly the working capital has become a negative of - $30.000.

And, in other scenarios, it is good to estimate what income can be generated from selling off all of the current assets. Cash will not count but will be used. Accounts receivable may have a margin of risk of 5% - 10% that not all of the clients will pay. So $ 160.000 – 5% = $ 152.000. And in practice inventory will hardly ever generate more than 45%. That leaves 45% of $ 180.000 = $ 81.000. Total result of selling off is: $ 250.000 + $ 152.000 + $ 81.000 = $ 483.000. A debt of $ 520.000 will not be fully paid in such a situation.

This is one of the reasons to introduce a third ratio for measuring liquidity:

3. THE QUICK RATIO or: THE ACID TEST

This ratio looks like the current ratio but excludes inventory in the calculation because of the risk it cannot be sold at short notice, leave alone at its book value.

The quick ratio from the above balance items would look as follows:

$$\frac{\$ 419.000}{\$ 520.000} = 0,80 \text{ which clearly is} < 1$$

Depending on the type of company and market circumstances a bank can "pull the plug" thus causing the company to go down.

In such situations a lifebuoy is needed desperately. There are several to be considered:

1. increase equity by issuing enough new shares against prompt payment
2. a subordinated loan. This altruistic type of loan is subordinated to all other liabilities when it comes to repayments. Such a loan is to be repaid only when all other creditors will have been satisfied. Such a loan may be recorded under equity for that reason.
3. an appraisal of the value of the company owned building, hoping the outcome will be substantially higher than its book value so that **borrowing capacity** will increase

It is important for any company to characterize their finished products and their raw materials realistically with a view of the chances to sell them at short notice and at good prices. If that is not the case such company can do its own quick ratio every now and then in order to take appropriate steps in time. Looking at the composition of the current assets the question is: how can a company succeed in keeping itself from such a horror scenario? This is not an easy question. What we are looking for is a much wider margin between current assets and current liabilities.

Under the assets accounts receivable may be stimulated upward by increasing sales. The revenue acquired will then have to be used for two purposes: increase the inventory which was depleted more quickly by higher sales volumes. But the increase must stay in a realistic proportion to the expected sales volume in the short term.

The second employment of the sales revenues would have to be to lower the current liabilities. In small steps a company can increase the working capital from $ 70.000 to well over $ 150.000. Most important is that as much of the inflow of cash as possible should be kept in the company in order to remain perfectly safe. Better still: treat inventory as a fixed asset by using the golden balance rule here below.

4. THE GOLDEN BALANCE RULE

Let us take a look at a company which succeeded in preparing a great safety against shortage of liquidity.

BALANCE SHEET

Building	$360 000 A	Share capital	$370 000 B
Equipment	180 000 A	Retained earnings	160 000 B
Office equipment	90 000 A		
		Mortgage loan	250 000 B
Inventory	180 000 A	Long-term loan	180 000 B
Accounts receivable	170 000 C		
Cash	110 000 C	Creditors	120 000 D
		Current Account credit	10 000 D
TOTAL	$1 090 000		$1 090 000

A = fixed assets + inventory = $ 810.000; B is long term financing = $ 960.000; C is current assets = $ 280.000 and D is current liabilities = 130.000.

We see that inventory now is listed under A for fixed assets. Their total value is $810.000.

Fixed assets should be financed by long term financing as much as possible in order to keep liquidity threats away. All of the items B fit here because their total of $ 960.000 not only financed all of the fixed assets, but also the inventory. B is larger than A which means that inventory was financed by long term financing.

There still is a margin to enlarge inventory of $ 960.000 - $ 810.000 = $ 150.000 So, even if inventory would increase by $ 100.000 then, still, the golden balance rule would apply.

By definition the above also means that if B > A then D can never be larger than C, so the current ratio cannot possibly be negative in this configuration. Check this by preparing a personal set of figures!

This company succeeded in creating this maximum of safety by leaving most of its profits in the company under retained earnings. The high amount of cash is a result of that policy.

If we look at the current ratio formula then we will notice how high that safety is: current assets : current liabilities is $ 460.000 : $ 130.000 = 3.5!

And also the **quick ratio** looks very attractive: current assets exclusive of inventory : current liabilities is $ 280.000 : $ 130.000 = 2.15.

And, finally, working capital is $ 460.000 - $ 130.000 = $ 330.000. This is an extremely favourable figure when it comes to building short term payment safeties.

After having seen how to test a balance sheet in relation to the ability to pay for the short term debts we now will investigate how the **STRUCTURAL ABILITY** to pay the debts in general looks like.

Corporate Solvency or Debt Ratio

The ability to repay ALL of the liabilities is a different matter in comparison to the ability to repay the current liabilities only.

Corporate solvency takes a broader view at the company's assets in comparison to liabilities in general. Let us take a look at a normal balance sheet.

BALANCE SHEET

Fixed assets total	$800 000	Equity total	$650 000
Inventory	400 000	Mortgage loan	500 000
		Long term loan	200 000
	--------------		--------------
TOTAL FIXED ASSETS	**$1 200 000**	**TOTAL LONG TERM CAPITAL**	**$1 350 000**
Accounts receivable	$300 000	Creditors	$140 000
Cash	100 000	Current account	110 000
	--------------		--------------
TOTAL CURRENT ASSETS	**$400 000**	**TOTAL CURRENT LIABILITIES**	**$250 000**
BALANCE TOTAL	$1 600 000	BALANCE TOTAL	$1 600 000

The question here is: if this company would sell all of the assets can it then pay off all of the liabilities? The answer is: Yes, if.... The "if" refers to the income which can be generated by selling all of the assets, of which we know that selling at book value hardly ever succeeds. Equipment, furniture, office equipment and inventory hardly ever are sold at book values but at distinctly lower prices.

The second question is: will the ratio equity – liabilities satisfy the bank? In the above balance sheet equity finances slightly more than 40% of the assets If the agreement with the bank allows 65% of liabilities for the financing of the assets then there will be no problem. If, however the limit to liabilities was agreed at 60% then the problem is imminent because there is only 0,625% more than the required equity.

The good thing about the above balance sheet is that the golden balance rule applies: fixed assets and inventory were financed by long term financing.

If we look at the total of the assets, $ 1.600.000 and all of these would be sold at book value then the balance equals total capital. The minimum figure to be obtained from the sale of all of the assets will have to equal the total figure of all of the liabilities of $ 950.000. It would mean that total assets should be sold for 60%+ of their book value.

Now, suppose the income from sales of all of the assets of $ 1.600.000 totals 70% of book value = $ 1.120.000 . Will that create a problem? No, because this income is higher than all of the liabilities of $ 950.000. As long as sale of all of the assets can generate 60% of their book value all of the liabilities can be paid.

Apparently, equity forms kind of a buffer to allow for lower revenues from total sales of assets. In fact, we now touch at **the essence of a bank's demand for a specific relation** between equity and liabilities. It all has to do with solvency in general.

Would a bank act conservatively by demanding that equity must represent 35% of the financing function then equity in the above balance sheet should have been 35% of $ 1.600.000 = $ 560.000 and liabilities should not be higher than 65% =$ 1.040.000.

In the above balance sheet liabilities finance almost 60% of the assets.

Solvency, now, is the foremost ratio to analyse a company's **structural ability to pay** all of its liabilities. The formula is simple: equity in %: liabilities in %. In the above balance sheet that ratio is 40.6: 59.4. Another way of analysing is to just find the percentage of one of the two. Because together the two are 100%, e.g. L(iabilities) : T(otal) A(sets) = L : TA = 59.4 So, equity must be 40.6

Every company has a choice in how far it intends to stretch its borrowing capacity of its allowed limit for liabilities. Smart companies take precautions by keeping a margin of at least 5% higher equity than demanded by it's bank (in the example: $ 720.000 in equity) so that an unfortunate event cannot create a crisis immediately.

Exercises of Chapter 7
Liquidity and Solvency

1. Analysing a company's liquidity has everything to do with

    a. the profit realized by the company
    b. the return on capital
    c. it's capacity to pay all of its current liabilities in time

2. The quick ratio, or acid test, calculates

    a. the capacity to pay debts also in the long run
    b. if the value of cash and of accounts receivables divided by total current liabilities is higher than 1 at any given time. That outcome indicates good payment capacity.
    c. the capacity to pay all of the current liabilities with the money equalling the value of the inventory at any time.

3. Here is a partial balance sheet

Furniture	$300 000	Long term loan	$280 000
Inventory	240 000	Creditors	400 000
Accounts receivable	180 000	Current account	190 000
Cash	120 000		

3.1 Calculate the current ratio

   a. 1.33
   b. 0,42
   b. 0.91

3.2 Calculate the quick ratio

   a. 0.508
   b. 0.61
   c. 0.580

3.3 Does this company seem to be solvent?

   a. yes
   b. no

3.4 What is the working capital?

   a. $ 90.000
   b. $ 50.000
   b. -$50.000

4. The current ratio is calculated on the basis of

   a. current assets
   b. all assets
   c. cash

5. To be sufficiently liquid

   a. the current ratio must by higher than 1
   b. return on equity must be higher than 1
   b. quick ratio must be higher than 1

6. Solvency informs about the capability to

   a. pay all of the debts in time
   b. repay the mortgage and the long-term loans
   c. have equity which is much higher than liabilities so that debts can be paid

Chapter 7
Ratio Analysis of a Company

7.2 Analysing Return Ratios

For specific parties it is of prominent interest to see what the return is of the capital such a party invested in the company:

- **The board of directors**, which looks for continuity but also for satisfaction on the side of the owners, the shareholders, with a view of the bonus it may expect for all the energy it put into the health of the company entrusted to them;

- **The shareholders** who took a risk of investing their money in a venture like the company whose shares they own. Their primary interest, after sharing the care for continuity of the company, is how high their reward =**DIVIDENDS** will be for taking the risks.

- **The bank**, by nature, is interested in the interest it earned by making loans available to the company

For every party it would be hard to accept that the return on its investment would be non existent or very modest. Such party might look for a different investment opportunity if the disappointing outcome would have been foreseen.
Let us discuss the various types of return now

1. Return On Total Capital

This return ratio is calculated from the **operating result** in the P & L statement. That is the result before deducting financing costs, provisions and tax. The reason behind this is that a board of directors hardly can influence the interest costs and the tax. In fact, this ratio ascertains the performance of the board and shareholders will, no doubt, compare the actual result with last year's results.
The ratio is calculated as follows:

$$\frac{\text{OPERATING RESULTS}}{\text{AVERAGE OF TOTAL CAPITAL}} \times 100\%$$

The ratio needs the **average of total capital** = the average of all of the financing in total. But how to find a correct outcome if, during the operating year, changes took place in the total of capital? New shares could have been issued. New loans could have been acquired. Or loans could have been repaid in part. A fair outcome can be reached by adding last year's total of capital to this year's total of capital and divide by 2:

$$\text{average total capital} = \frac{\text{last year's total capital} + \text{this year's total capital}}{2}$$

This may not be the ultimate fairness in computing because new shares may have been issued in November of the operating year and could not have contributed substantially to the operating results. The same applies to a partial repayment of a loan which took place in February of the operating year. But it would become too complicated to find the perfect average of the two values to be practical.

Let us suppose that the operating income for the operating year was $ 250.000 and that the average of last year's and this year's total capital would have been $ 2.000.000 then return on total capital would be ($ 250.000: $ 2.000.000) X 100 = 12.5%.

This ratio tells a board of directors much about the performance of the general manager. The higher the percentage the better general management proves to have succeeded in either increasing the operating income, or reducing total capital, or both. Reducing total capital could be achieved by keeping low inventory and low accounts receivable on the one side and reducing current liabilities. The risk of this ratio, apparently, is the continuous comparison to last year's performance. Boards generally are not happy with a lower performance than last year's. This may stir a general manager into dangerous directions, like keeping inventory levels which by far are not enough to satisfy clients.

2. RETURN ON EQUITY

This ratio calculates how high **net profit after tax is in a percentage of average total equity.**

Let us assume that last year's equity was $ 850.000 and this year's equity was $ 930.000 and that this year's net profit after tax amounted to $ 146.850. Then the ratio is calculated as follows

$$\$\,146.850 : \left(\frac{\$\,850.000 + \$\,930.000}{2}\right) \times 100 = \frac{\$\,146.850}{\$\,890.000} \times 100 = 16.5\,\%$$

This is a very favourable return on equity for the shareholders, the owners of the equity.

It does not mean that they can expect a dividend of 16.5%, because a part of this net profit will remain in the company under **"retained earnings"** but a dividend of 8% to 9% can be expected realistically. With interest percentages on a savings account at 3% this dividend percentage certainly will keep the shareholders satisfied.

Retaining earnings by a corporation stands for a solid and healthy policy because it lowers the need for liabilities. On the other hand, it widens the potential for additional loans should circumstances so demand. A possible negative implication of this policy could be the increase of the intrinsic value per share. This would make issuing new shares at the intrinsic value hardly possible.

We know that equity is the property of the shareholders. The higher the retained earnings the higher the value of their property: their individual shares. If, by retaining earnings during past years equity grew to a total of $ 970.000 and the total of outstanding shares was 800 at a par value of $ 1.000, then the excess value was $ 970.000 - $ 800.000 = $170.000.

The intrinsic value per share therefore grew to $ 970.000 : 800 = $ 1.212,50. This means that if additional share capital would be needed $ 1.212,50 instead of $ 1.000 would be the purchase price a (new) shareholder would have to pay as a minimum. If an existing shareholder would have earned a dividend of 15%, or $ 150,= then a new shareholder, having paid $ 1.212,50 per share would have had a return of ($ 150 : $ 1.212,50) X 100 = 12.3%. Such a percentage may draw some new shareholders, but also would scare others away.

The conclusion must be that a corporation would have to change retained earnings into shares before issuing new shares to the market of investors in order to keep their purchase price as close to the **par value per share** as possible. This can be done by offering bonus shares to the existing shareholders to the amount of retained earnings on the balance sheet.

3. RETURN ON LIABILITIES

This return does not benefit the borrowing corporation but it serves the lending bank. It also tells the company how much interest had been paid in a percentage of **ALL of the liabilities.**

The bank calculates the return by expressing the interest received during an operating year by 1% of the money it made available to the corporation.

The corporation itself uses **all of the liabilities**, including creditors who did not demand any interest payments. **It divides the total amount of interest paid during** an operating year by 1% of all of the liabilities figuring on it's balance sheet by the end of the year.

Example: we assume that a corporation has a mortgage loan on it's office building of $400.000 at an interest rate of 5%. Costs of interest during the year totals to $ 20.000. We also assume that the amount due to creditors was $ 280.000 during the previous year and $ 320.000 at the end of the current year. No repayments to the bank. The **average total of the liabilities** then was : ($ 680.000 + $ 720.000) : 2 = $ 700.000. This makes that the total of interest paid represented $ 20.000 : $ 7.000 = 2.587%.

The additional liabilities beside the mortgage caused the average percentage to drop to less than 3%. This is how many corporations calculate and analyse. This is done mainly to **compare the return on total capital with the return on liabilities.** This comparison teaches the corporation the **leverage in liabilities** from this comparison. It is true: if the return on total capital shows a figure of 10% and the return on liabilities shows a return of 2% then the ensuing reasoning will be: if every single $ invested in this company yields 10% (= $ 0,10) and every borrowed $ costs 2% ($ 0.02) then every such borrowed $ at not more than 2% yields a gain of 8% or $ 0,08!

It encourages a corporation to find more liabilities at not more than 2% of interest costs.

This phenomenon is called **LEVERAGE FACTOR or LEVERAGE EFFECT.**

It will be clear that such a positive leverage will be found only if and as long as return on capital is distinctly higher than return on liabilities. For that reason alone leverage never can be a part of the financial planning

Exercises Of Chapter
7.2 Return Ratios

1. For this exercise a Profit & Loss statement follows as well as two subsequent balance sheets

P&L statement yr. 2 X$1.000		balance sheets	year 1	year 2		year 1	year 2
Turnover	1 800	Buildings	600	570	Sharecap.	500	500
Costprice	900	Machinery	500	650	Retained earnings	200	300
Margin	900	Furniture	300	230	EQUITY	700	800
		FIXED ASSETS	1.400	1.450			
					Mortgage loan	600	600
Operating costs	300	Inventory	400	500	Long term loan	350	400
		Accounts receivable	300	400	LONG TERM LIABILITIES	950	1000
Depreciation	100	Liquidities	250	250	Creditors	400	450
OPERA-TING RESULT	500	CURR. ASSETS	950	1 150	Current account	300	350
Financial expenses	110				CURR. LIABILITIES	700	800
Net profit before tax	390						
Corp.tax 25%	97.5						
Net profit after tax	292.5						
		TOTAL	2.350	2.600	TOTAL	2350	2.600

Turnover is equally divided over the twelve months' period. Payment term both for suppliers and clients is 30 days. The figure of cost price on the P&L statement stands for purchases during the year. Delivery time of inventory is less than one month.

1.1 Calculate return on equity at the end of year 2

    a. approx. 41%
    b. approx. 36%
    c. approx. 39%

1.2 What was the return on all liabilities of year 2

    a. approximately 6.4
    b. approximately 6.6
    c. approximately 6.1

1.3 What was the percentage of the operating result in year 2?

    a. 19.4 %
    b. 20.2 %
    b. 21.7 %

1.4 How much of long-term total capital was invested in current assets in year 1

    a. $ 150.000
    b. $ 250.000
    c. $ 350.000

1.5 When 40% of net profit after tax would be paid to shareholders as a dividend and the shares all have a nominal value of $ 1.000 how much dividend per share would be paid in year 2

    a. $ 230
    b. $ 232
    b. $ 234

1.6 What was the yield per share in % of question 1.5

    a. 23.4%
    b. 21.4%
    c. 19.4%

1.7 Explain if there was a leverage effect in year 2

    a. Yes, by almost 18.5 %
    b. Yes, by almost 14 %
    b. Yes, by almost 16.8 %

1.8 Would it be wise policy in this company to borrow more money

   a. yes, because....
   b. no, because....

1.9 What was the turnover rate of the inventory in year 2

   a. 2.2
   b. 2.0
   c. 1.8

1.10 What was the payment term used by clients in year 2

   a. 3 months
   b. 2.8 months
   b. 2.6 months

1.11 What was the payment term used by the company to pay it's creditors in year 2 when the figure of total cost price stands for purchase total from suppliers.

   a. 6 months
   b. 5 months
   c. 4 months

Closing Assignment of Chapter 7

Here is a Profit & Loss statement of year 2 as well as balance sheets of years 1 and 2

P&L statement year 2		BALANCE SHEETS					
X $ 1.000			year 1	year 2		year 1	year 2
turnover	4 000	Buildings	2 000	1 950	Sharecapital	1 500	1 500
Costprice	2 320	Machinery	1 000	1 230	Retained earnings	228	450
MARGIN	1 680	Furniture	880	800	EQUITY	1 728	1 950
COSTS OF:		FIXED ASSETS	3 880	3 980	Mortgage	1 400	1 400
-personnel	300				Long term loan	700	700
-housing	160	Inventory	180	200	LONG TERM LIABILITIES	2 100	2 100
-sales	200	Accounts receivable	340	400			
-office	144	Cash	400	420	Creditors	400	450
-depreciation	200	CURRENT ASSETS	920	1 020	Current account	572	500
-transport	50				CURRENT LIABILITIES	972	950
OPERATING COSTS	1 054						
Operating Result	626						
Interest costs	330						
Net Profit Before Tax	296						
CORPORATE TAX 25%	74						
Net Profit After Tax	222 = 5.5%	TOTAL ASSETS	4 800	5 000	Total Capital	4 800	5 000

1.1 What was the solvency in year 1

　　a. equity 34%, liabilities 66%
　　b. equity 35% liabilities 65%
　　c. equity 36%, liabilities 64%

1.2 What was the quick ratio of year 2. Is liquidity of this company high, average or low?

　　a. 0,89 liquidity position is low
　　b. 0,86 liquidity position is low
　　b. 1.07 liquidity position is high

1.3 Does the "golden balance rule" apply in year 2

　　a. No. long term capital minus fixed assets is $ 70.000, which is far too low to finance the inventory OF $ 200.000
　　b. yes; current assets are much higher than current liabilities
　　c. yes; long term capital is much higher than the fixed assets

1.4 What was the return on Total Capital in year 2

　　a. 6.04%
　　b. 12.78%
　　c. 4.53%

1.5 What was the return on equity in year 2

　　a. 12,52%
　　b. 16.09%
　　b. 12.07%

1.6 Explain the leverage factor of year 2

　　a. Return on liabilities was 10,78% and return on total capital was 12.78%. There is a positive difference of 2%
　　b. Net profit after tax is 67% of the interest costs
　　c. Leverage comes from operating result and interest costs paid.

1.7 What was the turnover rate of the inventory in year 2

　　a. turnover: inventory = 20
　　b. cost price: inventory = 11.6
　　c. cost price total year: average inventory = 12.2

1.8 What was the payment term used by debtors in year 2

　　a. 1 month
　　b. 1.2 months
　　b. 1.5 months

1.9 How high was the working capital in year 2

    a. $ 70.000
    b. $ 65.000
    c. $ 72.00

Part 2
The Company and Its Business Activities

Chapter 8
Full Cost Price of a Single Product

Categories of costs and cost price calculation

As we learned from part 1, the start of a business, a company is making costs and expenses right after the start: costs of energy in the building, depreciation, financial costs, salaries etc. One of the goals of a company, obviously, is to earn enough to absorb all of such costs and more. Many of the costs a company incurs have a steady character. They are incurred and will have to be paid on preset times.

Costs of energy, financial interests and wages have to be paid month after month. They behave independently of the level of business activities. For that reason, such costs are called: **FIXED COSTS** or **INDIRECT COSTS**, while the costs immediately linked to the production activities are called **DIRECT COSTS**, like **raw material** used to make the final product and also **labour costs** of the people operating the equipment in the factory.

When we look at a manufacturing company a transformation from raw materials into finished products is the main activity of such a company. From various sources the company receives a number of raw materials which are transformed into finished products by means of people and equipment. The volume of these raw materials vary with the need of the company. This need in itself is based on the volume of finished products the company plans to make and sell. No company will order 1.000 exhaust pipes if it's planning shows that only 400 motorcars will be manufactured in the next 12 months. We can phrase this as follows: the costs of raw materials **VARY** with the planned output of the buyer of those raw materials. Hence, these costs are called VARIABLE **COSTS**

What we know, so far, is that a company plans and hopes, to sell a certain number of finished products to an unknown number of clients in a certain period. On that basis it plans the number of people to be employed and it buys adequate equipment. At the start of it's manufacturing process it orders certain quantities of raw materials.

It's goal (and it's hope) are that the planning was correct and that it will sell sufficient final products at such a **PRICE** that it will earn all of the fixed costs, all of the variable costs plus a nice profit, to secure it's future existence. (= **CONTINUITY**)

But how to correctly calculate a sales price? And how will the company be confident that it's market will accept the calculated sales price? This last question can be found in part 1 where we learned that every starting business can enlarge the chance of success by doing extensive research in the market it intends to serve: demand, competition and prevailing price levels etc.

The first question leads to an other question: **how to incorporate all of the costs of the company, both fixed costs and variable costs, into it's finished products?**

As for the variable costs it is not difficult to understand that if a single product in manufacture takes $ 4 of raw materials, then all other subsequently manufactured products require $ 4 of raw materials each. It is quite different when it comes to the fixed costs. Some of these fixed costs can be related to specific products, like the costs of equipment used to manufacture those products. But what about salaries of marketing personnel?

And yet, it is essential that a company can calculate the exact cost price in order to predict whether or not the products it manufactured will generate a profit when these are sold at a **pre-set sales price. Because that, precisely, is the function of calculating a cost price: find a firm as possible basis to calculate a realistic sales price.**

Another factor makes an exact calculation still more essential: what if changes occur in the fixed costs during the operating year. If additional employees were hired, if new equipment was purchased, if costs of energy changed, to what extent will it affect a pre-calculated cost price? If any and all of future changes in fixed costs could be predicted it would not be difficult. But practice shows very different situations. For that reason, the process of **budgeting** is extremely important to any business (see chapter 10). The whole organization is looking into the future together and translates the findings in a budget. It narrows the risk of strong deviations in the planning figures.

Let us focus on the calculation of a cost price by a simple example.

Bill won a sizeable price in a lottery. To celebrate this event, he would like to invite all of his 40 neighbours in his street to come to his large garden to eat pancakes. A colleague at work, Wilma, is a champion in baking excellent pancakes. She is willing to take on the job, provided she will have a profit of $ 0,50 for each pancake she will prepare. There is one restriction for Bill: he absolutely denies the cakes to be prepared in his own house because of the residual smell that will stay for weeks in every single room. Wilma has the same objection and so, they will have to find an other place. They find a small company with a kitchen of it's own in an adjacent street. They can use it at a modest fee of $ 200 during a Saturday. Wilma knows that it takes $ 0.80 of ingredients to prepare one pancake. Bill now knows almost all of the costs to calculate the cost price per pancake. Almost, because he does not know how many people in his street will accept the invitation, nor how many pancakes will be consumed by each of the visitors. He must make his best guess. He sits down with Wilma to calculate.

He reasons as follows: suppose you bake one pancake only. What would I have to pay to you to fill your $ 0.50 wish? He puts on paper:

Fixed costs	$200
variable costs/ ingredients	0,80
profit margin	0.50
	------------------
cost price of one pancake	$201.30

What if 20 out of the 40 neighbours will accept the invitation and each of them will eat one pancake only:

fixed costs $ 200: 20=	$10
variable costs (vc)=	0.80
profit margin=	0.50
	------------
cost price per pancake=	$11.30

Already at this point we notice that the **fixed cost component in the cost price goes down when production volume goes up.**

And what will be the cost price per pancake when all of the 40 neighbours accept the invitation and they will eat 100 pancakes in total: fixed costs $ 200: 100 = $ 2

variable costs (vc)   =0.80

```
                        profit margin      =0.50
                                           ------------
                        cost price per piece  =$3.30
```

From this example we learn a very important fact about full cost price calculation: the **portion of total fixed costs in a single product depends on the number of products manufactured.** The more products the less the relative portion of fixed costs per product. This means that **accurate calculation of a cost price depends on the accuracy of volume planning.** In a first production year this will be very difficult. But the longer the experience the higher the chance that a cost price will be calculated rather accurately.

Now, we know that the higher the volume manufactured the lower the portion of fixed costs per item. What if there are strong fluctuations in that volume? Would that force a company to re-calculate the cost price all the time? Most writers and scientists in business economics do not believe this is the right way to act. **The general acceptance is to base the fixed costs per item not on some planned volume, but on the volume the factory was equipped for. Let us call this the standard volume.**

In Business economics the following formula is used worldwide:

татаTOTAL FIXED COSTS

COSTPRICE = VARIABLE COSTS   +   ----------------------

STANDARD VOLUME

in short: TFC

$$CP = VC + \frac{TFC}{SV} \text{ is the FULL cost price per item manufactured.}$$

In the pancake example: cost price = $\frac{\$200}{100}$ + $ 0.80 + $ 0.50 = $ 3.30

The 100 in this example should be seen as the standard volume. A starting company did invest in manufacturing capacity. How did it define what the right capacity would have to be? The answer is that the capacity selected is based on the expectation of certain volumes in the future. The greater the insight in a market and what it can absorb of a product from all of the available manufacturers the easier it will be to decide on the capacity by the starting company.

Summarizing: **we know VOLUME now in terms of**

- **capacity selected to manufacture volume (A)**
- **the expected volume to be manufactured over a period of more years (B)**
- **the planned volume for the next twelve months (C)**
- **the volume realized by the manufacturer in practice (D)**

Of these four the only realistic volume is D. All the others are based on best guesses and are subjective. B is based on a decision by a company: it believes that this volume is a realistic one to cover all of the fixed costs. The advantage of this choice is that **frequent fluctuations in the cost price are avoided.** However, if at the end of a year the volume manufactured is much larger or much lower than B the initial cost price obviously was not correct. **The selected basis to carry all of the**

fixed costs proves to be larger or smaller at the end. Recalculating a cost price to repair the past is a useless exercise. In business economics a correction is made after the end of the year by **correcting the results of the period by a variance in the capacity really used versus the capacity originally planned = capacity variance.**

In this book we keep it simple. While three of the four volumes above are subjective, even A (if equipment is used longer than standard hours per day the capacity changes), the choice we make in this book is C, the volume planned for next year's manufacturing activities shows the shortest horizon and offers more certainty based on recent experience. So, instead of using STANDARD VOLUME **we will use the BUDGETED VOLUME (BV) to absorb all of the fixed costs.**

There is no clear reason to follow the fear of other authors that too many fluctuations in the cost price will occur. Experience evolves quickly in business leading to ever more realistic planning for a next period.

Variable costs for a **trading company** count from the moment this company receives a new shipment of products it intends to re-sell. For a manufacturing company **variable costs** only start from the moment the company sacrifices raw materials in its production process. As long as these raw materials rest in its warehouse, they constitute the current asset of inventory on the balance sheet.

An important difference between fixed costs and variable costs can be found when business slows down. The company can influence a part of it 's fixed costs but hardly it's variable costs. It can lay off some employees or sell off part of its equipment or economize on its marketing expenses. But it is not very likely that the company suddenly succeeds in lowering the purchase prices of its raw materials by a sizable percentage.

There are companies which use the direct relation between fixed costs and volume by manufacturing such a quantity that the cost price allows to make a profit on sales in its own market. When this market does not buy all of the products it manufactured it will sell these to a totally different market, where it tries **to break even** (see chapter 11). In every sizeable city we find "bargain stores". Many of these buy excess volumes at rock bottom prices. Consumers love these stores for their bargains. The stores are profitable.

This tactic of massive production to lower the cost price also explains why a company needs a very fair profit margin on each sale: if the planning of volume was not correct, or if an increase in fixed costs occurred during the operating year, then it still may absorb these costs and be profitable in the end.

Let us now explore what the meaning of cost price is for

1. a trading company,
2. for a manufacturer and
3. for a consulting agency.

1. COSTPRICE FOR A TRADING COMPANY.

We follow a trader, Jack, who sells at weekly markets in various places. He sells vacuum cleaner bags in which he is an expert. The weekly markets had been selected carefully and the local people had a choice of either buying in specialty stores or from his stand on the market square. Jack knows what the costs are for renting a stand, for a city license to sell to the public and he knows what the price per kilometre is for his van. He purchases the various brands of bags at a price of **$ 2.25** per bag. This is the variable cost **(VC)** per bag.

Like every other business Jack's goal is to yield a fair profit from the sales of his bags and he made a sales budget for every single market he visits.

His fixed costs are **$ 60** for the rent of a stand for one day and **$ 20** for the license. He also knows that the costs for the van are **$ 0.60** per kilometre. And he knows that on every market day he drives **50** kilometres in total. Finally, he pays **$ 800** per month for the lease of a warehouse where he stores all of his bags. He visits 3 different markets weekly. A month is assumed to have 4 weeks.

So, Jack incurs costs three times a week X 4 =12 times per month for: -renting a stand = 12 X $ 60, -a license = 12 X $ 20 -and he drives 50 kilometres X 12 X $ 0,60

We now can calculate his **total fixed costs, short: TFC** = (12 X $ 60) + (12 X $ 20) + (12 X 50 X $ 0.60) + 800 = $ 720 + $ 240 + $ 360 + $ 800 = **$ 2.120** per month.

These are the costs he incurs even if he does not sell a single bag!

Jack knows that on every day he was on the market he sold 102 bags per day at a sales price of **$7.50** each. That is 4 weeks X 3 markets X 102 bags = **1.224** bags per month. His cost price can be calculated now as follows:

cost price per bag =
$ 2.120 = **TFC**
+**VC of $ 2.25** > $ 1.73 + $ 2.25 = **$ 3.98**
1.224 = **PV** (planned volume)

For later use in this book the $ 1.73 will be called: **the fixed costs component** (FCC) in the cost price. In the calculation above we see three different amounts: the TFC in dollars, the PV in quantities and the VC in dollars. The TFC and the VC can be considered to be reasonably stable and constant. That does not necessarily apply to the PV figure. If weather conditions deteriorate for a longer period, Jack may not be able to match his historic sales volume. He runs the risk of losing money. If Jack reaches the PV during one month his yield would be: 1.224 X (7.50 - $ 3,98) = $ 4.308,48. Jack may operate a small business but, like the big corporations, Business Economics tells him to stay very alert: what are competitive threats? Can I lower my purchase price? Can I save on the fixed costs? Is there room for raising my sales price? Should I diversify by adding other products fitting the stall on the market place? These thoughts mean a constant factor for every business.

2. COSTPRICE FOR A CONSULTANCY COMPANY

People are not the same as equipment (although some are treated like that). And yet, they also have a cost price in their professional work if they are a consultant or have an other professional activity in servicing third parties at a price.

The difference with a manufacturing company is that there is no inventory, hardly ever equipment and that **an hour not worked needlessly is a lost hour**. Such a consulting company cannot store hours which can be delivered later.

We look at a consultancy agency in the field of tax assistance operating 4 professional tax advisors. Such a company also knows fixed costs for it's building, it's computers, furniture, clerks etc. We assume that the total fixed costs **(TFC)** are $ 380.000 and that each of the four consultants earn a total annual salary of $ 54.000. Working hours are 40 per week for 50 weeks per year.

What are the factors to take into consideration when calculating the correct cost price per consultant in order to set a **profitable fee** per hour of service to clients?

Most important is to plan the correct number of hours per year a consultant can use for services to clients. He can be absent because of illness, of meetings, seminars to be attended etc. We make the best possible estimate, like the company would do:

Max. number of hours available per year = 50 X 40 = 2.000
    estimated impediments> illness   80

office work	200		
seminars	90		
meetings	180	less =	550

available for work with clients = 1.450 hours

These are the hours **to be billed** to clients. The office pays an hourly salary per consultant of $ 54.000: 2.000 = $ 27. But that is not his cost price! **His hourly cost price** depends on the TFC. With four consultants rendering services to clients the total fixed costs will have to be absorbed in their individual cost price. So, each of the consultants will have to carry ¼ of the total fixed costs, $ 380.000: 4 = $ 95.000 plus his own salary costs which are his **variable costs of labour** (VC). We can now calculate the cost price per hour:

$$\text{cost price per consultant per hour: } \frac{\$380.000 \text{ (TFC)}}{4 \times 1.450 \text{ hours}} + \frac{\$54.000 \text{ (VC)}}{1.450 \text{ billable hours}} =$$

$$\frac{\$380.000}{5.800} = \$65,52 \text{ (\textbf{FCC}= fixed costs component)} + \$37,24 \text{ \textbf{VC}} > \textbf{CP} = \$102,76$$

Alternatively, we could have calculated the cost price for one consultant by having one consultant carry ¼ of the TFC: ($95.000: 1.450 hours) + his variable costs of ($54.000: 1.450) = CP > $ 65,52 + $ 37,24 = $ 102,76

Based on this cost price the company now can calculate the hourly fee to be billed to its clients. When it looks for a profit margin per hour of 45% the rate to be billed will have to be as follows: hourly fee = 100%, less cost price of $ 102,76 which must be 55% = profit margin (=45%). The fee therefore must be ($ 102,76 : 55) X 100 = $ 186,84 per hour. The margin in dollars will now be $ 186,84 - $ 102,76= $ 84,08 = 45% of the sales price of $ 186,84.

It is not difficult to see that the correctness of the cost price for a consultant hinge on the reality of the non-billable hours. If the number of hours of illness would be distinctly higher than estimated, then the number of billable hours would go down and the real cost price would be much higher. There are corporations which cover these contingencies by an (expensive) insurance.

For a consultancy like this Business Economics dictates thoughts like: is our fee competitive enough? A new company with lower fixed costs could offer distinctly lower fees even when their consultants work the same number of hours at equal salaries.

3. COSTPRICE FOR A MANUFACTURING COMPANY

In this chapter we will investigate the costing of a single product company. In the next chapter we will explore how cost prices best be calculated in a multiple product environment.

Where in the example of the trader his estimated sales volume played an important role to determine his cost price per piece, in a manufacturing company the **volume of production** plays a prominent role. That **volume must absorb all of the fixed costs.**

We visit a company making foamed plastic inlays for luxury pen sets. The TFC (total fixed costs) are **$ 480.000**. The VC per manufactured piece are **$ 0,32** and the planned volume for the full operating year is **8 million pieces**. The sales price is $0,50 each.

Let us calculate the **full cost price**:

$$\text{CP (cost price)} = \frac{\text{TFC}}{\text{PV}} + \text{VC} = \frac{\$480.000}{8.000.000} + \$0,32 = \$0,06 + \$0,32 = \$0,38 = \text{CP}$$

As long as this company meets a market willing to pay more than this CP it will make a profit. Based on their experience the sales price believed to be obtained in average is $0,50 and the profit margin then is $ 0,12 each, or ($0,12 : $0,50) X 100 = 24%

As long as this company will produce 8 million pieces its capacity is used optimally. If it produces more it will, obviously, make a more than **optimal use of its capacity.** If it produces distinctly less pieces there will be relatively much **idle capacity or underutilization. This plays a role when calculating annual profits (Ch. 11).** In both cases this company will watch the degree of utilization of its capacity very closely. An adjustment of the cost price may have to be made when a deviation of the planned utilization of capacity is starting to show a fairly **constant** annual fact.

In the case of the company above making foamed inlays we can ask the question what would happen to the cost price when in the course of the operating year a new truck was invested and essential equipment would have to be replaced for a total of $ 1 million. With a depreciation time of 10 years for both of these fixed assets the fixed costs of this company will go up from $ 480.000 to $ 580.000. When the same volume will be produced the fixed costs component in the cost price (FCC) would be $ 580.000 : 8 million pieces = $ 0,0725 per piece, which would be 1 and ¼ dollar cent per item higher than planned from the outset.

Here, Business Economics dictates different questions for this company to ask itself. With the same sales price the profit margin would go down to $ 0,50-(0,0725+0,32) = $ 0,1075/piece = 21.5%, a drop of 2.5%. Could we keep our customers happy by increasing our sales price to $ 0,52? Should we try to hold on to the same profit by increasing the production volume? Or would the solution be to strongly increase the sales volume? And, let us not forget to investigate how to economize in our fixed costs!

Customers will also have made their annual budgets based on the accepted purchase price of $ 0.50. So, a sudden price increase would not be appreciated at all! The best option for this company would be to increase the sales volume so that the profit margin per piece may drop while the annual profit in dollars would be affected hardly.

An other choice might be to increase the production volume to a level where the FCC (fixed costs component in the cost price) would be the same as in the original cost price: $ 0,06:

$$\frac{\text{TFC now } \$580.000}{\text{required volume}} = \$0.06 = \textbf{9.67 million pieces}: \frac{\$580.000}{9.67 \text{ million}} = \$0,06$$

By increasing the production volume from 8 million pieces to 9.67 million pieces the company succeeded in keeping the original cost price, but faces an over production of 1.670.000 pieces. If it's existing market is not large enough to absorb this excess quantity at the sales price of $ 0,50 the company may have to find a non familiar market and sell the quantity at a price which should be higher than the variable costs of $ 0,32 so as not to suffer a loss.

Business Economics also for a company like this will force to investigate if a market can be found to sell off the excess production volume without the risk of a boomerang. And also what it would take to lower fixed costs and to lower manufacturing costs by increasing the efficiency.

What we have seen in these calculations seems to require simple calculations. But it is much more than that. Careful and conservative work is needed to estimate possible volume sales, prices and costs. And all of these three are subject to unexpected changes, which require to make new and best possible economic decisions. The more stability of a national economy and the longer the experience of the company, the larger the chance to make planned cost prices a reality.

Exercises of Chapter 8

Full Cost Price

1. In a law firm five lawyers are employed earning $ 42.240 each per year. There also is a staff of 6 people. The annual fixed costs of the firm are $ 280.000. Work takes place 5 days of 8 hours each per week during 50 weeks per year. To each of the lawyers applies: 3 weeks off for holidays, 40 half days per year for meetings, 10 days off because of illness 8 half days per year for seminars and 200 hours per year for office work. Every lawyer invoices clients by the hour.

    1.1 What is the salary cost per lawyer per hour

    a. $ 22,12
    b. $ 21,12
    c. $ 20,12

    1.2 What are the variable costs per hour per lawyer
    a. $ 32
    b. $ 31
    c. $ 30

    1.3 Calculate the full cost price per lawyer per hour

    a. $ 69,77
    b. $ 67,72
    b. $ 65,77

2. Lee Wong obtained a license from San Diego city council to sell Asian spring rolls during the 50 weekly markets from his mobile kitchen. He has to drive 40 kilometres on each such day at the cost of $ 1,20 per kilometre. His gas consumption in his kitchen is 5 litres at $ 0,50 per litre and the cost of the license is $ 1.500 for 50 market days. His mobile kitchen cost $ 60.000 and will be written off in 5 years. The raw materials for a spring roll cost $ 0,60. He sells 200 spring rolls each week at $3.20.

    2.1 What is the total cost price per spring roll?

    a. $ 2.36
    b. $ 2,20
    c. $ 2.04

2.2 What is the profit margin in percentage of Lee's sales price

a. 31,25 %
b. 32,35 %
b. 33.45 %

3. At Watson's company desk lamps are assembled and sold to the trade. There are 4 workers under Mr. Watson as owner and they earn $ 12.000 per year. The rent of the building is $ 800 per month and the other operating costs are $ 15.000 per year. Raw materials are $ 3.30 per item. The PV (planned volume) is 20.000 pieces.

Calculate the full cost price of one desk lamp

a. $ 5,98
b. $ 6,23
c. $ 6,93

4. Derek works at an agricultural cooperative company which ploughs farmland at a rate per kilometre with its ploughing tractor. The equipment used costs $ 120.000 and is depreciated in 10 years, leaving a **residual sales value** of $ 10.000. The barn was an investment of $ 174.900, to be depreciated in thirty years. Derek's salary is $30.000 per year. Insurance costs are $ 120 monthly for the equipment. The fuel consumption of the tractor is 20 litres of $ 1.40 per 100 kilometres. Annual work covers 20.000 kilometres. Calculate the cost price per kilometre.

a. $ 2.86
b. $ 3.22
c. $ 2.69

5. In a photo lab for senior workers photo frames are constructed: 20.000 pieces of 20 X 25 centimetres and 20.000 of 30 X 40 centimetres. Ten seniors are employed earning $ 8.400 each per year. The rent for the lab is $ 1.500 per month. Every quarter the lab is cleaned for $ 1.000 costs. Material costs for the frames are $0,90 for the 20 X 25 and $ 1.20 for the 30 X 40 types. Each frame is packed in a little full colour carton box the costs of which are $ 240 per 3.000 pieces. The fixed costs apply to both dimensions equally. Calculate the cost price for each of the two dimensions.

a. 20 X 25 = $ 3.63 and 30 X 40 = $ 3.93
b. 20 X 25 = $ 3.48 and 30 X 40 = $ 3.74
b. 20 X 25 = $ 3.52 and 30 X 40 = $ 3.88

Closing Assignment of Chapter 8

Full Cost Price

1. In a small factory called Camping Life PVC pins are manufactured to fix tents to the ground. There are three lengths available and these are made in the following quantities: 700.000 pieces of 25 centimetres, 500.000 of 35 centimetres and 100.000 of 50 centimetres. Raw materials cost $ 0.08 for every 10 centimetre. The company owns the building of $ 416.400 to be depreciated in thirty years. There are two injection moulding machines of $ 175.000 each to be depreciated to a **residual value** of $ 20.000 each over a period of ten years. Twelve people are employed earning $ 23.760 each per year. There are two trucks of $ 150.000 each to be depreciated completely in five years. Office costs are $ 91.000 per year. Calculate the full cost price per type taking into account that each type absorbs a proportionate share of the TFC (total fixed costs) **disregarding** the difference in length.

Solution	a	b	c
25 centimetre	$ 0.55	$ 0.57	$ 0.52
35 centimetre	$ 0.60	$ 0.65	$ 0.65
50 centimetre	$ 0.75	$ 0.77	$ 0.72

2. A tax consultancy company employs four professional consultants. Each is earning $30.000 per year. On top of that the company pays 29.6% of the salary to a pension fund to take care of the time after retirement. The consultants work 50 weeks per year and 40 hours weekly on 5 days. They all attend tax seminars during 160 hours; their holidays total 5 weeks; meetings at the office cost 40 half days; average illness takes 6 days per consultant and office work takes 1 day per week.

   2.1 What are the total costs per consultant for the company per year

   a. $ 36.420
   b. $ 38.880
   b. $ 39.000

   2.2 In order to calculate an hourly fee to be charged to clients the company needs to know the hourly cost price per consultant. Calculate this cost price.

   a. $ 34.68
   b. $ 32.24
   c. 37.67

2.3 The company's goal is to earn 30% per billed hour. Suppose that the cost price per hour would be $ 56, then, what should be the hourly rate to be invoiced

   a. $ 80
   b. $ 78.82
   c. $ 78.57

2.4 If total fixed costs of this consultancy would be $ 185.400 and billable hours would be 1.030 and the costs per hour of each of the four consultants would be $ 32, then what would have been the full cost price per hour and what would have to be the hourly rate if the company wants a profit margin of 35%.

	Cost price/hour	rate per hour
a.	$ 72	$ 110.77
b.	$ 77	$ 118.46
c.	$ 74	$ 113.85

3. In a carpentry factory wooden garden chairs are made. The PV (planned volume) is 60.000 pieces. TFC (total fixed costs) for personnel, energy, depreciation etc are $900.000. Variable material costs per chair are $ 14. Calculate the full cost price.

   a. $ 31
   b. $ 32
   c. $ 29

Chapter 9
Full Cost Price of Multiple Manufactured Products and Services

(Activity Based Costing)

Whenever products are manufactured or services provided all of the costs of the company must be incorporated in those products and services first. If not, or if not done correctly and completely, there is no **sound basis to set a sales price.**

Earlier we learned that costs incurred consist of two categories: variable costs and fixed costs. For product variable costs consist of raw material, labour and, in many cases, also costs of packing. For a service **the true costs <u>directly</u> related to a consultant per billable hour are the variable costs.** (salary plus extras; annual hours less non billable hours)

We also saw how the fixed costs are incorporated in the cost price of a product or of an hour of service. The normal volume or the PV (planned volume) of a product and the planned volume in hours respectively are the carrier of all of the fixed costs. From the pancake example we saw that the portion of fixed costs per pancake decreases as more pancakes are prepared. Or: the higher the PV, the lower the portion of fixed costs (**Fixed costs component**, or FCC) per product. And in the servicing industry the same applies: the more hours to carry the fixed costs, the lower the portion of fixed costs per hour. Suppose a company would manufacture twice as much products compared to its PV. It would be significantly cheaper to make the products and the profit margin would grow correspondingly. However: **the market and the manufacturing capacity are the limit** for such quantities to be made. And no company makes progress if manufactured volumes pile up in the warehouses instead of being sold.

How should a company, manufacturing more than one product type, make sure that each of the product types absorb **their proportionate share of the fixed costs** in their respective cost prices?

The easiest way would be to establish a direct connection between a product type and parts of the fixed costs. If a company manufactures two product types but uses expensive equipment for only one of these types, it is obvious that the costs of that equipment should become part of that product type only. It has a **direct** link to one specific product. Hence the distinction between **DIRECT COSTS and INDIRECT COSTS**. This is an important aid to narrow down the approach to the calculation of cost prices.

But in most cases, such a close connection cannot be found. A more general approach must be used in such cases.

Another question is: which data linked to each of more product types should be leading in incorporating the fixed costs in their respective cost prices? The price of their raw materials? The volume planned for each of their manufacturing process? And which data are completely known to the company? Planned volume, in principle, is the best guess in most cases. Let us see which data a company knows before starting it's calculation of the cost prices of two products to be made for the next twelve months

1. **The total fixed costs** show a high degree of certainty. Not 100%, because unpredictable situations can occur, forcing to make additional investments in people and/or in equipment. Example: a nation by law forces all companies to bring down their noise to a certain level or to limit their emission of toxic gasses. A company can be forced to invest in equipment to obey the new law. The investment will lead to higher fixed costs.
2. **The variable costs** per product type also show a high degree of certainty.
3. **The PV for the year**. Of the three this shows the lowest certainty. However, to increase that certainty most companies rely on historic sales volumes and on intelligence from their markets in terms of growth or decline. A good example comes from the motor car industry. When economy in a country or in a continent slide into a recession the volume of cars purchased will go down substantially. **Relying on the volume of** manufactured **numbers in the past is no option any more.** And yet, the motor car manufacturer has no choice than to make a calculated guess about future demand. Not only to make a good manufacturing schedule, but also to determine where costs can be and must be cut in order to contain losses to a minimum.

Let us investigate how to calculate the cost prices of two products.

We make the guess that 10.000 pieces of product A with $ 8 in variable costs and 6.000 pieces of B with $ 20 in variable costs are planned to be made during the year. And the fixed costs are $ 96.000

From these data we could divide the **fixed costs** over the two products in proportion to their respective variable costs: 8 : 20, or 2 : 5. But in that case we would miss out on the respective volumes which should be the carriers for the TFC.

Should we, then, look at the volumes to be made only ? That would be 10/16 or 5/8 and 6/16, or 3/8. The danger would be that in such choice the sales price of one of the products would be disproportionately higher than the other. Product A would carry 5/8 of $ 96.000 = $ 60.000 and product B $ 36.000. The FCC for A would then be $60.000 : 10.000 = $ 6.00 and the FCC for B would be $ 36.000 : 6.000 = $ 6,0. Their full cost prices would then be: $ 6 + $ 8 = **$ 14** for product A and $ 6 + $ 20 = **$ 26** for product B. The cost price of one of these would be too low, the other would be too high.

The optimal choice to be made is to use **ALL OF THE KNOWN DATA: both volumes and variable costs as the basis** for allocating the fixed costs to the two products. In other words: we will be comparing **TOTAL VARIABLE COSTS** with **TFC**. Let us work this out and let us assume TFC (total fixed costs) will be $ 96.000 again; of product A 10.000 pieces of production are planned at $ 8 in variable costs and of product B 6.000 are planned at variable costs of $ 20.

First step: the total of variable costs are: product A 10.000 X $ 8 = $ 80.000 and B 6.000 X $ 20 = $120.000, totalling $ 200.000. This latter figure now forms the basis for allocating the fixed costs. It works as follows in

step two: we calculate how much % TFC is of the total of variable costs. ($ 96.000 : $200.000) X 100 = **48%**.

Step three is to increase the **variable costs per piece per product** type by 48%. A: $8 + 48% = **$11.84**. B: $ 20 + 48% = **$ 29,60. We call this 48% the "cost plus percentage" or "cost plus method"**.

Step four serves to check if all of the costs were absorbed in that way by both of the product types: Total fixed costs are

		$96.000
	Variable costs	200.000

	Total costs	$296.000
A = 10.000 X **$ 11.84**	$118.400	

B = 6.000 X $ **29.60**   177.600   296.000

Remember: at the start, above, A found a full cost price of $ 14 and B $ 26!

We have confirmed that all of the costs are now allocated to the two product types in proportion to their total variable costs. This is the **most general way** to apply the **COST-PLUS METHOD**. We could also us the term: **SURCHARGE METHOD**. In both cases a company tries to establish how much percentage **total indirect costs** are of total variable costs of the PV (planned volume) for **allocating these indirect costs to each of the products made as accurately as possible**.

As said earlier a company can increase the accuracy of this cost-plus method if it can **break down all of the indirect costs** of the company into specific categories and if it knows which category of such costs applies more to one than to both products to be manufactured. This is a logical refinement. It would not make sense when expensive equipment with it's costs of energy, maintenance and depreciation would be allocated 50/50 to two products if this equipment is used exclusively for only one of these products.

For the purpose of examining how this works we look at a company having been manufacturing coffins for the past 80 years but saw it's markets stagnate because of increased health and longer life. Ten years ago it decided to fill the gap by manufacturing wooden chairs for outdoor use as a second product line.

Wood Comfort Inc. plans to manufacture 120.000 coffins and 300.000 wooden outdoor chairs for the next twelve months. Variable costs for raw material and labour per coffin: $ 40, and for chairs: $ 50. The company had made a fair estimate of the proportion in which indirect costs were to be allocated to the two product groups:

	coffins			chairs	
Depreciation of equipment	$140 000	40%	=$56 000	60% =	$84 000
Personnel	$200 000	30%	=60 000	70% =	140 000
Other indirect costs	$1 000 000	50%	=500 000	50% =	500 000
Total of **INDIRECT COSTS**	$1 340 000		=$ 616 000		+$724 000

Total variable costs	120.000 X $ 40	=	**$4.800.000**
	300.000 X $ 50	=	**$15.000.000**
TOTAL COSTS:	$1.340.000 + $19.800.000	=	**$21.140.000**

We now can express the **indirect costs** in a percentage of each of the two products' respective variable costs: indirect costs of $ 616.000 is 12.83% of total variable costs of the coffins of $ 4.800.000; indirect costs of $ 724.000 of the chairs is 4.83% % of $15.000.000

This will work out as follows:

	Coffins	**Chairs**
Variable costs	$ 4 800 000	$15 000 000
Cost plus% 12.83% =	615 840	4.83% =-724 500
	$5 415 840	$15 724 500

Cost price of a coffin will be $ 40 + 12.83% = $45.13 = total $5.415.840
Cost price of a chair will be $ 50 + 4.83% = $52.42 = total $15.724.500

Check proves a small difference only to the total costs above: **$ 21.140.340**

We safely can say that ALL of the fixed and ALL of the variable costs have been allocated properly to the coffins and the chairs. By working with percentages tiny deviations can occur.

We have seen how a fairly accurate cost price can be calculated for more than one product in a general or in a more precise way of allocating fixed costs to either product. The proper ingredients are: the PV (planned volume) of both products, their correct variable costs and the fixed costs, split in categories, which are roughly split in portions for either product as best as possible. And if such a split is not possible, the cost plus percentage will have to be equal for both products.

The cost plus method can be refined even further. From the basic calculation method we know that a manufacturing company makes fixed costs, most of which are indirect costs and it makes variable costs, which are direct costs. The indirect costs can be expressed in a cost plus percentage of the total of variable costs of more than one product.

When we look at these **variable = direct costs** it seems logical that these consist not only of material, but of **material plus labour**. These two are **DIRECT MATERIAL COSTS** and **DIRECT LABOUR COSTS**. It is not illogical that many companies make **INDIRECT material costs** as well. We can imagine that handling of incoming raw material, storing and working it by equipment are indirectly connected to the variable material costs of a product. And when we could allocate the costs of these actions to the product made from these raw materials we would have succeeded in **fine tuning** these indirect costs. The same applies to direct labour costs: also here we can imagine that people in the purchase department and in the production planning could be linked in a more refined way to the direct labour costs of each of the products to be made.

Example: we take two products made of oak: cabinets and garden chairs. The selection of oak for cabinets by quality managers is more critical than that for garden chairs. Also, in storing oak for cabinets climate control and careful handling by warehouse management are more critical than they are for garden furniture. When we understand this then the question can be raised: is it accurate enough to allocate all of the indirect costs in equal cost plus percentages to the two so different products? The answer is NO. **If we can fine tune such costs than we should fine tune them.** And the same applies to costs of indirect personnel = not directly involved in the production process. We can think of people in the purchase department who will have to place many more purchase orders for garden furniture in spring and summer than they have to place in autumn and winter. Sloppy purchase planning can lead to many sales orders missed. We can imagine also that making a cabinet is a more critical process than that for making garden furniture and that in the latter less highly qualified people are involved compared to the cabinet making process.

Let us now take the manufacturer of cabinets and garden chairs. We use different figures, however.

The planned volume for cabinets is 300.000 for the next twelve months and 600.000 for the garden chairs. Te direct costs are for

Volume	300 000 cabinets	600 000 garden chairs
Costs of raw materials	X $ 80 = $ 24 mln	X $ 24 = $ 14.4 mln
Labour costs	X $ 42 = $ 12.6 mln	X $ 28 = $ 16.8 mln

TOTAL DIRECT COSTS are raw material $ 24.000.000 + 14.400.000 = $38.400.000
Labour costs   - 12.600.000 + 16.800.000   = $29.400.000

TOTAL DIRECT COSTS $ 36.600.000 + $ 31.200.000   = $67.800.000

Indirect Costs

Indirect material costs	cabinets	garden chairs
Depreciation ware house	$48 000	
to be allocated to direct material costs	70%	30%
depreciation main building	$120 000	
to be allocated to direct material costs	60%	40%
energy and depreciation of equipment	$280 000	
to be allocated to direct material costs	32%	68%
Indirect personnel production	$148 000	
to be allocated to direct labour costs	44%	56%
indirect personnel planning and quality $ 92 000	64%	36%
Other indirect costs $600 000	50%	50%
Total indirect costs are	$1 288 000 to be allocated to all direct costs	

The allocation percentages, obviously, are based on careful splitting cost creating actions between the cabinets and the garden chairs. Computerized systems facilitate such fine tuning. We now know two kinds of direct costs and we know their total.

It would be easy now to allocate the indirect material costs and the **indirect costs of labour** to the two products proportionately and divide the total of direct and indirect costs by the respective volumes. We then would miss out on the cost-plus percentages, which tell more than just large figures. So we will apply percentages to the variable costs as follows:

	cabinets	garden chairs
Direct material costs of $38 400 000	$24 000 000	$14 400 000
Indirect material costs		
$ 48 000 depreciation 70/30=	$33 600	$14 400
$ 120 000 depreciation 60/40=	72 000	48 000
$ 280 000 energy etc 32/68=	89.600	190.400
total indirect material costs	$195.200	$252.800
in % of total direct material costs:	0.8133%	1.76%
Direct costs of labour $ 29 400=	$12 600 000	$16 800 000
Indirect labour costs		
$148 000 personnel 44/56 =	$65 120	$82 880
$92 000 personnel 64/36 =	58 880	33 120
total indirect costs of labour	$124 000	$116 000
in % of total direct labour costs	0.984%	0.69%
$ 600 000 other indirect in 50/50	$300 000	$300 000
in % of total variable costs	0.82%	0.962%

Now, the cost-plus method works in the way we explained earlier: indirect material costs and indirect labour costs are allocated to the two products by expressing these costs in a percentage of the variable material costs and of the variable labour costs per product.

	Cabinets	Chairs
Direct material costs per piece	$80	$24
Cost plus percentage	0.8133%=-0.65	1.76 %-0.42
total material costs per piece	**$80.65**	**$24.42**
direct labour costs per piece	$42.00	$28.00
cost plus percentage	0.984 %-0.41	0.69 -0.19
total labour costs per piece	**$42.41**	**$28.19**
provisional cost price per piece	$123.06	$52.61
cost plus % other indirect costs	0.82%-1.01	0.962%-0.51
TOTAL COST PRICE PER PIECE	**$124.07**	**$53.12**

Finally, we always must check if total annual costs were allocated properly.

Total cost prices   Cabinets   Chairs   **Total**
300.000 X $ 124,07 $ **37.221.000**   600.000 X $ 53,21 $ **31.926.000** = **$ 69.147.000**
Total direct costs were $67.800.000
Total indirect material costs were $448.000
Total indirect labour costs were $240.000
Other indirect costs were $600.000

total costs $69.093.000

A slight difference occurs when applying percentages. But we can safely say that all of the costs were allocated to the two products properly.

The advantage of percentages is the possibility to compare and to analyse. One of the questions could be: why is the cost-plus percentage for indirect material more than two times higher for chairs than for cabinets? This may give a company reason to reconsider the flow, the destination and the proper costs of materials. The cost price of a chair might create a sales price which discourages a number of clients to buy. Every selected method deserves to be checked and re-checked.

Cost plus method to calculate the cost price of services

Earlier we saw that not only products have a cost price. Also, professional people have a cost price from which an hourly billable rate can be established. The office from where these professionals operate will know fixed costs just like manufacturing companies do. And depending on the accuracy of breaking down these fixed costs into categories and allocating these proportionately to the different groups of professionals the cost price per professional can be calculated in a more precise manner. Let us examine an example.

ICT Galore Inc. renders two types of services to its's clients: developing tailor made software by designers and making applications operative by assistants. There are three designers, earning $ 60.000 each per year and five assistants earning $ 32.400 each per year. The total fixed costs of ICT Galore: $ 900.000. Total billable hours are 1.200 out of 2.000 for designers and 1.800 out of 2.000 for assistants. We now can calculate their respective cost price per hour.

	Designer	**assistant**	**total**
Total variable costs per year	$ 60.000	$ 32.400	
VC/hr $ 60.000: 1.200 hours	- 50 at 1.800 hrs.-	18	
Total variable costs are	X 3 = $ 180.000 +	X 5 = $ 162.000 =	**$ 342.000**

(TFC: TVC) X 100 = ($ 900.000: $ 342.000) X 100 = 263.158% = cost plus %.
Cost price per type $ 50 + 263.158% =   **$ 181.58** $ 18+263.158%=**$ 65.37**
Check: Total costs per year are $ 900.000 + $ 342.000 =   **$ 1.242.000**
Cost price all designers 3 X 1.200 X $ 181.58 = $ 653.688
Cost price all assistants 5 X 1.800 X $ 65.37 = - 588.330
                                                                                       $ 1.242.018

As we can see the total costs were allocated accurately to the two categories of people.

Let us explore what the respective cost prices would be if ICT Galore could specify and allocate the indirect costs fairly accurately. These were $ 900.000 and we assume that their breakdown looks as follows:

	Assistants	**Designers**	**Depreciations**
	$120.000 in 40/60 relation	$48.000	$72.000
Office costs	$480.000 in 35/65 relation	168.000	312.000
Other fixed costs	$300.000 in 30/70 relation	90.000	210.000
	-------------	-------------	-------------
total	$900.000	$306.000	$594.000

These allocated totals can now be expressed in a percentage of total variable costs of the two groups. ($ 306.000: $ 180.000) X 100   = 170%
           ($ 594.000: $ 162.000) X 100   = 366.67%

We now apply these cost-plus percentage to the individual variable costs:

Designers $ 50 + 170%	= **$ 135**	X 3 X 1.200	is per year	$486.000
Assistants $ 18 + 366.67 %	= **$ 84**	X 5 X 1.800	is per year	$756.000

Total   **$1.242.000**

As the total costs per year for ICT Galore were $ 1.242.000 we see that these have been completely covered by the respective cost prices. The difference in the hourly cost prices between this more specified example compared to the earlier example is, however, significant: the designer's cost price per hour now is **$ 135 instead of $181.58** and the cost price for an assistant now is **$ 84 instead of $ 65.37**. From the point of view of competitive pricing in the market it makes a great difference for a client who should at least pay $ 280 per hour for a designer in the earlier calculation compared to $208 in this last calculation at a profit margin of 35% for ICT Galore. The conclusion for any company making more than one product or employing two kinds of professionals is that it makes very good **sense to break down the total fixed costs into categories** and then try to express these categories as accurately as possible in **cost plus percentages** of the total variable costs of either product or of either professional.

Exercises of Chapter 9

Cost Prices for Multiple Products And Services

1. Mary bought herself a knitting machine and sells socks and knitted baby shirts. The socks contain wool for $ 2 per pair, de shirts wool for $ 5. Her expectations for the next twelve months are to sell 2.000 pairs of socks and 1.000 shirts. The machine had cost her $ 3.000 and will be depreciated in five years with no residual value. Annual costs of electricity are $ 300.

    1.1 What are the total variable costs of the two products together

    a. $ 8.000
    b. $ 9.000
    c. $ 10.500

    1.2 What is the cost price for the socks using the cost plus method

    a. $ 2.20
    b. $ 3.10
    b. $ 2.40

    1.3 What is the cost price for the baby shirts

    a. $ 5.00
    b. $ 5.25
    c. $ 5.50

2. Gary is a trader at local weekly markets selling jeans which he buys at $ 35 each and sweat shirts with a purchase price of $ 18. The rent and the license cost him $ 70 per week. His travelling costs 60 kilometres at $ 1.80 per kilometre per market day. He stores his products in a warehouse the rent of which is $ 600 for every 4 weeks period. He visits the market place fifty times a year. Like last year he believes to sell 3.000 jeans and 1.800 sweatshirts.

    2.1 Calculate the cost-plus percentage and the cost price for jeans. Use three decimals behind the comma.

    a. Cost plus percentage is 10.3%. Cost price for jeans is $ 35 X 110.3% = $ 38.60
    b. Cost plus percentage is 12.6%. Cost price for jeans is $ 35 X 112.6% = $ 39.41
    c. Cost plus percentage is 11.936%. Cost price jeans is $ 35X111.936% = $ 39.18

2.2 Calculate the cost price for the sweat shirts using the cost-plus percentage

a. Cost plus percentage is 10.3%. $ 18 + 10.3% = $ 19.85
b. Cost plus percentage is 11.936%. $ 18 + 11.936% = $ 20.15
b. Cost plus percentage is 12.6%. $ 18 + 12.6% = $ 20.27

2.3 Demonstrate that the total of annual cost prices covers both the variable and all of the indirect costs. A rounding variation of $ 300 is allowed.

a. Total of cost prices is (3.000 X $ 38.60) + (1.800 X $ 20.27) = $152.286
   Total variable costs jeans is 3.000 X $ 35.00   =$105.000
   Total variable costs of shirts 1.800 X $ 18.00   =-36.400
   Booth and license is 50 X 70   =-3.500
   Travelling is 50 X 60 X $ 1.80   =-5.400
   Warehouse rent is 12 X $ 600   =-7.200 $157.500

b. Total cost prices jeans 3.000 X $ 38.60   =$115.800
   Total cost prices shirts 1.800 X $ 19.85   =35.730, totals $ 151.530
   Total indirect $15.900
   Total variable costs   137.400 totals $ 153.300

c. Total cost prices 3.000 X $ 39.18 + 1.800 X $ 20.15   =$153.780
   total variable costs 3.000X$35 + 1.800X$18   =$137.400
   total indirect costs: $ 3.500 + $ 5.400 + $ 7.500   16.400
   totals   =$153.800

3. At a tax consultancy company four tax specialists are employed to submit tailor made advice to corporate clients. Also, six tax declaration assistants are employed supporting small retail and private clients to fill out their tax declarations correctly. The specialists earn $ 70.000, the assistants $ 40.000 per year. The billable hours of a specialist are 1.400 hours and of the assistants 1.600 hours. Total indirect costs of the company are $600.000 of which following elements relate to:

	specialists	assistants
ICT external support costs	$120.000	$72.000
Other personnel	160.000	148.000
Other fixed costs	30.000	70.000
TOTAL	$310.000	$290.000

3.1 Calculate the cost price per hour for a specialist with the cost-plus method.

a. $ 110.46
b. $ 105.36
c. $ 102.26

Calculate the cost price per hour for an assistant using the cost-plus method.

a. $ 55.21
b. $ 52.48
b. $ 46.80

3.2 Demonstrate that all of the costs of the company have been incorporated in the respective cost prices correctly. (Ignore minor rounding variation)

a. 4 X 1.400 X $ 102.26 = $ 572.656 + 6 X 1.600 X $ 52.21 = $ 501.216, totalling $1.073.872. Total salaries + total indirect costs = $ 1.120.000.

b. 4 X 1.400 X $ 105.36 = $ 590.016 + 6 X 1.600 X $ 55.21 = $ 530.0016, totalling $1.120.032. Total salaries + total indirect costs: $ 70.000 X 4 = $ 280.000 + 6 X $40.000 = $ 240.000 + indirect costs of $ 600.000 = 1.120.000.

c. 4 X 1.400 X 110.46 = $ 618.576 + 6 X 1.600 X $ 46.80 = $ 449.280, totalling $1.067.856. Total indirect plus total salaries is $ 1.120.000

4. In a knitting workshop woollen berets and woollen scarves are made on **four** large knitting machines. The berets contain wool at $ 3 each plus $ 2 for direct labour costs, the scarves have wool at $ 4 each plus $ 1.50 for direct labour costs. Depreciation of the machines is $ 6.000 each per year, 1/3 of which to be allocated to the material costs of the scarves and 2/3 to those of the berets. Indirect labour costs are $ 120.000, 60% of which to be allocated to the direct labour costs of the scarves, 40% to those of the berets. The budget shows that 30.000 berets and 40.000 scarves will be made during next twelve months. What is the cost price for one beret and one scarf?

a. berets $ 7.20, scarves $ 6.98
b. berets $ 7.28, scarves $ 6.84
c. berets $ 7.35, scarves $ 6.73

5. In a wood processing factory wooden pallets and wooden bird feeders are made. Pallets contain $ 4.50 of wood material and bird feeders $ 2.40. Budgeted volumes are: pallets 100.000 pieces, bird feeders 200.000. Indirect material costs are $ 380.000, 25% of which to be allocated to the pallets, 75% to those of the bird feeders. Calculate the total of material costs of the two products

a. Pallets $ 5.40, bird feeders $ 3.95
b. pallets $ 5.45, bird feeders $ 3.83
c. pallets $ 5.28, bird feeders $ 3.20

6. In the NIRVANA wellness centre eight cosmeticians are employed earning $ 68.880 each per year. There are four assistants available earning $ 33.300 each per year. The cosmeticians have 1.640 billable hours the assistants 1.800 hours. Indirect costs of labour are $ 273.696 covering administration and management. 65% of this amount is to be allocated to the cosmeticians, 35% to the assistants.

7. Calculate the hourly cost price per type of employee and demonstrate that all of the costs were absorbed by the cost prices.

    a. cosmeticians $ 55.56, assistants $ 31.81
    b. cosmeticians $ 57.60, assistants $ 34.76
    b. cosmeticians $ 60.40, assistants $ 36.54

Closing Assignment of Chapter 9

Cost Prices of Multiple Products and Services

1. In a wood processing company, The Singing Saw both climbing racks and ladders are manufactured. The racks require $ 58 of materials and the ladders have materials for $72. Indirect costs of The Singing Saw are $ 380.000. The planned volumes are 1.200 racks and 3.000 ladders.

   1.1 Calculate the cost price for the climbing racks with the cost-plus percentage

   a. $ 130
   b. $ 133.55
   b. 135.17

   1.2 Calculate the cost price for the ladders using the cost-plus percentage

   a. $ 172.22
   b. $ 167.80
   c. $ 170.80

2. The Isolation technique Inc. manufactures metal jugs and metal coffee tumblers for consumers. Variable costs of the jugs are $ 9.40 and of the tumblers $ 11.60. The indirect costs of Isolation technique are specified and have a relation to the two products as follows:

		jugs	tumblers
costs of management	$120 000	40%	60%
costs of marketing	$260 000	70 %	30%
office costs	$90 000	20 %	80%
personnel	$430 000	45%	55%
depreciation	$110 000	30%	70%
financial costs	$172 000	50%	50%

   The PV of the products is: jugs 150.000 and tumblers 230.000 pieces.

   2.1 Calculate the cost price of one jug with the cost-plus percentage

   a. $ 14.52
   b. $ 13.14
   b. $ 13.88

2.2 Calculate the cost price of one tumbler with the cost-plus percentage

a. $ 14.52
b. $ 14.48
c. $ 14.30

2.3 Demonstrate that all of the costs were allocated to both products completely.

a. Total costs are **$ 5.260.000**. (indirect $ 1.182.000 + variable costs jugs 150.000 X $ 9.40 = $1.410.000+ variable costs tumblers 230.000 X $ 11.60 = $2.668.000). Cost price X volume is 150.000 X $13.14 plus 230.000 X $ 14.30 = $ 1.971.000 + $ 3.289.000 = **$ 5.260.000**
b. Total costs are $ 5.260.000. 150.000 jugs at $ 13.88 plus 230.000 tumblers at $14.48 = $ 5.410.000
c. Total costs are $ 5.260.000. 150.000 jugs at $ 14.52 plus 230.000 tumblers at $14.52 = $ 5.217.600

3. At a large wellness centre in the hills, called Nirvana, 30 people are busy daily for improving the wellness of their clients. There are four diet specialists earning $ 4.000 per month and twelve masseuses, earning $ 2.800 per month. Both salaries are increased by 8% of a pension premium. Total indirect costs of Nirvana are $ 1.800.000. Both specialists and masseuses work 1.950 hours per year. Billable hours are 1.500 for the diet specialists and 1.768 hours for the masseuses.

3.1 What is the hourly cost for the company of a diet specialist and of a masseuse

a. specialist $ 27.00, masseuse $ 24.00
b. specialist $ 26.85, masseuse $ 18.61
b. specialist $ 25.90, masseuse $ 18.20

3.2 What are the total variable costs of the specialists and the masseuses

a. $ 642.816
b. $ 648.422
c. $ 644.678

3.3 Calculate the cost price of a specialist using the cost-plus method

a. $ 130.28
b. $ 125.90
b. $ 131.33

3.4 Nirvana succeeded in allocating all of the indirect costs to the diet specialists and to the masseuses as follows

	spec./mass		specialists	masseuses
Management costs	$200 000 in	40/60	$80 000	$120 000
Personnel	$680 000 in	70/30	476 000	204 000
Cosmetic products	$320 000 in	20/80	64 000	256 000
Energy and cleaning costs	$120 000 in	30/70	36 000	84 000
Marketing expenses	$340 000 in	65/35	221 000	119 000
Depreciation	$140 000 in	50/50	70 000	70 000
	$1 800 000=		$947 000	+$853 000

Calculate the cost price per hour per specialist and per masseuse

a. specialist $ 202.58, masseuse $ 63.54
b. specialist $ 192.39, masseuse $ 60.72
c. specialist $ 198.76, masseuse $ 62.48

3.5 Nirvana intends to make profit margins on the hours billed by specialists of 35% and billed by masseuses of 30%. Assume that hourly cost prices are $ 190 and $ 60 respectively. What will be billed by Nirvana for the two categories.

a. Specialists will cost consumers $ 291.56/hour, masseuses $ 84.06
b. Specialists will cost consumers $ 290.80/hour, masseuses $ 84,28
b. Specialists will cost consumers $ 292.31/hour, masseuses $ 85.71

Chapter 10
Budgeting Process and Analysis of Variances

Nobody with an income has a duty to make a periodic budget. But every sane individual with an income will not start a holiday trip without any kind of preparation: where would we like to go? When could we go there? Is there accommodation for us all? What way of transportation will we choose? Will there be activities for all of us? What will all what we want cost us in the end and can we really afford this? We think this is absolutely a sane preparation for families planning a trip together. In many cases this preparation is finalized by some kind of a budget, telling the family what it can and cannot afford.

This is not different from commercial companies, nor from heads of state. A company asks itself periodically: "where are we now and where do we want to go"? Because profit, necessary to ensure continuity, plays a dominant role, it is essential that a company takes time to answer numerous questions very carefully. The slogan for a company could be phrased as follows: **"we make goals and our mission is to reach these goals with as little sacrifice as possible" That is economic thinking.**

Also the owner of a small business will know a budgeting process and will ask himself questions like "what was my turn over last year", what are the changes that will or could affect my market? Is the market growing, stagnant or even declining? And what should I do to go with the flow? He looks at his range of products asking himself if he should abandon slow moving items and which alternative items would fit his range. He looks at income and expenses and what kind of changes lay ahead. **His drive is to minimize economic insecurity as much as he can.**

The difference between a small private business and a large company can be found in the time needed to come up with an ocean of questions and answers. The small business can go through this process in several weeks. And **most of these constantly are thinking about the future and how to survive.** The larger a company the more managers will have to be consulted and, hence, the more time it will take. And this requires a strict scenario and time frame.

Let us look at a company employing five hundred people and having many departments:

BOARD OF DIRECTORS

Marketing	purchase	production	research	administration	Personnel dept.
Market research	Raw materials	Planning	Research raw materials	Bookkeeping	Planning
Product management	Final products	Production line 1	Development of final products	Payroll administration	Social security
Sales management	Packaging materials	Production line 2	Testing lab.	accountancy	Safety regulations
Area managers	planning	Production line 3	Quality Control		Hiring
Sales force		Technical support	Claim handling		Update of individual files
		Inventory Management			
		Quality Control planning			

It would be very strange when a general manager would ask the production how large the production volume for next year will be. The production manager would answer that his production volume will depend on how much sales there will be. The same strange question to the purchasing manager could sound like: how much volume do you think to buy next year? The answer would be that this would depend on the need of the production department entirely. We could go on, but the message behind this is: budgeting is a planning process which has a **logical beginning and a logical end**. It will be obvious that the beginning will be in the sales department. If this department would not consider the chances and risks for sales very carefully it would cause a problem, ranging from annoyance to complete disaster.

The advantage larger companies have is that they know a management team where all the heads of all of the departments are members. This team is the heart of the company; all of the leads in the planning process come together in this team at the end. These managers inspire their respective departments to fill out their estimation folders; he reads them, he checks them with historic figures and data; he sits together with his people to ask numerous critical questions to be informed properly. His one goal is to picture the one year's future of his department. That picture, once complete, will be shared with his fellow managers in the management team. The team's goal is to present a next year's budget with the highest possible degree of realism. So much will depend on this realism: if sales will start the year with a monthly increase of 15% unexpectedly then chaos and heated discussions will take place: purchase department did not fill the warehouse in time, production could not fill the need of the sales department and, what is worse, the market will complain that the company is not reliable enough. **So, very careful budgeting is crucial!**

Let us demonstrate the relativity of the foregoing immediately: if a chemical company budgeted to produce 800.000 tons of oil based raw materials and India and China suddenly would increase their purchase of crude oil by thirty percent then the rest of the world will have a shortage for six to eight months. The chemical company will hear that supply of raw material will be lower because of unforeseen circumstances. **The solidity of a budget depends on uninterrupted flows of needed products over the world.**

Before going into the process of budgeting it is good to know the difference between **"estimates" and "budgets"**. Budgets always start by estimations. The latter are always open for discussions and amendments. The responsibility of managers is to discuss the estimates with their people. They will always have questions like: "did you take factor A or B into consideration?" 'Can you explain why your estimate is so much different from historic figures?" "Did you take into account the new competitive activities we saw in the market lately?" Etc.

When all of the estimations have been put on paper by all of the departments and have been adjusted many times they will become final, a budget, by the approval of the board of directors, or **the management team**. This approval means that the budget is **AN ASSIGNMENT, AN ORDER, AUTHORIZING THE FUNDS AND EXPENDITURES ASKED.**

As said earlier it is the sales department where the budgeting process starts upon the signal of the management team. When this department intimately knows what is going on in it' s market, among large clients, among their competitors and in terms of innovations and, last but not least, about the historic trends of turnover then we may say that it's estimations will be very reliable. This sales department will trigger the start of the process by consulting the production department about the required production output if the sale estimates would become budget. The production department will consult among it' s people the required capacity in terms of people and equipment. If the number of people will have to change it will consult the personnel department about the hiring or firing within a certain time frame. The production manager will present the management team a survey of the required investments in the production department if it is to meet the needs of the sales department. The sales department will also consult it 's colleagues in the development centre about the desired innovations within a given time frame. This development department will ventilate it' s knowledge about new raw materials and new final products during the year among the colleagues in the management team.

Many companies have a habit of so called **"rolling forecasts"**. The sales department uses realized sales to plot future sales in a continuous sales plan. The merit of such rolling forecast is that when the budgeting process starts the sales department has the most recent sales experience already extrapolated in a sales estimate for always twelve months. This system reduces the time the department needs to produce it's best estimates for next year.

Because all of the departments are involved in the process and because these departments need sufficient time to consult the other departments frequently it will be clear that the total process is time consuming. In most of the larger companies, therefore, the budgeting process starts before June of every year. The disadvantage of this is that many external changes to be expected on a national scale e.g. tax rates, import duties to be decided by national governments, and salaries and wage levels for the next year still are unknown when a company starts it' s process of budgeting. Here best estimates and extrapolations, are mostly done at top level by consulting the authorities, the unions and employers' platforms and the outcome will be communicated to the various departments within the company.

Finally: a budget should be as accurate and detailed and in line with future reality as humanly possible. The **details will enable the company to analyse variances** that occur afterwards and learn lessons from it. It intends to avoid such variances in future by improved management and control. But also: the more detailed a budget is, the larger the chance of variances. But despite this, budgeting is an unavoidable necessity for any and all of the larger companies. And the value of preparing it carefully will prove to be greater than the disadvantages.

ANALYSING VARIANCES

"Treasure the measure" is a saying with a meaning. Every company can benefit from analysing discovered variances, because it allows for better control and improved results. Also, since a budget is a command, accepting any result whatsoever is no option. So, analysis is as necessary as the budgeting itself. **A budget without an analysis at the end of the budget period loses it's value.**

What is there to analyse? In a production environment it is important to know if the volume of raw materials used matched the budgeted volume for the output realized. And also, it is important to check if the costs of the raw materials matched the budgeted prices. The production budget will also show how many equipment hours were needed and after the planning period the production ledger must show if the budget was correct or not.

In sales it is important to analyse realized sales versus budgeted sales as well as the average prices realized versus the budgeted price level.

We know that every manufactured item contains variable costs of material and labour and indirect costs. When at the end of a planning period it is found out that production had cost more or less than the preset volumes times prices it is extremely important to find out what it was that caused these variances. It could have been volume; it could have been price or it could have been both. Not knowing the real cause could mean a financial disaster for companies manufacturing millions of tons of a product.

When the analysis shows a variance in volume used for the production, we speak of an **EFFICIENCY VARIANCE**: the volume used was higher or lower than the budget promised. This variance is measured by the following formula: **(PV-RV)X BP**, meaning: **planned volume less volume realized times the budgeted price**. In every such formula it is important that there is **one debatable factor only**. In the formula above we would not know if the variance was caused by a deviation from the anticipated volume, the preset purchase price, or both, if the price realized instead of the budgeted price would have been used. Hence, when measuring a volume variance we use standard, = budgeted, price

To find out if a **PRICE VARIANCE** occurred the formula reads as follows: **(BP-RP) X RV**, which means that the budgeted price (BP) is compared with the realized (and measurable) price (RP) for the volume (RV) **realized** in practice. Here the **budgeted** volume would confuse the analysis. The realized volume is a fact.

Finally, there is a third variance: **CAPACITY VARIANCE** which compares the basis to absorb all of the costs as foreseen in the budget with the realized basis. This requires a separate chapter 10. But here it is noted that more production volume and/or higher sales volume than budgeted increases the operating result. And that is because volume determines how much of the fixed costs really were absorbed by one single item. Remember the example of the pancakes. The more pancakes prepared, the lower the portion of the fixed costs of rent per pancake.

It is time for an example. In a catering company for prefab meals sold to super markets and nursing homes the total fixed costs are $ 10.000 per month. According to budget 1.000 meals per month are to be sold. This is the PV, planned volume. We already can see that $ 10 of fixed costs are absorbed by each meal if the PV is realized. Each meal always contains 500 grams (= PV) of ingredients at a budgeted purchase price (= BP) of $ 2 per kilogram. Given the 500 grams per meal (= half of one kilogram) we can see that each meal was budgeted to have $ 1 of ingredients. Preparation of one meal takes 10 minutes at a wage of $ 30 per hour. So, six meals in one hour will cost $ 5 per meal. Total budgeted costs:$ 10,00 + $ 1,00 + $ 5,00 is **$ 16 per meal.**

At the end of a month the facts are reported: production volume was 1.200 meals (=RV, Realized Volume), 600 kilograms of ingredients had been bought at a total price of $ 1.100 (=RP, realized price) and the costs of wages had been $ 5.400. The report compared to budget:

	According to budget	in reality
Total fixed costs	$10 000	$10 000
Variable cost of material:	1 000x0.5x$2 =1 000	600 kilogram* =-1 100
Wages 1 000 X 1/6 X $ 30=	5 000	-5 400
	---------------	--------------
Total costs for **1 000 meals**	$16 000	1 200 meals $16 500
Cost price per meal	$16	$13.75

* **600 kilogram was needed to prepare the 1.200 meals.**

There is a benefit of **$ 2.25** per meal. Analysis should tell where this advantage came from. It could not come from less raw material, because every meal contains one half of a kilogram. So, either an efficiency variance or a price variance must have caused the difference. We can see that when 1.200 meals are prepared this would cost according to budget (1.200: 6 meals per hour) X $ 30 = 200 X $ 30 = $ 6.000 in costs of labour. Apparently, there was more output than expected, because wage costs for the month were $ 5.400. Divide by $30 = 180 hours. The budget says that in 180 hours 1.080 meals could have been prepared. In fact, 1.200 had been prepared. We analyse:

Efficiency Variance	Allowed	Realized	Variance +/-
Raw material per meal 500 kilogram: 1 000	500 grams		
600 kilograms used: 1 200 meals		500 grams	0
Hours (RV-BV) X BP of $ 30= (180-200) X $30	$ 6 000	$5 400	- $ 600
1 200 meals allowed for 200 hours. In fact, 180 hours were needed			-
Price (RP-BP) RV= ($ 1.833 - $ 2) X 600 kilograms ($ 1.100 for 600 kilograms)	$ 1 200	$ 1 100	-$ 100
Capacity ratio 200 meals more at $ 10 per meal for fixed costs			-$ 2 000
REALIZED ADVANTAGE			$ 2 700

The advantage achieved per meal: $ 2.700: 1.200 = **$ 2.25** as announced above

After such an analysis **the next logical step** is to draw conclusions and re-plan for the future. What did the catering company learn from it 's analysis?

1. **Efficiency**. No variance in weight per meal was found. If so, it would have been a disadvantage either for clients, or for the company.
2. It was a discovery that less hours were needed to prepare meals. Instead of 200 hours (1.200:6 per hour = 200 hours) only 180 hours were needed. A saving of 20 hours. 180 X 60 minutes = 10.800 minutes. This is per meal 10.800: 1.200 = 9 minutes per meal! This is **significant when the company produces 100.000 meals a year!** The conclusion must be that the company should **re-set the standard time allowed for the meals.** Instead of 10 minutes per meal the employees are allowed 9 minutes per meal. The company can enforce this standard by not paying salaries per hour but a standard wage per 10 meals prepared.

3. The next conclusion is that savings can be made in the raw materials. The budget was 500 grams per meal at $ 1. In practice 600 kilograms had cost $ 1.100: 1.200 = $0.9167 per meal instead of $ 1.00. The conclusion can be that solid price agreements with the supplier(s) are in order.
4. The largest advantage was made by producing 200 meals more than in the budget. It offers the **next options** to the company: a. try always to make 1.000 meals or more than before. This would work if demand is large enough. Streamlining the production by better engineering could help here. b. to enlarge the basis for the fixed costs a larger volume proved to be possible. If the existing market cannot absorb larger quantities the alternative would be to open up new markets for the excess production, even at lower sales prices. The lower price will be compensated generously by the larger cost carrying basis.

Reading and re-reading the above should confirm the importance to make an analysis always, especially where huge volumes are involved.

Here is another example concerning sales. The bicycle factory Gazelle shows a sales budget for the month of May of 8.000 bicycles. Standard sales price to dealers is $ 110 and the budgeted cost price is $ 72. In early June the records show that 8.200 bicycles were sold in May at an average sales price to dealers of $ 115. How to analyse the variances.

The profit margin realized in May versus the margin in the budget is calculated:

8.000 X ($ 110 -$ 72) = $ 304.000 budgeted profit margin
8.200 X ($ 115 -$72) = $ 352.600 realized profit margin. Variance: **+$48.600.**

This amount must equal volume variance + price variance. Volume variance is (RV-BV) X (BP-Cost price) = (8.200 – 8.000) X ($ 110 - $ 72)   **=$7.600**

Note that in this calculation the standard price must be used. If not, it will not be clear what the real cause was for the amount of $ 7.600

The price variance for May was:(RP–BP)XRV= ($115-$110) X 8.200   = **$ 41.000**
Totalized: $ 48.600 of which the price variance was the largest contributor.

We see that variances can occur both in the field of production and in the field of sales. This makes analysis in both fields necessary.

Example. The sales budget indicates a sales volume of 1.000 pieces at an average sales price of $ 10. This means a turnover of $ 10.000. After the planning period the records show that turnover was $ 14.000. It would be too easy and also incorrect to draw the conclusion that 1.400 pieces were sold in that period. Who can say that there was no variance in the price level? Let us assume that the sales records show a volume variance of + 250 pieces. That would indicate a variance of 250 X $ 10 = $ 2.500 while the real variance totalled **$4.000.** Let us analyse.

a. volume variance was (RV – BV) X BP (real volume – budget volume) x budget price. = (1.250 – 1.000) X $ 10 = 250 X 10 = **$ 2.500**

b. price variance was (RP –BP) x RV (realized price – budget price) x real volume) What was the realized price? This must have been $ 14.000: 1.250 = $ 11.20. So, (14.000: 1.250) = RP = $ 11.20 ($ 11.20 -$ 10) X 1.250 =   **$ 1.500**

Total variance of $ 4.000 proves to consist of $ 2.500 volume variance plus $ 1.500 price variance.

The conclusion of this chapter of budgeting and analysis is that every company, large or small, would be wise to accept the burden of doing both. The time sacrificed may create a higher profitability. And it certainly will enable better **economic choices** in the future.

Exercises of Chapter 10

Budgeting Process and Analysis of Variances

1. What is the meaning of a budget versus an estimate

   a. a budget is made once every year, an estimate is made frequently
   b. an estimate is provisional, a budget is a binding assignment with authorizations
   b. an estimate is for all of a company, a budget is made per department

2. The monthly budget for PANNED CHICKEN DELICIOUS where complete chicken containing meals are prepared indicates that 3.200 meals must be prepared. Every meal always contains ¼ of a kilogram of raw materials with a cost of $ 2,40/kilogram. The budgeted production standard is 20 meals per hour. Hourly wage is $ 40 and 160 hours of labour are planned. Indirect costs of the company are $ 19.200 per month. After the end of the month it is found that 4.000 meals were completed and that $ 2.160 was paid for raw materials. Budgeted working hours of 160 showed no variance.

   2.1 Calculate the total variance for the month

   a. budget shows (3.200 X $ 0.60 of material) + (160 hours X $ 40) + $ 19.200 = $27.520; Real costs were $ 26.600. So, variance totals $ + 600
   b. budget totals $ 27.200 in costs; real costs were $ 26.400 – variance of -$800
   c. c. budget for 3.200 meals totals $ 27.520 in costs =$ 8.60 per meal; costs of 4.000 meals would have been $ 34.400. Real costs were $ 27.760 ($ 19.200 + $ 2.160 for raw materials + $ 6.400 of wages) = $ 6,94. Variance totals 4.000X($8,60-$ 6,94) = $ 6.640

   2.2 Calculate the efficiency variance

   a. $ 1.600 because 4.0000 meals took 40 hours less than in budget
   b. $ 1.800 because 4.000 meals took 45 hours less than in budget
   c. $ 1.400 because 4.000 meals took 35 hours less than in budget

   2.3 Calculate the price variance for the raw materials

   a. $ 280
   b. $ 240
   b. $ 220

2.4 What was the capacity variance

a. $ 4.800
b. $ 4.600
c. $ 4.400

3. At Gazelle Bicycles the sales budget for June reads 6.000 bicycles with an average sales price to dealers of $ 120. Standard cost price of a bicycle is $ 80. After June the records show a realized sales volume of 5.800 at an average price of $ 132

3.1 What is the volume variance in dollars

a. -$ 18.800
b. -$ 17.900
b. -$ 24.000

3.2 What was the price variance

a. $ 69.600
b. $ 68.800
c. $ 67.700

3.3 Calculate the variance of proceeds

a. + $ 62.400
b. + $ 61.600
b. + $ 63.100

Closing Assignment of Chapter 10

Budgeting Process and Analysis of Variances

1. At GAZELLLE BICYCLES INC. the budget for August shows that 7.200 bicycles will be manufactured, of which the material costs are $ 48. Standard is three hours of labour per piece at $ 32 per hour. The sales budget commands that 7.400 bicycles will be sold in August at an average sales price of $ 210. Monthly indirect costs are $ 108.000. After the budget month the records tell that 7.400 bicycles were made with a total of material costs of $340.400 and that 19.800 hours were needed with a total of $ 594.000 in wages. In reality 7.600 bicycles were sold at a total proceed of $ 1.626.400.

   1.1 Calculate the difference in cost price per bicycle between production budget and reality.
   - a. Cost price was $ 19.28 lower than budget
   - b. Cost price was $ 18.14 lower than budget
   - b. Cost price was $ 19.66 lower than budget

   1.2 What was the difference in profit margin per piece between budget and reality.
   - a. Profit margin was $ 22.14 higher than budget
   - b. Profit margin was $ 25.20 higher than budget
   - c. Profit margin was $ 27.40 higher than budget

   1.3 What was the efficiency variance in material costs
   - a. Savings on materials was $ 9.800
   - b. Savings on materials was $ 10.200
   - b. Savings on materials was $ 9.600

   1.4 What was the price variance of materials
   - a. Savings on material costs were $ 12.600
   - b. Savings on material costs were $ 14.800
   - c. Savings on material costs were $ 13.400

   1.5 Calculate the volume variance of sales
   - a. Positive difference is + $ 32.800
   - b. Positive difference is + $ 40.400
   - b. Positive difference is + $ 42.000

   1.6 What was the price variance of sales
   - a. Better price total was + $ 30.400
   - b. Better price total was + $ 30.200
   - c. Better price total was + $ 32.400

1.7 What was the efficiency variance in labour
- a. Positive difference was $ 56.400
- b. Positive difference was $ 56.800
- b. Positive difference was $ 57.600

1.8 Calculate the price variance of labour
- a. Positive variance was $ 15.400
- b. Positive variance was $ 14.800
- c. Positive variance was $ 14.200

1.9 What was the capacity variance
- a. $ 3.000
- b. $ 3.380
- b. $ 3.330

Chapter 11
Profit Calculations and Break-Even Point

In earlier chapters (4 and 8) we saw how a profit & loss statement is made and what the lessons are we can learn from the details of it and we saw how to calculate a full cost price. Normally, a P&L statement shows the total turnover and deducts the **costs of raw materials** to result in a profit margin. From the latter all other costs a company makes, including all of the costs of personnel, are deducted to end with a net profit figure. **We know that a full cost price contains both variable costs of material plus labour, and fixed** costs. Once a correct cost price is made a sales price can be calculated. **This practically is the main purpose for cost price calculations.**

It is not logical at all to calculate a full cost price of the products to be made, multiply the cost price by the volume of products sold and deduct this figure from the turnover realized in the P&L statement. ALL of **the known costs** had been incorporated in (or: **ABSORBED** by)the full cost price already. It does not make sense to deduct these again from the profit margin. If we would do that **then costs of labour were deducted twice:** the first time by means of the labour costs absorbed by the full cost price, the second time by deducting costs of personnel as one of the operating costs.

What we see is that in the P&L statement the fixed costs were detailed and deducted from the profit margin. This was possible because only the variable costs of the products sold were deducted from the turnover figure. An other variable cost is labour. **While this factor is important to calculate a cost price it is nearly never mentioned under the variable** costs in the P&L statement, **because the total cost per year of a worker hardly ever equals this worker's costs under the variable costs of labour in the cost price.** All of the costs of personnel belong to the operating costs, just like housing costs and office costs. This is different from the variable cost of materials used in manufacturing a product: an exact record can be kept on the volume of each raw material used during a certain period.

In the P&L statement we used the **VARIABLE COSTING METHOD (VC method)**, meaning that only the variable costs of raw materials are deducted from the turnover figure. The difference is called: **CONTRIBUTION MARGIN**, which means that this margin is meant to contribute to compensate for all or part of the fixed costs. One advantage we mention here at this point is that contribution margin plays an important roll in setting sales prices in a slow market where sales had been dropping. A company then will stimulate the sales force to sell at any price **as long as there is a positive contribution margin.** And this contribution margin plays a main role in finding the breakeven point.

The other way to calculate the periodic profit is called **ABSORPTION COSTING**. This method intends to correct the provisionally calculated profit by a capacity variance. The principle behind it is that a correction is justified when much more or much less was produced compared to the normal annual volume, since this changed the basis for absorbing all of the fixed costs.

We demonstrate the difference between Absorption costing and variable costing method by the following example.

We use a company with volume sales and a normal production volume 20.000 pieces at a sales price of $ 40. The raw materials cost are $ 18. The total fixed costs are $ 380.000. In practice 20.000 pieces were made and sold.

Using the full cost price method or **ABSORPTION COSTING** method to calculate the result we have to calculate the full cost price first:

$$\text{COST PRICE} = \text{VARIABLE COSTS} + \frac{\text{TOTAL FIXED COSTS}}{\text{BUDGETED VOLUME}}$$

Cost price = $ 18 + ($ 380.000: 20.000) = $ 18 + $ 19* = $ 37 (* is fixed cost component)
Let us now fill out the statements below.

	P & L statement **Variable costs method**	Full cost price method **absorption costing method**
Turnover 20 000 X $ 40	$800 000	$800 000
Less: variable costs 20 000 x $ 18 =	$360 000	full cost price-740 000(20 000x$37)
CONTRIBUTION MARGIN	$440 000	**net profit $60 000**

costs of housing	$80.000
Salaries and wages	120.000
Marketing costs	140.000+=-340.000
OPERATING RESULT	$100.000
Financial costs	40.000
net profit	**$60.000**

In the absorption costing the turnover figure was decreased by deducting all of the costs: the variable costs plus all of the fixed costs that were **ABSORBED by the cost price earlier**. Hence, the term **ABSORPTION COSTING. (AC method).** In this example there was no difference in results. That is because the volume produced equalled the volume sold. We shall discuss this later.

Believers in the variable costing method defend their method by claiming that

1. visibility of all of the costs is greater;
2. sudden and unexpected changes in the fixed costs are reported clearly in the P&L statement and do have an impact on the final profit figure. It means that the fixed costs in this method are treated as **costs of a given period.**
3. For decision making purposes variable costing is used in general.

Believers in the absorption costing extend the purpose of pre calculating a **full cost price** by also using that full cost price to be deducted from the turnover figure.

1. Their claim is that if the full cost price is based on a certain volume to be manufactured and sold that volume is the basis to support all of these costs. If, however much **more is manufactured and sold than the normal volume** then the basis to cover for fixed costs was, in fact, **wider than anticipated**, decreasing the portion of fixed costs in the full cost price

(=the fixed costs component). Because it does not make sense to adjust a cost price after the turnover was realized, the AC method must use a correction, **CAPACITY VARIANCE,** in the calculation of the profit, which benefits from the advantage of higher production figures. The principle of this method is that not only the variable costs but also the fixed costs are an **integrated part** of the costs of each product.

2. In external reporting of financial statements full costing should be used in declaring a company's profit or loss.
3. What happens in this method is that **raw materials in stock** may be recorded at variable costs basis. But once raw materials are transformed into a **finished product**, ready to be sold, any such finished **product** returning to **inventory will be recorded at full cost price, since it absorbed fixed costs plus** variable costs **during the production cycle. This (higher) inventory is then recorded in the balance sheet.**

This also means that the costs made during the production period are not treated as costs to be recorded in the P&L statement but as **an integrated part of the products** moved to inventory.

In the calculation above we saw no difference in profit between the VC and the AC method. That is because no variance in sales volume compared to production volume occurred. If production would be higher than sales then, in the AC method, a correction would have to take place because profit should benefit from this wider basis to carry all of the costs. We use the following example.

A manufacturer of surf boards manufactures a normal quantity of, and plans to sell, 40.000 boards in one year. The material costs of one board are $ 80. The total fixed costs are $ 1.600.000. After the end of that year the records show that 52.000 boards were made and **48.000** sold at $300 each. We calculate the results using the VC and the AC method. First, we calculate the full cost price: $ 80 + ($ 1.600.000: 40.000) = $ 80 + $40 = **$ 120**

	Variable costing method	Absorption costing method
Turnover 48 000 X $ 300	$14 400 000	$14 400 000
Material costs 48 000 X $80	- 3 840 000	full cost price -5 760 000*
contribution margin (for fixed costs)	$10 560 000	transaction result $8 640 000
total fixed costs	-1 600 000	capacity variance -480 000**
result of the period	$8 960 000	result of period $9 120 000

* 48.000 X $ 120 = $ 5.760.000

In the AC method more products made than normally means better coverage of fixed costs. This **capacity variance is calculated as follows: RV(= REALISED VOLUME) –BV (= budgeted volume sold X (total fixed costs : BV)= (52.000 – 40.000) X ($ 1.600.000 : 40.000) = 12.000 X $ 40 = **$ 480.000.**

What we see is a difference between the two systems of $ 912.000-$ 8.960.000 = **$160.000**. More boards were made than boards sold: 4.000. These 4.000 will stay in inventory until they will have been sold. In the AC method these 4.000 pieces will be in **inventory on the basis of the full cost price; in the VC method this inventory is reported on the basis of variable costs.** The difference is in the **fixed costs component** of the cost price of the volume not sold. That FCC **(fixed costs component)** is $ 40 as we could see above. 4.000 pieces were unsold X $ 40 = **$ 160.000 and this exactly is the difference in financial results between the two systems.**

In the AC method we also see "transaction result". This is done since it does not indicate the total result of a period since the **"capacity variance"** will have to be calculated first to then be reported together as the result of the booking period.

We can conclude that such a capacity variance **only occurs when a change in inventory** occurs caused by the difference between volume produced and volume sold. So, when production and inventory increase, lower costs of goods sold will be reported as well as more gross profit.

Let us explore if the capacity variance can be negative and will lead to a different result. We use the same company producing surf boards.

A manufacturer of surf boards normally manufactures and sells 52.000 boards in one year. The material costs of one board are $ 80. The total fixed costs are $ 1.664.000. After the end of that year the records show that 48.000 boards were made and 52.000 sold at $300 each. We calculate the results using the VC and the AC method. First we calculate the full cost price: $ 80 + ($ 1.664.000 : 52.000) = $ 80 + $ 32,00 = **$ 112,00.** We see the following results

	AC METHOD		VC METHOD
Turnover 52 000 X $ 300	$15 600 000		$15 600 000
Cost price 52 000 X $ 112.00	-5 824 000	X variable costs $80	-4 160 000
result of transaction	$9 776 000	Contribution margin	$11 440 000
capacity variance	- *128 000	Total fixed costs	-1 664 000
Result of the period	$9 648 000		$9 776 000

*Capacity variance is negative by (48.000 – 52.000) X $ 32.00 =   **- $ 128.000**

The difference in profit in the AC method now is lower than in the VC method. The difference is $ 9.776.000 - $ 9.648.000 = **$ 128.000.**

This difference occurred because the production volume was lower than the sales volume: 4.000 pieces less manufactured than normally. There is a **decrease in inventory** of 4.000 X FCC of $ 32 = **$ 128.000**. The basis to cover fixed costs, therefore, was lower than planned. The consequence is that, in fact, the full cost price in the AC method was lower than justified. And since the inventory in the AC method was at full cost price and the costs were, therefore, on the balance sheet and not in the P&L statement, the costs now are treated as costs. Hence the negative capacity variance.

Finally, there is a hidden risk in the AC method. Higher production volume than sales volume generates a positive capacity variance. This improves the final profit. Where general managers in large corporations are rewarded by a big bonus, depending on the final profit one or more of these general managers could be tempted to stimulate their bonus by taking this AC method to extremes. An example.

In a chemical conglomerate general managers enjoy a bonus system, promising $ 20.000 for every $ 1.000.000 of profit. Fixed costs are **$ 15.000.000**. The budgeted volume is 2.000.000 kilogram of a special polyurethane chemical with a raw material cost of **$ 60** per kilogram. Sales price is $ 90. In a given year 1.800.000 kilograms are sold at an average price of **$ 92**. But the production was boosted up to 3.125.000 kilograms.

First, we calculate the full cost price: $ 60 + ($ 15.000.000: 2.000.000) = $ 60 + $ 7.50 totals **$ 67.50.**

The result in the Ac method: Turnover 1.800.000 X $ 92 = $ 165.600.000

Full cost price	1 800 000 X $ 67.50 = -121 500 000
result of transactions	$44 100 000
capacity variance*	8 437 500
result for the period	$52 537 500

* Capacity variance is (RV – BV) X $ 7.50. (3.125.000 – 2.000.000) = 1.125.000 X $ 7.50 = $8.437.500

The consequences are fairly dramatic:

1. Because of a massive over production there is an excess inventory of 3.125.000 kilograms – 1.800.000 kilograms = 1.325.000 X full costs of $ 67.50 = $89.437.500 which is a gigantic increase on the balance sheet.
2. Because assets increased additional financing is required. If the interest rate would be 8% it would cost the company $ 7.155.000 in financial costs per year.
3. The advantage of more than $ 8 million as a result of the enormous capacity variance does not promise any additional dividends to the shareholders because this extra profit is hidden in the warehouse.
4. The responsible general manager earns a bonus of 52,5 X $ 20.000 = $ 1.050.000.

This example looks extreme. Fortunately checks and balances in most internationals are finely tuned and applied. It is natural that a general manager is rewarded for a better performance than expected. But in most cases, there are strict conditions, e.g. a firm control of working capital and a limited level of liabilities.

A final conclusion of the two methods is that even when in AC over production took place in one year production level will be lowered in the next year until inventory will be back at a normal level. Lower production than under normal circumstances leads to a negative capacity variance. Over a longer period both methods will, therefore, show equal results.

Break Even Point

In many situations a company likes to predict at **which volume of sales** it's company will not incur a loss nor a profit. Such data tell the company how much more volume must be sold in order to make a profit. Starting companies or companies considering to add a new product are prime examples for this need.

We give a simple example of the sales man working on weekly markets to sell bags for vacuum cleaners. He buys these at $ 3 and sells them at $ 6.90. His fixed costs per market day are licence plus rent plus travelling, totalling $ 156 per market day. At which volume will he have no loss and no profit?

The solution is not so difficult when we look back at the variable costing method above. In fact, the question he will ask himself is: "how many times must I pocket the difference between sales price and purchase price to cover all of these costs?" In economic terms he asks what the **CONTRIBUTION MARGIN** must be per day. When his daily costs are $156 and he pockets $3.90 per bag he obviously must sell 156: 3.90 = 40 bags per day. Every bag **in excess of that volume will mean a profit.** The formula: **fixed costs: contribution margin per piece = number of pieces to be sold to cover fixed costs. That result is called: the breakeven point.**

The term "contribution margin" is easy to understand: it's amount in dollars **"contributes to cover for the fixed costs".** Many larger companies use this exercise for there business, depending on their circumstances. If a company for its turnover depends on one significant client for the larger portion of the turnover there is the risk of pressure or even blackmail. The client cannot be blamed; he acts in his financial interests. When he finds a competitor with a better offer for equal quality his first step will be to confront his supplier with a choice. When this happens the supplier's choice is to accept or to reject an adjustment of his sales price. In such a case middle sized companies will accept as long as the sales price **covers more than the variable costs** of its product and, thus, will generate a **contribution margin.** If it rejects it loses a significant part of it's turnover. By accepting it can buy time to vigorously looking for new and smaller clients until these will have matched the proceeds generated by the one large client.

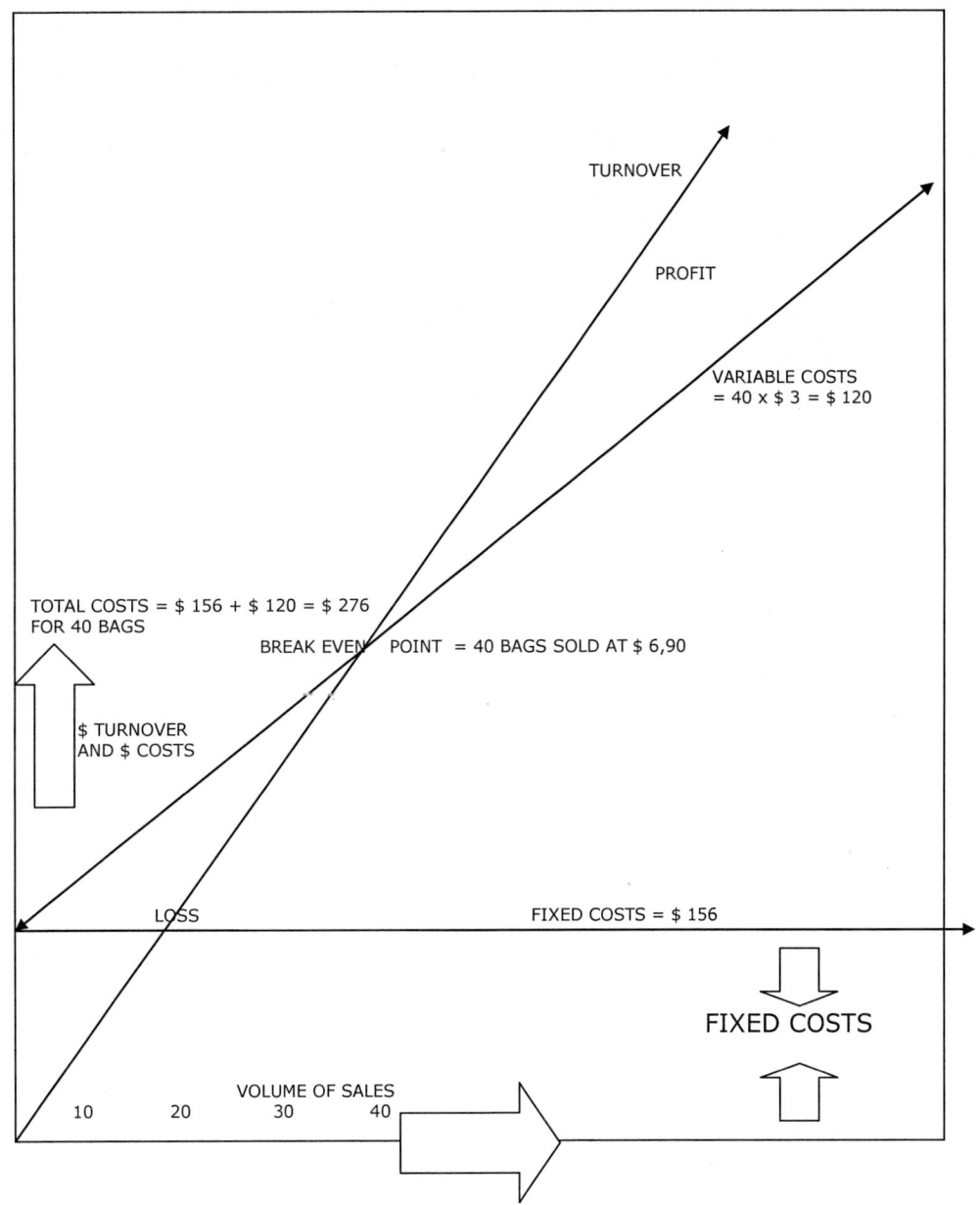

Another situation where this breakeven point can play a large role is when a company has excess capacity in it's factory. We demonstrate this with the following example.

The capacity of the factory is 800.000 pieces. The budgeted volume of production and sales is **600.000** pieces. Variable costs are $ 6. Sales price is $ 14.86 The total fixed costs are **$ 3.000.000.** We calculate the full cost price for the actual situation as well as for full use of the capacity.

1. If the budgeted 600.000 pieces are made and sold the full cost price would be ($3.000.000: 600.000) + $ 6 = $ 5 + $ 6 = $ 11.
2. If 800.000 pieces could be made and sold: ($ 3.000.000: 800.000) = $ 3.75 + $ 6 = $9.75 A difference of $ 1.25 per piece.

The P&L statement with 600.000 in sales volume.

	600 000 X $14.86 =	$8 916 000
Variable costs	600 000 X $ 6=	- 3 600 000
		-----------------
contribution margin		$5 316 000
Total indirect costs		- 3 000 000

Profit is 25.9%		$2 316 000

A client in a remote market is found and would accept to buy 180.000 pieces in one year under the condition that the price will be $ 10. Should this be accepted?

This is how the P&L statement would look. Sales

	600 000 X $14.86	$8 916 000
Additional sales	180 000 X $10	1 800 000
		-----------------
total sales		$10 716 000
total variable costs	780 000 X $6	- 4 680 000
		-----------------
contribution margin		$6 036 000
total indirect costs		- 3 000 000
		-----------------
profit is 28.33%		$3 036 000

We see an increase in profit of $ 720.000, so the additional sales is a welcome thing. Also, because of the increased production volume the basis to cover for indirect costs will be much stronger. In fact the full cost price of $ 11 would be lower: the fixed costs component in the cost price would decrease to ($ 3.000.000: 780.000) = $ 3,85 and the cost price would be $ 3.85 + $ 6 = $ 9.85 instead of $ 11,00.

We see that excess capacity can be turned into a profit maker as long as the manufactured excess quantities are **sold at a price HIGHER than the variable costs.**

A last example: a starting company incurs $ 200.000 in fixed costs per year. It wants to introduce electrically heated gloves to areas with a Siberian climate. A charged pair of gloves will keep a temperature of 25 degrees Celsius. (= F 77) for 3 hours. He can make these at variable costs of $ 15 per pair. Now, he believes he must be able to sell 4.000 to 5.000 pairs, but he has no idea what his maximum sales price should be to achieve those volumes. There are no competitive data available to him.

When we start from 4.000 as a realistic goal he needs to break even with $200.000 in fixed costs, selling 4.000 pieces. Obviously, each pair should contribute 200.000 : 4.000 = $ 5 to break even. If each pair must contribute $ 5 then the sales price must be $ 15 + $5 = $ 20. Check: $ 200.000 : contribution margin = volume to be sold. $ 200.000 : 5 = 4.000 pairs of gloves. He now knows that his minimum price must be $ 20. Depending on how much profit he needs to generate he will have to increase that price. Every dollar in excess of $ 20 will mean $ 1 of profit or more.

After a while of slowly growing sales volumes his buyers give the feedback that the warm time of 3 hours just is not enough. He re-designs his product by a different circuit resulting in a warm time of six hours. Recalculating the costs he finds that the material costs grew **to $ 18** and it takes 0.75 hours to manufacture a pair on his sowing machine. He sets his hourly costs at $ 16, so it will **cost $ 12** in labour costs. Now, he is not certain about sales price and sales volume. He knows that his fixed costs are $ 200.000 per year.

He needs a breakeven point again. But to find that without a clue about a sales price he cannot set a contribution margin. He must make some intelligent and realistic estimates. First of all he knows that to earn back his variable costs he would need to sell $ 200.000: $30 = 6.667 pairs in which case his sales price would equal the variable costs. He would do wise to calculate various sales prices by setting profit margins, like 25%-30% and 35% by using different volumes of potential sales. That exercise would tell him what his projected sales prices would have to be. And having found these he will have to decide which of the projected volumes and sales prices probably would be realistic:

First, he projects sales and production volumes of 4.000, 5.000 and 8.000. His variable costs are $ 18 for materials and $ 12 for labour = **$ 30**. Fixed costs still are $ 200.000. This means that the FCC (fixed costs component) in his cost price will be $50, $ 40 and $25 for these pre-set quantities. He finds three **cost prices: $ 80 - $ 70 and $ 55** The sales price will have to be: with 25% margin 106,67 93,33$ 73,33 and with 30% margin 114,21 100,00 78,57 and, finally, with 35% margin 123,07 107,69 84,62 and these figures belong to his projected volume sales of 4.000 5.000 and 8.000

The manufacturer is inclined to go for the $ 78,57 but, since he is not sure if the quantity of 8.000 can be generated, he calculates his breakeven point again with this sales price: his contribution margin will be $ 78,57 - $ 30 of variable costs = $ 48.57. The volume needed to break even now is $ 200.000: contribution margin of $ 48, 57 = 4.118 pieces. He decides that this is a viable option to him and decides to move forward at this price

SUMMARIZING: to find the breakeven point this formula is used: FIXED COSTS: CONTRIBUTION MARGIN = SALES VOLUME NEEDED. Sales price – variable costs = contribution margin. The formula simply tells how often the contribution margin in dollars has to be earned to cover the fixed costs dollars.

Exercises of Chapter 11
Methods to Calculate Profits and The Break-Even Point

1. A manufacturer of non-alcoholic drinks has a capacity of 30 million bottles and cans. For next year the budget indicates a sales volume of 24 million pieces. Variable costs per piece are $ 0,20 including packaging. Sales price to dealers is $ 0.29. Fixed costs are $1.200.000. in practice 28 million pieces were made and 22.800.000 pieces were sold.

1.1 Calculate the full cost price
   a. $ 0,24
   b. $ 0,25
   b. $ 0,26

1.2 Calculate the annual result with the absorption costing method.
   a. $ 1.160.000
   b. $ 1.020.000
   c. $ 1.112.000

1.3. Calculate for the volume sold the contribution margin (CM) and the final profit.
   a. CM is $ 2.052.000, final profit is $ 852.000
   b. CM is $ 1.980.000, final profit is $ 890.000
   b. CM is $ 2.230.000, final profit is $ 998.000

1.4. An foreign party shows an interest to buy 4 million pieces, provided that the price will not exceed $ 0.23. He then will pay in cash. Should the company accept or reject. In case of an acceptance what would be the contribution margin and the final profit according to the variable costing method.
   a. Reject because a profit margin of only $ 0.03 will generate a result of only $960.000
   b. Accept, because the end result will be $ 972.000
   c. Accept, because there is sufficient capacity, the CM will increase and the final profit will be $ 1.040.000

2. A competitive producer of non alcoholic sodas knows variable costs of $ 0.23; $ 0,20 for ingredients and $ 0.03 for a one litre bottle. The capacity is 20 million litres. Fixed costs are $ 875.000. For next year a production volume of 17.5 million litres is planned. At the end of that year the records show a realized production volume of 18 million litres and a sales volume of 17.2 million litres in bottles with an average sales price of $ 0.48. In the last quarter an Indonesian hotel chain, not a client, asks to make him an offer for 1.5 million bottles provided the price will not be higher than $ 0.28

2.1 Calculate the full cost price per bottle of one litre
   a. $ 0,32
   b. $ 0.30
   b. $ 0,28

2.2 Calculate the result for the period with the AC method and use a full cost price of $0,28
   a. $ 3.465.000
   b. $ 3.225.000
   c. $ 3.184.000

2.3 Calculate the result of the period with the AC method

   a. $ 3.340.000
   b. $ 3.238.000
   b. $ 3.425.000

2.4 Explain the difference in outcome between the two methods
   a. Difference of $ 125.000 because 2.5 million bottles X $ 0.05 went to inventory
   b. Difference $ 40.000 in AC method because (RV-BV)X$0.05 went to inventory
   c. Difference $ 227.000. 4.54 million litres at $ 0.05 went to inventory

2.5 If the Indonesian order will be accepted, then what would be the final result in AC
   a. $ 3.500.000
   b. $ 3.480.000
   b. $ 3.460.000

2.6 f the Indonesian order would be accepted then what would be the result in VC
   a. $ 3.840.000
   b. $ 3.460.000
   c. $ 3.500.000

2.7 What is the breakeven point if the sales price would be $ 0,48
   a. At 3.640.000 bottles
   b. At 3.500.000 bottles
   b. At 3.580.000 bottles

3. In a chemical factory special mixture of chemicals is made for use in aeroplanes. Each kilogram of the mixture has variable costs of $ 78. Fixed costs are $ 4.800.000. For next year a production volume of 384.000 kilograms is planned and a sales volume of 390.000 kilograms at an average sale price of $ 146 per kilogram. At the end of the period the recorded production volume was 320.000 kilograms and the sales volume 400.000 kilograms.

   3.1 What was the full cost price of one kilogram of the mixture
   a. $ 88.80
   b. $ 90.50
   c. $ 89.50

3.2 Calculate the result of the period with the VC method
   a. $ 21.800.000
   b. $ 24.600.000
   b. $ 22.400.000

3.2 What would have been the full cost price if production- and sales volume would have been 400.000 kilograms in the budget and in reality.
   a. $ 88
   b. $ 84
   c. $ 90

3.3 Calculate the breakeven volume for this company at a sales price of $ 146 and at variable costs of $ 78
   a. at 70.588 kilograms
   b. at 61.200 kilograms
   b. at 70.820 kilograms

3.4 What would have been the result of the period in AC method when 320.000 kilograms would have been made and 400.000 kilograms would have been sold at the sales price of $ 146.
   a. $ 22.300.000
   b. $ 21.400.000
   c. $ 15.960.000

Closing Assignment of Chapter 11

Methods to Calculate Profit and the Break Even Point

1. A factory of non-alcoholic drinks in one litre packaging has a production capacity of 5 million bottles. Fixed costs of the company are $ 504.000. The average historic volumes produced were 4.2 million bottles. For next year the company plans to produce and sell 4.6 million bottles. Variable costs per bottle are $ 0,15. After year end the records show that 4.7 million bottles were produced and 4.4 million bottles were sold at an average sales price of $ 0,38.

1.1 Calculate the full cost price per bottle
   a. $ 0,30
   b. $ 0,27
   c. $ 0,28

1.2 What was the annual result in the Absorption costing method
   a. $ 536.000
   b. $ 530.000
   b. $ 544.000

1.3 And what was the annual result in the variable costing method
   a. $ 508.000
   b. $ 506.000
   c. $ 504.000

1.4 Explain the difference in outcome of questions 1.2 and 1.3
   a. The 300.000 unsold bottles went to inventory at $ 0,15 = $ 45.000
   b. The 300.000 unsold bottles went to inventory at the full cost price of $ 0,27 in the AC method or at variable costs of $ 0,15. Difference is $ 0,12 X 300.000 = $36.000
   c. The unsold 300.000 bottles went to inventory at the cost price of $ 0,27 = $81.000

1.5 At which sales volume will this company meet its breakeven point
   a. At 2.114.000 bottles sold
   b. At 2.220.000 bottles sold
   c. At 2.191.304 bottles sold

1.6 An unknown party from Saudi Arabia shows an interest to buy 350.000 bottles in one shipment only, provided the price will be $ 0,20. Should the company accept the order and, if so, what would be the financial result in total
   a. Yes, because the price is higher than variable costs and the sale would mean $17.500 more proceeds.
   b. Yes, because capacity is large enough and the sale would bring $ 19.200 in extra profits
   b. No, because the price limit is too much lower than market price.

Chapter 12
Pre-Calculation Methods for Investment Options

All companies in the world at one time or another face the question whether or not a proposed investment will be profitable or not in the end. It requires to search for answers. Answers that are hidden in the future. When mentioning **"investment" this situation takes place for machinery, for buildings, but also for people.**

In chapter 1 investment was the important issue. The investments in that chapter were needed to start a company. A real calculative method where most of the uncertainties could be excluded was not in order at the start of a company, except to make a well-considered selection from more investment options like trucks. The starting business man could not use historic data, because there were none. The only data he could use were the purchase price and the annual costs of investments. And the limit for his investments was dictated by the equity and his borrowing capacity.

During the life of a company **investment dilemmas** present themselves from time to time. Equipment which can generate savings in the labour costs. There is never a water tight security about the profitability of an investment. So, companies will have to find instruments to reduce the insecurity as much as possible. **Business Economics offers a helping hand.**

How to judge if an investment in new equipment with a purchase price of $ 500.000 will be wise to undertake if savings in costs of labour seem to be in the order of $ 10.000 per year? In internal management discussions it is likely that people will draw a conclusion rather quickly that there will be not enough savings when the life time of the equipment will be ten years. Depreciation will cost $ 50.000 per year and that figure will not be compensated by savings of $ 10.000. **The key to such an investment issue is the question if financial advantages will outweigh the added costs from an investment within a certain time limit.**

Right here and now one of the facts of life is uncovered: governments at occasion make a law prohibiting sound above a certain limit, emissions of toxic gases etc. which make investments necessary beyond the control of a business. Such regulations demand investments by a company and it certainly will have nothing to do with business economics. The investment will have to take place, disregarding financial results.

The key question in investment options a company faces is: what must be the **FUTURE** financial advantages to **compensate for a capital expenditure TODAY plus the annual costs of an investment**? In such cases two different time factors present themselves: an immediate out of pocket payment for an investment versus a range of advantages in the near and far away future. **The economic value of these advantages decreases with time needed for the advantages to happen.** In other words, $ 10 to be received in one year has less economic value than $ 10 today. And $ 10 in five years' time have less value than $ 10 to be expected in two years. The reason is the prevailing rates of interest and the costs of capital in companies. If there is a choice to receive $ 10 to day or to receive these $ 10 at an extreme interest rate of 50% in one year everyone would gladly wait for one year. People expect a certain advantage over time when investing in a share in a business, or after having filled a savings account which advantage is needed to compensate for not having the invested sum at his disposal any more. The reverse is also true: when someone asks for a loan which will be paid back in one year's time the financier expects a certain compensation for not having the sum at his disposal. He expects a fair interest rate. Reversely, when a company can create future advantages and income by investing to day it will have to determine what the value today is of the future economic values it hopefully will gain.

How to compare economic advantages that can be expected during a period of ten years with the cash expenditure today? These **advantages will have to be discounted** methodically. There is no other way than to calculate **THE PRESENT VALUE** OF FUTURE ADVANTAGES.

This working toward the present value can be compared to bringing an amount to a bank with the question to which level this deposit would grow in a period of ten years. Example: a lady asks this question before depositing $ 200.000 on a savings account for a period of five years. The interest rate is 4%. The bank calculates for her: ($ 200.000 X 1.04) X 1.04 X 1.04 X 1,04 X 1.04 = $ 243.330,57. We can see immediately that the announced final amount in five years does not have that value today.

The lady could have asked a different question: "what would I have to deposit today to receive $ 320.000 five years from now with your interest rate of 5%?" The bank would calculate for her as follows: we divide the amount of $ 320.000 by (1.05x1.05x1.05x1.05x1.05) = $ 320.000: 1.27628 = $ 250.729. And he would also show how to check: $ 250.720 x 1,05x1.05x1.05x1.05x1.05= $ 320.000

So, $ 320.000 five years from now has a **PRESENT VALUE** of $ 250.720. The future accruals to the deposit were discounted to their value today. In an investment discussion this would not be much different. There the first step would be to set an economic lifetime for the investment. In equipment this mostly is ten years during which the equipment is depreciated. The method calculates the **NET PRESENT VALUE (NPV-METHOD)** The **added word "net" is significant**: all of the future annual financial **advantages should be reduced by the amounts of annual depreciations and other added costs which would not exist if there would be no investment.** If all of these net advantages are added up and the total figure still is higher than that of the investment then that investment is viable enough to undertake.

Here is an example from practice. Chocolate factories during a very long time used to work with assembly lines where three to five people filled boxes with various tastes of chocolate. At Droste chocolate in The Netherlands five ladies worked the assembly line, four of which had been doing and loving that work for more than twenty-five years. Now, under new owners the management was ordered to calculate the viability of an investment in a fully automatic filling machine of $ 400.000 which demanded one operator only. The five ladies earned $ 28.000 each per year. The economic lifetime of the equipment was ten years. The interest rate is 4%.

The management went to work: the annual savings would be 4 X $ 28.000 = $ 112.000 less the depreciation costs of the new equipment of $ 40.000 = **net savings of $72.000**. It had to calculate the net present value of this annual amount in savings every year during ten years. The next step was to calculate the factor by which every year's saving had to be divided:

year	1	2	3	4	5	6	7	8	9	10
1.04 x 1.04 etc.=	1.04	1.0816	1.1249	1.1699	1.2167	1.2653	1.3159	1.3686	1.4233	1.4802.

We see that by multiplying the interest rate year after year the factor by which every year's saving must be divided is higher than the last one, thus reducing every year's saving drastically till all of the amounts have reached their present value:

year 1 = $ 72 000: 1.04 =$69 230		year 2 = $72 000: 1.0816 =$66 568	
year 3 = $ 72 000: 1.1249 =$64 005		year 4 = $72 000: 1.1699 =$61 543	
year 5 = $ 72 000: 1.2167 =$59 176		year 6 = $72 000: 1.2653 =$56 903	
year 7 = $ 72 000: 1.3159 =$54 715		year 8 = $72 000: 1.3686 =$52 608	
year 9 = $ 72 000: 1.4233 =$50 586		year 10= $72 000:1.4802 = $48 642	
------------- +		------------------	
$297 712		$286 264	

total future savings of 10 X $ 72.000 = $ 720.000 show a <u>present</u> value of $583.976. And since these accrued savings are higher than the out of pocket expenditure for the new machine **the investment is proven viable:**

present value of all of the savings	$583 970
price of the investment	- 400 000
	------------------
net present value	$183 976

So: sum of the investment less the total of the savings = <u>net present value.</u>

This technique is very useful for a single investment, but also if for the same purpose more investments are optional. With the present value method, the best of the options can be selected. In the chocolate example there could be an alternative assembly line with a lower price but to be handled by two operators. That really asks for a comparative calculation.

In a case like described we miss a number of questions Droste Chocolate could, and should, have asked itself: do we need an additional loan, and, if so, would we still match the demands of the bank in terms of our solvability ratio? Apart from energy, what would be the annual costs of maintenance? And if there would be a standstill of the equipment do, we then still have the option to go back to hand work temporarily?

Apart from investments in equipment the method also can be very useful to better balance the different age groups of employees. An example: in a factory of one hundred employees sixty of them are earning $ 37.000 in average. These sixty are older than fifty-five years. Their total costs exceed $ 2 million every year. If this group could be replaced by sixty young employees, earning an average wage of $ 18.000 then savings of $ 1 million per year could be expected. This fact makes it attractive for any company to consider a fund from which it could offer older employees an attractive farewell premium.

But how much could the company afford to feed such a fund. It asks the personnel department to make a financial sound proposition for consideration by the board of directors. The department is advised to use the average return on total capital of the past five years and use ten years of savings as a basis. Let us suppose this average is 6%.

The possible annual savings are 60 X ($ 37.000 - $ 18.000) = $ 1.140.000. In a period of ten years it would total $ 11.400.000. The question now is: what is the value today and how much can we offer to people in order to volunteer and leave with a premium.

This can be calculated by the **net present value** method as follows. First, the growing annual factor is calculated by 1.06 X 1.06 etc.

1	2	3	4	5	6	7	8	9	10
1.06	1.1236	1.1910	1.2625	1.3382	1.4185	1.5036	1.5938	1.6895	1.7908

Then $ 1.140.000 is divided by the relevant annual factor per year as follow

Yr.1 1 140 000: 1.06 = $ 1 075 472	yr.	2 1 140 000: 1.1236= $ 1 014 596
Yr.3 1 140 000: 1.1910 $ 957 179	yr.	4 1 140 000: 1.2625 = $902 970
Yr.5 1 140 000: 1.3382=$ 851 891	yr.	6 1 140 000: 1.4185 = $803 666
Yr.7 1 140 000: 1.5036=$ 758 180	yr.	8 1 140 000: 1.5938 = $715 272
Yr.9 1 140 000: 1.6895=$ 674 756	yr.	10 1 140 000:1.7908 = $636 587
-------------------	+	-------------------
$4 317 478	+	$4 073 091

The **total present value** of savings of ten years is $ 8.390.569. When all of this money was to be spent as a farewell premium for all of the sixty older employees it would mean that per person $ 139.842 could paid. That equals $ 139.842: $ 37.000 = 3.8 years of salary per person. The personnel department wisely recommends the board to offer two years of salary to every older employee prepared to leave voluntarily. That is a very generous offer which hardly anyone could resist. Should all of the sixty people accept the offer then it would cost 60 X 2 X $ 37.000 = $ 4.440.000, leaving total savings for the period of $8.390.569 - $ 4.440.000 = $ 3.950.569 = **$ 395.057 per year in savings for the company**

The **net present value** discussed so far is not the only way to assess the viability of an investment. The following methods are also used in practice: 1. Cash flow method 2. the payback period and 3 the average profitability.

1. In the **cash flow method,** the calculation starts with the negative amount of the investment. Then the **cash flow (= net profit after tax + depreciation costs)** is estimated for the next years. The last cash flow which turns the negative into a positive is the time it takes to earn back the investment by cash flows. In this method there could be one factor making the results uncertain: are all of the cash flows that are measured the result of the investments or did other actions create cash flows as well? This method, therefore, requires a precise recording of cash flows directly linked to the investment.
2. The **pay back method** is the most simple of all: it adds future savings on the basis of an estimate (or: provisional budget). It is not difficult to guess in which year the investment will have been earned back. Also, here only the savings in terms of **cash savings** are to be taken into account. Many companies want to allow for a payback period of 5 years maximum. Some even shorter. This is a contrast with Japanese business philosophy. Japanese weigh the strategic importance of an investment, e.g. a takeover abroad, and think long term in that respect. They seem to have much more patience, but, in fact, their philosophy differs from that of western companies.

Here is an example. Invested equipment of $ 400.000 leads to savings in labour costs of five people with a total salary of $ 140.000 per year. The annual costs of the equipment are $ 8.000 in maintenance and energy. Depreciation period is ten years. In how many years will the investment have been earned back?

Annual savings in labour costs		$140 000
Additional costs per year $8 000=cash outflow		
Costs of depreciation	$ 40 000 = no cash outflow	8 000
		----------------
additional cash flow as a result of the investment		$132 000
Payback period will be $ 400 000: $ 132 000 = 3 years.		

3. **The average profitability method** expresses the average of invested capital in a percentage of the average net profit per year. Management picks a period and by setting up provisional budgets for the next four years the four amounts of net profit will become visible. Then the total investment amount is divided by four and the result is expressed in a percentage of the average profits. It is up to a decision of the board what the minimum percentage should be before it can give green light for the investment.

Exercises Of Chapter 12

Pre-Calculation Methods for Investment Options

1. In WILLIAM CIGAR COMPANY boxes are filled with cigars by hand on an assembly line by five workers. Their total salary is $ 110.000 per year. The company can buy a filling machine for $ 380.000 where no operator is needed. Question is whether the savings of five people make the investment a viable one if interest rates are 6% and the depreciation time is ten years. The residual value of the equipment will be $ 10.000 then.

1.1 Calculate the net present value of this investment (2 figures behind the comma)
   a. $ 160.972,34
   b. $ 157.297,12
   b. $ 154.485,86

1.2 Calculate the payback period expressed in years and months
   a. 5 years plus 4 months
   b. 4 years and 3 months
   c. 3 years and 7 months

2. In an old factory of STORK MACINERY 75 people are employed. 30 of them are older than 55 years. They earn $ 52.000 each per year. They could be replaced by young people of under 25 and these would earn $ 23.000 per year each. The financial department is asked to calculate the savings in labour costs for the next yen years. Interest rate to be used is 4% . Calculate the present value of the savings of this period of 10 years. No figures behind the comma.

   a. present value of the net savings is $ 7.056.666
   b. present value of the net savings is $ 7.556.788
   b. present value of the net savings is $ 7.224.936

Closing Assignment of Chapter 12

Pre-Calculation of Investment Options

1. In an assembly company of mobile phones four people are doing manual assembly functions. They earn $ 26.000 each per year. Wages are increased by 3% every year. There are two robots who could do their work. Robot A costs $ 170.000 and requires maintenance costs of $ 8.000. It can replace three of the four people. Depreciation time is five years. Interest rate to be used is 4% . Robot B costs $ 200.000 and requires maintenance costs of $ 10.000. It can replace all of the four people. Depreciation time also five years and 4% of interest rate.

1.1 Calculate the net present value of both the robot investments and indicate which deserves to be purchased. No figures behind the comma.
   a. NPV (net present value) of investment A is $ 10.882 and of B $ 67.890. B wins.
   b. NPV of investment A is $ 12.264 and of B $ 60.178. B wins.
   b. NPV of investment A is $ 13.586 and of B $ 61.442. B wins

1.2 Calculate the payback period in years and months and indicate which robot wins.
   a. A= 1 year and 4 months; B=2 years and 5 months. A wins.
   b. A=2 years and 2.5 months; B=1 year and 8 months. B wins.
   c. A=1 year and 7.4 months; B=1 year and 4.5 months. B wins.

Solutions of the Exercises Chapter 1

The Investment Plan

1. Answer b is the correct one.

   Let us total the investments Peter is considering:

	building	$300000
	equipment	180 000
	furniture	90 000
	computers	24 000
	TOTAL	$594 000

   The bank requires that Peter's own capital represents 40% of the value of all of these investments = $ 237.600 Since Peter owns $ 220.000 only, he cannot afford this total amount.

   So, he either tries to save on equipment or furniture so that his $ 220.000 will do the job, or he must decide not to buy the building yet.

2. The correct answer is: b (vehicle B)

There is a choice from 2 vehicles	A	B
purchase	$85 000	$105 000
less: residual value	-20 000	-15 000
to be depreciated in 5 years' time	$65 000	$90 000
COSTS PER YEAR		
depreciation	13 000	18 000
maintenance	8 000	5 000
insurance	1 600	1 100
fuel consumption	(700X12X$1.30)10 920	(700X9X$1.30) 8 190
Annual operating costs	$33 520	$32 290

3. The correct answer is b. Explore:

	A	B
Purchase price	$120 000	
Cost of lease per year		$26 400
Depreciation 1/10th.	12 000	
Costs of energy	6 000	3 600
Costs of maintenance	18 000	12 000
TOTAL OPERATING COSTS	$36 000	$42 000

Since Derek was prepared to select the lease option if the additional costs would not exceed $ 10.000 equipment B will meet his demand.

4. Here is a list of items needed by a company.

Fixed assets	Current Assets	Operating costs
1 = X		
2 = X		
		3 = X
		4 = X *
	5 = X **	
7 = X		
8 = X		
6 = X		
	9 = X	

Place an X in the column indicating to which category each item belongs

1. architect's drawing table
2. waste containers
3. 500 markers
4. 200 packs of letter paper *
5. a container with packing cartons **
6. tooling in a workshop
7. forklift truck
8. 10 2d hand computers
9. money in the bank account .

* Letter paper is for office use only and are considered as operating costs
* * the packing cartons, however are meant to be part of products to be shipped to clients and, therefore, are part of the current assets

5. The correct answer here is b!
When Tracy needs 5.000 bottles of lotion each month and delivery time to her is 2 weeks only, then her need totals to 2.500 bottles in stock. Total purchase price: 2.500 X $ 10 =$25.000.
Financing of this amount during 2 weeks is based on her average stock level: at the beginning of the two weeks, she will have 2.500 bottles in stock. At the end of the two weeks her stock will be 0. Average stock 2.500: 2 = 1.250 bottles which will cost her $12.500. The financing costs will be 14% of $ 12.500 = $ 1.750/yr : 26 = $ 67,60 for 2 weeks, assuming she will pay back the loan on a weekly basis. This would bring the total costs per bottle ($ 25.000 + $ 67,60) : 2.500 = $ 10.03
If she would accept the rebate offer, she would have to buy a stock of 40.000 bottles which will cost 40.000 X $ 10 = $ 400.000 less 3 % rebate = $ 388.000 investment in inventory. It would take her 40.000: monthly sales volume of 5.000 = 8 months of total stock which will decrease every month.

Her average stock level would be half of that, because in that period of 8 months that stock will decrease to 0 So, 50% of $ 388.000 would be her average stock to be financed at 14%/yr. This would cost her 8 months of interest: 14% of $ 388.000 per year = $54.320. Divide by 12 and multiply by 8 to arrive at 8 months of interest = $ 36.213,33
Total investment: $ 388.000 + $ 36.213,33 = $ 424.213,33 : 40.000 bottles = $ 10.61 per bottle. Each bottle will cost an additional $ 0.58 = 5.7% more expensive

There are more reasons for not accepting the offer: 1) Tracy may stretch her credit limit too heavily, so that she may not have credit enough should she be faced with an unexpected investment that may bring the relation between her equity and liabilities amount in danger and 2) should the offer of the supplier come to the end of a financial year then, if she ended up with a profit, the percentage of this net profit from total assets would be much lower than it would have been with a stock not higher than necessary, based on the short delivery time. That profit in % may, as a consequence, be so slim that her financial creditors may become too nervous to extend her additional credits. It is as if someone invested $ 50.000 in a building project where every investor expected over 10% of return and would find themselves harvesting $ 50 only = 0.1%

6. machine A machine

	A	B
a. The costs of depreciating	$15 000/yr.	$25 000/yr.
divide by annual volume of 12X5 000 pieces=60 000= $0.25/piece		$0.42
b. maintenance costs A is 18 days of $ 10 00	$180 000/yr.	
maintenance costs B is 36 days of $ 3 500		$126 000/yr.
costs of maintenance per item: divide by 60 000	$3.00/piece	$2.10/piece
c. total operating costs	$195 000	$151 000
operating costs per piece (divide by 60 000) =	$3.25	$2.52

d. Conclusion: machine B presents the lowest annual operating costs and is the best choice. Solution 2 is the correct answer

7. The correct answer is a.

The need of capacity is expressed per calendar quarter; the capacity of the equipment is expressed per calendar year. A match can be found only if the quantities can be compared. This should be done by treating the highest quarterly need as the standard and extrapolate it to a full calendar year: the 3d. quarter is the highest with a need of 20.000 litres. Per year 80.000 litres. Add the desired extra need of 20% = 96.000 litres. This is the capacity really needed. Machine C is of no use. Machine B brings the full 96.000 litres exactly, but the cheaper A deserves to be selected because of the lower price and lower depreciation costs. The fact that it produces more than needed is acceptable. In BE it is called **"rational excess capacity"**

8. The correct answer is b)

When annual sales are $ 480.000 and all of the clients pay within 2 weeks then the balance figure for debtors will be $ 480.000: 12: 2 = $ 20.000. The balance sheet shows a figure of $ 120.000, which means that clients pay in $ 120.000: ($ 480.000: 12) = 3 months.

9. The correct answer is C

Annual consumption of 4.200 tins equals a weekly quantity of 84 tins. With an extremely short delivery time a stock of a ½ week would be adequate = 42 tins. So, a sound balance figure would have been 42 X $ 12 = $ 504

10. The correct answer is b)

When a company decides on a fixed annual amount for depreciation costs of $ 20.000 then, total depreciation in 10 years would be $ 200.000, so residual value would be $40.000

Solutions of the Exercises of Chapter 2.1

The Financing Plan: Equity

1.1 The correct answer is c. Equity will rise by 50 X $ 1.000 and since shares were paid in cash so will the amount of cash under current assets: $ 50.000. In fact the current asset of cash was financed by equity.

1.2 The correct answer is b.
With total equity of $ 177.000 and 150 shares issued earlier to Jack and his wife the intrinsic value per share is ($ 177.000: 150) = $1.180. Hank receives 20 shares and pays 20 X $ 1.180, to be recorded as follows: cash 20 X $ 1.180 = +$ 23.600, common share capital 20 X $ 1.000 = $ 20.000 and APIC (additional paid-in capital) 20 X $ 180 = $ 3.600. Assets (cash) grew with $ 23.600 and equity grew with $20.000 + $ 3.600= $ 23.600

2. The correct answer is a. During a first year without earnings and depreciating costs of ($ 210.000: 30) = $ 7.000, the correct changes in the balance sheet are: fixed assets - $ 7.000 and under equity: operating loss - $ 7.000, thus lowering total equity.

3. The correct answer is b. After 5 years of depreciation of ($ 210.000 : 30 years) = $ 7.000/year the book value of the building was decreased by 5 X $ 7.000 = $35.000. As a consequence its book value now is $ 175.000 which is the figure on Gordon's last balance sheet. The difference with the appraised value of $ 300.000 will be recorded correctly as follows: fixed assets + $ 125.000 ($ 300.000 - $175.000); revaluation reserve + $ 125.000

4.1 The correct answer is c. Common share capital amounts to 60 X $ 1.000 = $60.000. Add retained earnings are $ 120.000. Add a reappraisal reserve of $ 60.000 and this will total the equity to $ 240.000.

4.2 The correct answer is b. When the corporation has 60 shares among its shareholders and equity totals $ 60.000 for the shares + $ 120.000 retained earnings + $60.000 reappraisal reserve = $ 240.000, then value per share is 1/60 = $ 4.000

5. The correct answer is c. First fixed assets will grow by $ 600.000 - $ 240.000 = $360.000 and reappraisal reserve will grow with the same amount. After the sale of the building fixed assets decrease by $ 600.000 and cash will grow with $ 600.000

6. The correct answer is c.

INVESTMENT PLAN		FINANCING PLAN	
Fixed assets: building	$350 000	Suppliers payment term	$110 000
fixtures	85 000	40% required equity	222 000
racks	10 000	(40% of $ 555 000)	---------
	---------	Available finance	$332 000
Total fixed assets	$445 000		
Current assets		Still needed	$555 000
inventory shop	80 000	less	332 000
inventory warehouse	30 000		---------
	---------	Mortgage loan	$223 000
total current assets	$110 000	Financing complete	
TOTAL ASSETS	$555 000		

7.1 The correct answer is b. When the Profit & Loss Statement shows a net profit after tax and there also was depreciation among the operating costs, then clients will have paid for those depreciation as well. No outgoing cash is involved when depreciating fixed assets. As a consequence, the cash flow amounted to $ 80.000 of net profit + $25.000 of total depreciation = $ 105.000

7.2 The correct answer is c. Retained earnings under equity will increase by the figure of net earnings of $ 80.000. Building will decrease by its depreciation of $ 15.000 and so will warehouse equipment with its depreciation figure of $ 10.000. Since depreciation will never cause an outgoing cash flow the cash under current assets will increase by net earnings + depreciation = $ 105.000. Increase of total balance: $ 80.000

8. The correct answer is b.

INVESTMENT PLAN			FINANCING RESOURCES	
Building		$ 180 000	Mortgage 75% =	$ 135 000
			Equity 25% =	- 45 000
Racks $ 18 000			5-year loan 60% =	- 18 000
Furniture $ 8 000			equity 40% =	- 12 000
Computers $ 4 000	total $ 30 000			
			Balance of equity now: $ 125 000	
			less already used	- 57 000
			Left for current assets = $ 68 000	
			= 80% of investment in tools and lotions	
Tools 80% of $ 60 000 =	$ 48 000		Equity must finance at least 40% of investments of $	
Lotions 80% of $ 25 000 =	$ 20 000		278 000 = $ 111 200.	
			So, his $ 125 000 meets that demand.	
Total assets =	$ 278 000		Financed by equity $ 45 000	
			+ 12 000	
			+ 68 000	

			$ 125 000	
			(= 44,96% of assets total)	
			liabilities - 153 000	
			Total $ 278 000	

10.1   The correct answer is c

The building's market value is $ 150.000 higher than book value. So revaluation reserve + $ 150.000. This extra value of equity belongs to the shareholders.

10.2   The correct answer is b.

Equity grows with the difference between appraised value and book value of the building > $ 238.000 + $ 150.000 = $ 388.000: 150 = $ 2.586,67

10.3   The correct answer is a.

Equity grew from $ 238.000 with $ 150.000 to $ 388.000 which represents 40% of total balance. Total assets may, therefore, grow to ($ 388.000: 40) X100 = $ 970.000. This is $ 970.000 - $ 675.000 = $ 295.000 higher than the original balance sheet.

Solutions of the Exercises of Chapter 2.2

The Financing Plan: Liabilities

1.1 The correct answer is c

	Assets			financing sources
Building $ 0				equity -175 000
equipment – 240 000		5-year loan	$65 000	
furniture etc – 40 000				equity-40 000
inventory - 30 000		suppliers	$30 000	
cash - 10 000				equity -10000
Investment $ 320 000		liabilities	$95 000	equity $225 000

$ 225.000 is 70% when the building is leased.

1.2 The correct answer is a.
   40% of the investment of $ 620.000 is $ 248.000. Shortage of equity is $ 23.000

   2.1 The correct answer is c

Assets		financing sources			
Fixed assets					
Building	$300 000	mortgage loan	$300 000		
Equipment	-240 000	5-year loan	-65 000	equity + 175 000	
furniture etc	-40 000			equity	40 000
inventory	30 000	suppliers	-30 000		
cash	-10 000			equity	10 000
	$620 000		$395 000		$225 000

The best economical choice is to use as much equity for equipment to save higher interest rates of the long-term loan

   2.2 The correct answer is b:
      Total assets are $ 620.000. Equity finances $ 225.000; so ratio equity : liabilities will be 36,3 : 63,7

   2.3 The correct answer is c
      When Vincent uses $ 175.000 of equity for the equipment, he will need $ 65.000 of the long term loan only. Mortgage will then be 4% of $ 300.000 plus 7.5% of $ 65.000 =$16.875

3.1 The correct answer is b

With annual sales of $ 90.000 at purchase price monthly need of inventory was $7.500. His inventory of $ 30.000 will last for 4 months

3.2 The correct answer is a

Monthly sales were $ 10.000 per month. When accounts receivable are $ 40.000 the clients used a payment term of 4 months

3.3 The correct answer is c

At annual sales against purchase price of $ 90.000- and one-week delivery time the allowed inventory for two weeks is 1/25 of $ 90.000 = $ 3.600. Excess therefore $26.400. Accounts payable on the balance sheet should be ($ 120.000: 50) X 2 = $4.800. Excess is $ 35.200. Total excess therefore: $ 61.600. Interest to be paid in excess is 16% of $ 61.600 = $ 9.856.

4. The correct answer is b.

If equity is $ 300.000 and finances 40% of all assets, total assets cannot be higher than ($ 300.000: 40) X 100 = $ 750.000. Liabilities maximum therefore $ 450.000

5. The correct answer is b

Ownership of shares in another corporation is meant to stay for a long time, contrary to the amount of accounts receivable. Therefore, such share ownership is an **intangible fixed asset.**

Solution of the Exercises of Chapter 3

The Opening Balance Sheet

1.1 The correct answer is b
Assets total: $ 280.000 + $ 110.000 + $ 80.000 + $ 75.000 + $ 35.000 = $ 580.000 Equity of $ 220.000 constitutes 37,9%

1.2 The correct answer is a
Mortgage is $ 250.000 at 5% = $ 12.500 and long-term loan of $ 35.000 at 8% = $2.800. So, total comes to $ 15.300

1.3 The correct answer is c.
Only the mortgage of $ 250.000 and the long-term loan of $ 35.000 are long term liabilities

2. The correct answer is c
   The figure of ordinary shares of $ 100.000 remains unchanged as long as no change takes place in the number of outstanding shares. The only way to report the loss is to put it under the phrase "retained earnings" with a minus: - $ 20.000

3. The correct answer is b
   If sales of 7.800 pieces per year are budgeted, then the inventory to cover two weeks of delivery time should be 7.800: 24 = 325 pieces. Inventory then is X $ 130 = $42.250 The opening balance sheet shows excess inventory of $ 44.850

4. The correct answer is c
   First a long-term loan is obtained: cash + $ 15.000, long term loan + $ 15.000. Then the computers are added to the balance sheet: fixed assets + $ 25.000 and cash -$10.000, creditors + $ 15.000

5. The correct answer is b
   The fixed assets grow by $ 60.000 and so does the only one correct credit booking: revaluation reserve + $ 60.000

6. The correct answer is a
   First fixed assets decrease by $ 45.000; the net loss is booked directly under equity: net earnings - $ 25.000 and since depreciation does not create a flow of cash we book under cash + $ 20.000. We see that retained earnings can show a negative figure.

7. The correct answer is c
   Inventory decreases by 10 pieces at cost price $ 510 = - $ 5.100. Sales price was $7.500 of which 50% is paid in cash, so cash + $ 3.750 and accounts receivable + $3.750. The profit made was $ 240 per piece, so retained earnings 10 X $ 240 = $2.400

8.1 The correct answer is c

Ordinary share capital is $ 125.000. Add $ 45.000 of retained earnings and revaluation reserve of $ 95.000 = total equity = $ 265.000. Divide by 125: $ 2.120 intrinsic value

8.2 The correct answer is a

10 shares were sold at the intrinsic value of $ 2.120. This leads to cash + $ 21.200, share capital + $ 10.000 and additional paid in capital + $ 11.200

8.3 The correct answer is b

Besides share capital the extra equity amounts to $ 45.000 + $ 95.000 = $140. 000.So, 140 bonus shares are issued. Share capital mounts from $ 125.000 to $ 265.000 Retained earnings and revaluation reserve disappear.

9. The correct answer is a

With annual sales of $ 2.064.000 of which half was paid in cash the other half: 12 would have been the correct figure on the balance sheet for accounts receivable per month = ($ 2.064.000: 2) : 12 = $ 86.000. The difference to the $ 154.000 is $68.000. This exercise shows how we can relate figures from the P&L statement to the balance sheet

10.1 The correct answer is b

Fixed assets of $ 927.000 + inventory of $ 253.000 = $ 1.180.000 is smaller than the long-term financing by equity of $ 480.000 + mortgage loan + long term loan of $705.000 = $ 1.850.000. So, the golden balance rule applies.

10.2 The correct answer is c

5,5% of $ 440.000 = $ 24.200 + 8,5% of $ 265.000 = $ 22.525.000 + 15% of $125.000 = $ 18.750 = total of $ 65.475. This is another relation between a balance sheet and the related Profit & Loss statement (or also: financial statement)

Solutions of Exercises of Chapter 4

P&L STATEMENT

1. The correct answer is b

   Before the price increase turnover was 15.000 X $ 840 = $ 12.600.000. After the price increase of 5% to $ 882 its sales would drop 4% to 14.400. So, 14.400 X $ 882 = $12.700.800

2. The correct answer is a

   Sales of 75.000 pieces at $ 42 or Sales + 10% = 82.500 pieces at $ 39.90 (-5%)
   Sales 75.000 X $ 42   = $ 3.150.000. 82.500 X $ 39,90   = $ 3.291.750
   Cost 75.000 X $ 28,56 = - 2.142.000 = 68% 82.500 X $ 28,56 = - 2.356.200 71.5%
   ----------------   ----------------
   Profit margin $ 1.008.000 = 32 % $ 935.550 28,4%
   The manager correctly saw the sales man's pitfall: a drop of more than 7% in dollars.

3. The correct answer is b

   If purchase price is $ 42 and profit margin is $ 8 then sales price is $ 50 = 100%. The purchase price of $ 42 is 84% of the sales price (so, the profit margin is 16%)

4. The correct answer is a

   When profit margin is 25%, then purchase price must be 75% because sales price is 100%. The purchase price of $ 15 therefore is 75%. 100% = (15 : 75) X 100 =sales price = $ 20.

5. The correct answer is c

   Depreciation does not create a flow of cash and a mortgage decreases only by paying back. So: equity will decrease (unless net profit was higher than depreciation!)

6. The correct answer is b.

   Costs of housing are not easily controllable because of ongoing costs of energy; costs of depreciation are not controllable and nor are the financing costs

7. The correct answer is c

   When 60 people could make 90.000 bikes then this is 1.500 bikes/person. In 2008 the company should have 54.000: 1.500 = 36 employees. 24 are redundant = $ 768.000

8. The correct answer is a.

   Trucks serve more than 2 years and , thereby, belong to fixed assets. So depreciation costs should be reported on the P&L statement: (6 X $ 320.000) : 5 = $ 384.000. The other costs belong under "transportation costs": (6 X 60.000) : 100 = 3.600 X 8 X $1.2 = $ 34.560 (or:

360.000 X .096 =) + 6X $ 9.500 = $ 57.000 for maintenance plus insurance. Total $ 34.560 + $ 57.000 = $ 91.560.

9. The correct answer is b

   Under depreciation it will record (2X$18.000):5 + (2X$12.000):10 = $ 9.600 and as office costs it will book (4 X 10 X $42) + (4 X 25 X $ 24,50) = $ 4.130

10. The correct answer is c

    8% net profit means $ 806.400, which requires $ 326.400 in economizing. The costs of personnel plus marketing total $ 2.344.000. $ 326.400 is 13,925% of that figure. So, both these costs have to decrease by that percentage.

Solutions of the Exercises of Chapter 5

Liquidity

1. Put an X under Balance Sheet or P & L Statement, depending on the relative action in the first column. Place a V in one or more of the columns 1 to 4 reporting the meaning of the actions.

ACTION	Balance sheet	P & L statement	1 revenue	2 costs	3 receipt	4 expenditure
Example: client pays his bill	X				V	
payment of $ 4.000 in wages		X		V		V
client buys for $ 100 and may pay after 30 days	X	X	V			
a printer is purchased for the office and paid in cash	X					V
a client purchases a product and pays cash		X	V		V	
A contractor repairs the roof; payment in 30 days	X	X		V		
equipment is purchased; payment in 60 days	X					
10 Christmas presents are bought for employees and paid in cash		X		V		V
Depreciation of building of $ 30.000	X	X		V		
20 new shares are issued; buyers pay in cash	X				V	
interest on mortgage is paid		X		V		V
the bill of a supplier is paid	X					V
An employee lends $ 1.000 from						

the company to buy a computer privately	X	V
Long term loan is increased by $ 50.000; money received one day later	X	V
credit in current account is lowered buy paying back $ 10.000 to the bank	X	V

2. The correct answer is a

   An invoice must be paid on or before the end of the term allowed and so must a tax notice and the periodic interest. Depreciation is a cost but never an expenditure.

3. The correct answer is c

   Profit leads to income partially: accounts receivable already contributed to the profit before payments are received. The foremost advantage is to anticipate possible liquidity shortages which will require additional financing

4. The correct answer is b

   Even the largest corporations can get into financial trouble, especially when they stretched their borrowing capacity to the limit and see that growth requires additional financing

5. The correct answer is a

   Income was $ 125.000 and payments were $ 135.000. So a shortage of $ 10.000 From this exercise it can be seen that good planning of liquidity is not difficult and will contribute to sound financing of a company

6. The correct answer is c

   Positive cash flows were: $ 15.000 available balance by the end of May, plus $ 70.00 plus $ 22.000 sales in cash, less wages of $ 70.000 in June = $ 37.000
   We see that a solid liquidity plan can help setting limits to certain expenditures

7. The correct answer is a

Sales in July will yield: 10 tastes X 30 containers X $ 300 =		$90 000
10 tastes X 20 containers X $ 300 =		60 000
20 tastes X 10 containers X $ 300 =		60 000
Total income July		$210 000
Less: tax payment of	$10 000	
Purchases	25 000	
Wages	4 000	
desired balance end of July	150 000	
total expenditure	$189 000	$189 000
Balance available to hire part time employees		$21 000
A part time employee will cost 31 days X $ 50 = $ 1.550		

Giovanni therefore can afford $ 21.000 : $ 1.550 = 13.5 part time employees

8.1 Fill the format here below for Johnson Controls

ACTION	2d QUARTER	3d QUARTER
Cash balance begin of period	100 000	+ 84 698
payments received from clients	1) 571 200	571 200
other payments received		120 000
TOTAL PAYMENTS RECEIVED	671 200	775 898
To be paid to suppliers	336 000	336 000
Salaries and wages paid (=70%)	42 000	42 000
Holiday bonus paid	11 520	
pay-roll tax to be paid	2) 25 680	18 000
pension premiums to be paid	12 000	12 000
balance of value added tax to be paid	3) 37 552	37 552
corporate tax to be paid	4) 56 250	56 250
interest to be paid	18 000	18 000
marketing expenses to be paid	28 500	28 500
purchased assets to be paid	15 000	58 000
maintenance costs to be paid		10 000
office appliances	4 000	2 000
TOTAL EXPENDITURES	586 502	618 302
Surplus or shortage of CASH	+ 84 698	157 596

Explanatory notes
1. Annual turnover is $ 1.920.000 + 19% value added tax of $ 363.800 = $ 2.284.800 which is $ 571.200 per quarter to be received from clients.
2. Salaries and wages per quarter are $ 240.000 : 4 = $ 60.000. 70% of this is paid = $42.000. Pay-roll tax must be paid on regular salaries and on the holiday bonus. So, 30% of $ 60.000 = $ 18.000 and in the second quarter the holiday bonus was 8% of annual salaries and wages. 8% of $ 240.000 is $ 19.200 of which 60% is paid to the employees = $ 11.520 and 40% or $ 7.680 is added to the pay-roll tax due in the second quarter which, therefore will be $ 18.000 + $ 7.680 = $ 25.680

3. Sales are $ 1.920.000 : 4 = $ 480.000. Value added tax to be declared is 19%: $91.200 Purchases are $ 1.344.000. Per quarter: $ 336.000. Without value added tax this is : divide by 119% = $ 282.352 per quarter. The difference of $ 336.000 - $ 282.352 = $ 53.648 is value added tax to be paid to suppliers and to be deducted from the tax declaration: $91.200 - $ 53.648 = $ 37.552. This amount must be declared.
4. 25% Corporate tax of $ 450.000 is $ 112.500. The 4 installments start in May. So twice in the 2d quarter and twice in the 3d quarter $ 56.250 must be paid.

8.2 The correct answer is b

9. The correct answer is c

Quarterly fixed costs are 3 X $ 27.400 = $ 82.200. In the first quarter earnings were 1.500 X ($ 30 - $ 12) = $ 27.000 and in quarter 4 3.000 X ($30 -$ 12) = $ 54.000

Solutions of the Exercises of Chapter 6

The Closing Balance Sheet

1. The changes to be made on the closing balance sheet are

DEBIT SIDE		CREDIT SIDE	
Building	$15 000 A	equity + $180 000 D	
Equipment	$20 000 A		
new investment	+$50 000 B	mortgage loan-$20 000 E	
new printers	+$60 000 C	long term loan+$40 000 B	
furniture and fixtures	-$25 000 A		
Cash for equipment	-$50 000 B	creditors	+$60 000 C
Long term loan cash	+$40 000 B		
cash to repay mortgage	-$20 000 E		
cash flow in: profit	+$180 000 D		
+depreciation	+$60 000 A		
	---------------		------------------
Total change	+$260 000	Total change	+ $260 000

Watch B. We see that B is recorded four times. It could have been done in three times: **debit side**: equipment + $ 50.000 and cash - $ 10.000; **credit side**: loan + $ 40.000

1.2 The correct answer is b

On the opening balance sheet cash was $ 90.000. To be added is the cash flow = net profit of $ 180.000 + depreciations of $ 60.000 plus the $ 40.000 from the loan and to be subtracted the cash for equipment of $ 50.000 and the repayment of the mortgage of $ 20.000 = $ 300.000
Note that the interest payments do not affect the cash flow: interest paid was part of the P&L statement, which resulted in a net profit. It does not make sense to take these interest payments into account again when calculating the cash flow.

1.3 The correct answer is c

Mortgage was partly paid back by $ 20.000 = $ 380.000. Long term loan was increased for an investment by $ 40.000 = $ 280.000

2.1 BALANCE SHEET

Factory building	$325 000	Ordinary share capital	$340 000
Equipment	-150 000	Retained earnings	120 000
Furniture and fixtures	-96 000		
		Mortgage loan 5%	170 000
Inventory of products	-120 000	Long term loan 8%	130 000
Accounts receivable	-140 000	Provision maintenance work	-20 000
Cash	-279 000	Creditors	140 000
		Current account credit 14%	-190 000
TOTAL	$ 1 110 000	TOTAL	$1 110 000

The changes in the balance sheet are explained as follows: The fixed assets are decreased by their respective depreciations which total figure of $ 64.000 adds to the cash figure (cash flow) of $ 90.000. Additional equipment increased this asset by $60.000 and it increased the figure of creditors with the same figure. The furniture purchased at $15.000 must be added to this asset and cash must be decreased by the same figure. Profit is to be added to cash for $ 120.000.

A new item appears on the credit side under long term liabilities: provisions $ 20.000 which did not create a flow of cash and therefore must be added to the cash flow. Share capital increased by the stock dividend of $ 80.000 which 80 shares created a $0 in retained earnings. This last item is then filled by the net profit of $ 120.000.

2.2 The correct answer is

Cash started with $ 90.000. Add the depreciations of $ 64.000 and the provision of $ 20.000 plus the net profit and decrease it by the expenditure for furniture of $ 15.000 = $ 279.000

2.3 The correct answer is b

To be added to the starting figure of $ 90.000 are: net profit of $ 120.000, total depreciation of $ 64.000 plus the provision of $ 20.000, less $ 15.000 for furniture. Cash on closing balance is $ 279.000

2. The correct answer is c
   This exercise is made best in 3 steps.

Opening balance

DEBIT	DEBIT	CREDIT	CREDIT
inventory	cash	retained earnings	current account credit
$80 000	$40 000	$0	$120 000
		Step 1	
-$ 80 000	+ $125 000	+$45 000	
inventory	cash	retained earnings	current account credit
		step 2	
+ $ 1 036 800 (=64% of sales)*		+ $1 036 800	
- $ 1 036 800	+$1 620 000	+ $583 200	
		step 3	
+ $259 200			+ $259 200
---------------	---------------	---------------	---------------
$259 200	$1 785 000	$628 200	$1 416 000

Debit side and credit side are equal. To realize the annual turnover $ 1.036.800 of inventory was needed and was financed by the current account credit. During the year profit margin was 36% of $ 1.620.000 = $ 583.200 which belongs under equity. And the inventory in step 3 is one quarter of the annual need = three months of inventory = 64% of $ 1.620.000 is $ 1.036.800. Divide by 4 to find three months of needed inventory = $ 259.200 and record the same figure under current account.

4.1 The correct answer is b

Depreciation, being not an expenditure adds to the cash $ 212.000 and decreases the respective fixed assets by the same amount. Cash decreases with the amount of the loss of $ 40.000 and closes at $ 172.000. Retained earnings created a negative of the credit side of - $ 40.000, and the debit side closes at $172.000-$ 212.000 = - $40.000.

4.2 The correct answer is c

Cash flow is annual profit + depreciation: - $ 40.000 + $ 212.000 = $ 172.000

5. The correct answer is a

Monthly turnover should have been the figure for accounts receivable : $ 480.000 : 12 = $ 40.000. Compared to the figure on the balance sheet this is too high by $ 15.000. Inventory on a monthly basis should have been ($ 480.000 X 68%) : 12 = $ 27.200. The figure of $ 42.000, therefore was too high by $ 14.800

6. The correct answer is c

Repayment on a loan is never recorded in a P&L statement; depreciations of two or more types of fixed assets are recorded in one total figure on a P&L statement and, therefore, cannot be transferred from P&L statement directly to the balance sheet.

7. The correct answer is c

Since depreciation does not cause expenditures, Cash will grow by $ 102.000 and fixed assets decrease by the same amount. No profit, no loss; so nothing under retained earnings

Solutions of the Exercise of Chapter 7.1

1. The correct answer is c
   Liquidity has everything to do with the potential to pay current liabilities

2. The correct answer is b
   Acid test or quick ratio calculates the liquidity whereby inventory is left out from the current assets. If then, still, a company reaches current assets: current liabilities = > 1, then it has a solid potential to pay all of its current liabilities.

3.1 The correct answer is c
   Current ratio is Current assets: Current liabilities. If > 1 then liquidity looks sufficient to pay all of the current liabilities. In this case the current ratio is $ 540.000: $590.000 = 0,91, which does not look solidly enough.

3.2 The correct answer is a
   Quick ratio excludes inventory from the current assets because inventory is hard to turn into cash quickly. In this case $ 300.000: $ 590.000 = 0.508 which by far is not enough to pay the current liabilities.

3.3 The correct answer is b
   This company will not be able to pay it's current liabilities at short notice.

3.4 The correct answer is c
   The working capital shows a negative: $ 540.000 of total current assets less $590.000 of current liabilities = - $ 50.000. There is no room to add more liabilities in the short run.

4. The correct answer is a
   Current ratio is calculated by dividing current assets by current liabilities.

5. The correct answer is c
   There is a solid liquidity when the quick ratio is > 1

6. The correct answer is a
   Solvability indicates the power to pay ALL of the liabilities.

Solutions of the Exercise of Chapter 7.2

1.1 The correct answer is c

First, we calculate the average equity: ($ 700.000 + $ 800.000):2=$ 750.000. Net profit after tax was $ 292.500, which is 39% of $ 750.000

1.2 The correct answer is a

Average of liabilities is ($ 1.650.000+$ 1.800.000) : 2 = $ 1.725.000. Interest paid during the 2d. year was $ 110.000, which is 6.4% of this amount.

1.3 The correct answer is b

Average total capital is ($ 2.350.000 + $ 2.600.000) : 2 =$ 2.475.000. The operating result in year 2 was $ 500.000, which is 20.2 % of that average.

1.4 The correct answer is b

In year 1 long capital consisted of equity of $ 700.000 + long term liabilities of $950.000 = $ 1.650.000. This portion had to finance fixed assets in the first place, which amounted to $ 1.400.000. The positive difference of $250.000 could, hence, be used to finance current assets. An other approach to this question could have been: current assets totalled $950.000 and current liabilities were $ 700.000. So, $ 250.000 must have come from long term capital.

1.5 The correct answer is c

40% of net profit after tax is $ 117.000 and when nominal value per share was $1.000 then there are 500 shares. Yield per share was $ 234

1.6 The correct answer is a

When a share of $ 1.000 yields $ 234 then the return was 23.4%

1.7 The correct answer is b

First, we calculate the return on total capital from the operating result of $500.000. Average of total capital was ($ 2.350.000 + $ 2.600.000) : 2 = $2.475.000. The operating result of $ 500.000 is 20.2% of that average. On every $ 1 invested 20.2 cents were earned. The average total of liabilities was ($1.650.000 + $ 1.800.000) : 2 = $ 1.725.000. The interest paid in year 2 was $110.000, which is 6,38%. Every $ of liabilities cost 6.4 cents. The positive leverage was 20.2% - 6.38% = 13.82 %. The relative indication is that every dollar borrowed will yield a benefit of $ 0,138, or almost $ 0,14.

1.8 The correct answer is a

There is ample room for more borrowings because the yield on every invested dollar was 20% (= $ 0,20) whereas the yield on liabilities was 6% only (=$0.06). In other words: every dollar invested yields $ 0,20 at a financial cost of $ 0.06. We have to bear in mind that more borrowings depend on the agreement with the bank on how large the equity percentage of all investments has to be. And, more borrowings should be considered carefully in advance and promise positive growth.

1.9 The correct answer is c

The turnover rate of inventory from the balance is calculated as follows. The annual purchases according to the P&L statement were $ 900.000. This is $75.000 per month, which should be the amount of inventory on the balance sheet if all suppliers can deliver within several weeks. The balance, however shows an amount of $ 500.000, which is enough to keep deliveries going for 6.6 months. The turnover rate, therefore is 12 : 6.6 = 1.8 which is, by all standards, a very poor performance.

1.10 The correct answer is c

Sales were $ 1.800.000, which comes down to $ 150.000 per month. If debtors would pay their bills within the standard 30 days this would have been the amount on the balance sheet, more or less. In practice the balance shows an amount of $400.000. Apparently, clients use a payment term of $400.000: $ 150.000 = 2.6 months, which indicates that somebody on the accounts receivables department has been asleep constantly.

1.11 The correct answer is a

Purchases were $ 900.000 for the year. This is $ 75.000 per month, which would have appeared on the balance sheet if the corporation would have the habit of prompt payment at 30 days. In fact creditors appear on the balance sheet at $450.000. The company smartly got away with a payment term of $450.000 : $75.000 = 6 months.

Solutions of the Exercise of Chapter 8

1.1 The correct answer is b

$ 42.240: 2.000 hours (50 X 5 X 8) = $ 21.12

1.2 The correct answer is c

Net hours in one year are 2.000 – 120 – 160 – 80 – 32 -200 = 1.408 billable hours. $ 42.240 of salary: 1.408 net hours = $ 30

1.3 The correct answer is a

First the hours not worked are to be deducted from the 2.000: = - 592. Working hours which are billable are 1.408. $ 42.240: 1.408 = $ 30 = variable costs. Lawyers can bill 5 X 1.408 hours per year. The FCC (fixed cost component) in their cost price is, therefore: $ 280.000: (5 X 1.408) = $ 39,77. Together with their variable costs of $ 30 the cost price now is $ 69,77

2.1 The correct answer is b

Lee's fixed costs are kilometres (40 X $ 1,20) + gas consumption (5 X $ 0,50) + license ($ 1.500: 50) + depreciation ($ 60.000: 5) : 50 = $ 48 = $ 2.50 + $ 30 + $ 240 = $320,50 per market day. The fixed cost per piece are $ 320,50 : 200 = $1,60. The variable cost are $ 0,60, so cost price is $ 2,20

2.2 The correct answer is a

When the sales price is $ 3.20 and the cost price is $ 2.20 then the profit margin is $ 1,00 each which is 31,25% of the sales price (= 100%)

3. The correct answer is c

Fixed costs total: (4 X $ 12.000) + (12 X $ 800) + $ 15.000 = $ 72.600, so the FCC (fixed costs component) is $ 72.600 : 20.000 = $ 3.63. CP is $3,63 + $3.3 = $6.93

d. The correct answer is c.

Fixed costs are: depreciation equipment is ($ 120.000 - $ 10.000) :10 =$11.000 + depreciation barn $ 5.830 + annual salary Derek $ 30.000 + insurance of 12 X $ 120 = $ 1.440 totals: $ 48.270. This is $ 2.41/km. Add the variable cost of fuel = (20 X $ 1.40) : 100 = $ 0.28. Cost price per kilometre is $ 2.41 + $ 0.28 = $ 2.69.

b. The correct answer is a

Fixed costs are $ 84.000 for salaries + $ 18.000 for rent + $ 4.000 for cleaning   totalling $ 106.000. Fixed Costs Component per piece is $ 106.000 : 40.000 pieces = $ 2.65. The variable costs per dimension are 20 cm. X 25 cm. = $ 0.90 and for 30 cm. X 40 cm. $ 1.20. Add $240 : 3.000 per carton box = $ 0.08. Cost price 20 cm. X 25 cm. therefore $ 2.65 + $ 0.90 + $ 0.08=$3.63 and 30 cm. X 40 cm. : $2.65 + $ 1.20 + $ 0.08 = $3.93

Solutions of the Exercises of Chapter 9
Cost Prices for Multiple Products and Services

ACTIVITY BASED COSTING

1.1 The correct answer is b

Socks contain wool for 2000 X $ 2 = $ 4.000, shirts 1.000 X $ 5 = $ 5.000

1.2 The correct answer is a

Indirect costs are $ 3.000: 5 = $ 600 for depreciation of the knitting machine plus $300 for electricity = $ 900. Total variable costs for the two products are $ 9.000. Indirect costs are ($ 900 : $ 9.000) X 100 = 10% of the variable costs. By adding 10% tot the variable costs we arrive at the correct cost price for the socks: $ 2 + 10% = $ 2.20

1.3 The correct answer is c

Indirect costs are $ 600 + $ 300 = $ 900. The cost plus percentage must be ($900 : $ 9.000) X 100 = 10%. So, cost price for the shirts is $ 5 + 10% = $ 5.50

2.1 The correct answer is c

First, we calculate total variable costs: 3.000 jeans X $ 35 = $ 105.000
                             1.800 sweatshirts X $ 18 = -32.400

                            Total of variable costs = $ 137.400

Indirect costs: 50 X 60 kilometres X $ 1.80 = $ 5.400
Rent of his booth + licence: 50 X $ 70   = - 3.500
Warehouse rent is ($ 600: 4) X 50   = -7.500

          Total indirect costs $ 16.400 = 11.936% of $ 137.400

Cost price jeans therefore $ 35 + 11.936 % = $ 39.18

2.2 The correct answer is b

From 2.1 we know that the cost plus percentage is 11.936%. Cost price of a sweat shirt therefore is $ 18 + 11.936 % = $ 20.15

2.3 The correct answer is c

The cost price totals were 3 000 X $ 39.10 + 1 800 X $ 20.11=	$153 498
The variable costs totals were 3 000 X $ 35 + 1 800 X $ 18 =	$137 400
Total indirect was: $ 5 400 (car)+$ 3 500 (booth) + $ 7.200 =	16 100

Total costs	$153 500

3.1 The correct answer is b

The four specialists earn $ 70.000 per year each. At 1.400 hours this is $ 50 per hour. Total variable costs of specialists is 4 X $ 70.000 per year = $ 280.000. The portion of indirect costs having a relation with specialists is $ 310.000. (Indirect costs : variable costs) X 100% = ($ 310.000 : 280.000) X 100% = 110.71%. Variable cost per hour + 110.71% = $ 105.36

3.2 The correct answer is a

The six assistants earn $ 40.000 each. At 1.600 hours this is $ 25 per hour. The total variable costs of the assistants is 6 X $ 40.000 = $ 240.000. The portion of the indirect costs with a relation to assistants is $ 290.000. (indirect costs: variable costs)X100% = ($ 290.000 : $ 240.000) X 100% = 120.83%. Variable costs per hour per assistant are $ 25. Increased by 120.83 this makes $ 55.21

3.3 The correct answer is b

It is clear that $ 310.000 of indirect costs must be incorporated in the hourly rate of specialists: ($ 310.000 : $ 280.000) 100% = 110.71% For assistants this is ($ 290.000 : $ 240.000) X 100% = 120.83%. Hourly cost price specialist will be $ 50 + 110.71% = $105.36 and for an assistant $ 25 + 120.83% = $ 55.21. Total cost prices: 4 X 1.400 X $105.36 = $ 590.016 + 6 X 1.600 X $ 55.21 = $ 530.016 is $ 1.120.032 Indirect costs + total salaries: $ 600.000 + $ 520.000 = $ 1.120.000

4. The correct answer is c

BERETS	**SCARVES**	**TOTAL**
TOTAL VARIABLE COSTS	TOTAL VARIABLE COSTS	TOTAL FOR TWO PRODUCTS
Material 30 000 X $ 3 =$ 90 000	Material 40 000 X $ 4 = $ 160 000	Material $ 250 000
Direct labour 30 000 X $ 2 =$ 60 000	Direct labour 40 000 X $ 1.50 = $ 60 000	Labour $ 120 000
TOTAL DIRECT COSTS $ 150 000	TOTAL DIRECT COSTS $ 220 000	**TOTAL DIRECT** $370 000
Cost plus % of depreciation 2/3 of $24 000 = $ 16 000 = 17.78% of $90 000. **Material cost is $ 3 + 17.78% = $3.53**	Cost plus % of depreciation is 1/3 of $24 000 = $ 8 000 = 5% of $ 160 000 **Material cost is $ 4 + 5% = $ 4.20**	Depreciation $24 000 Indir.labour $120 000 **Total indir.$144 000**
Cost plus % labour is 40% of $ 120 000 = $ 48 000 = 80% of $ 60 000 **Direct labour is $ 2 + 80% = $ 3.60**	Cost plus% labour is 60% of $ 120 000 = $ 72 000 = 120% of $ 60 000. **Direct labour is $ 1.50+120%=$3.30**	TOTAL COST **$ 514 000**
Cost price $ 3.53 + $ 3.60 = $ 7.13 TOTAL COST PRICE ONE YEAR: 30 000 x $ 7 13 =$ 213 900	Cost price is $ 4.20 + $ 3.30 = $ 7.50 TOTAL COST PRICE ONE YEAR: 40 000 x $ 7.50 = $ 300 000 =	TOTAL COSTS **$ 513 900**

The correct answer is b

	pallets	bird feeders	total
direct material 100 000X$4.50=	$450 000	$480 000 (200 000 X $ 2.40)	= $930 000
share for indirect material of $ 380 000	25%	75%	
indirect material costs	$95 000	$285 000	$380 000
total			**$1 310 000**

cost plus percentage
$ 95.000: $ 450.000   21.11% $ 285.000: $ 480.000   59.375%
direct material will be
$ 4.50 + 21.11% = $ 5.45 $ 2.40 + 59.375% = $ 3.83
Check: 100.000 X $ 5.45 = $ 545.000 + 200.000 X $ 3.83 = $ 766.000 = **$ 1.311.000**

6.1 The correct answer is a

First we calculate the total variable costs of the cosmeticians: 8 X $ 68.880 = $551.040 and of the assistants 4 X $ 33.300 =$ 133.200. Then we can calculate the cost plus percentage: 65% of $ 273.696= $ 177.902,40. ($ 177.902,40 : $ 551.040) X 100% = 32.2848% for the cosmeticians and 35% of $ 273.696 = $ 95.793.60. ($ 95.793,60 : $133.200) X 100% = 71.92%. Hourly cost price of the cosmetician is ($ 68.880 : 1.640) = $ 42. $ 42 + 32.2848% = **$ 55.56**. And for the assistants ($33.300:1.800) + 71.92% = **$ 31.81**

Check: total costs were $ 273.696+(8X$68.880)+(4X$33.300)   = $ 957.936
Cosmeticians 8 X 1.640 X $ 55.56   = $ 728.947
Assistants   4 X 1.800 X $ 31.81   = $ 229.032 +   = $ 957.979

Solutions of the Exercise of Chapter 10

The Budgeting Process and Analysis of Variances

1. The correct answer is b.

An estimate in a larger to very large company is provisional in nature. Nobody can be held accountable if the estimated goals were not achieved. Only after all of the estimates of all of the departments were integrated and calculated to a provisional P&L statement and there are no reasons left for any changes in figures the final stage of approval is reached. This **approval by the board or by the Management Team turns estimates into firm assignments** for all of the departments: budgets, meaning the **assignments** to reach the goals and **authorization** for the anticipated costs and expenses.

2.1 The correct answer is c.

	budget	reality
Indirect total cost	$19 200	$19 200
Variable costs of materials	1 920	2 160
Labour costs	6 400	6 400
Costs of 3.200 meals	$27 520 and 4 000 meals	$27 760

There were 800 more meals at additional costs of $ 240. Normal costs would have been: $27.520 : 3.200 meals = $ 8.60. In reality the costs per meal were $ 27.760 : 4.000 = $6.94. Positive variance totals 4.000 X (8.60 - $ 6.94) = **$ 6.640**.

2.2 The correct answer is a

(RV – BV) X $2 ($ 40 is hourly wage : 20 meals per hour) = 4.000 – 3.200 X $2 = $1.600. There are 160 hours available for the month. The BV for 4.000 meals would have been: 4.000 : 20 meals = 200 hours. In reality 160 hours were needed; a saving of 40 hours X $ 40 = **$ 1.600**.

2.4 The correct answer is b

(BP – RP) X RV (budgeted price less real price x real volume)

Budgeted price is ¼ of a kilogram X $ 2.40 = $ 0.60 per meal. In reality $ 2.160 was paid for the raw materials of 4.000 meals = $ 0.54 per meal. 4.000 meals took 1.000 kilograms which cost $ 2.160 : 1.000 = $ 2.16. Per meal this is ¼ = $ 0.54. The price variance therefore is ($ 0.60 - $ 0.54) X 4.000 = **$ 240**.

2.5 The correct answer is a

The indirect costs per meal according to budget would be $ 19.200 : 3.200 = $ 6, where 3.200 meals are within budget = BV. Because 800 meals more had been prepared the carrying basis for these indirect costs was distinctly larger than budgeted. (RV – BV) X (total indirect costs : BV) = (4.000 – 3.200) X ($ 19.200 : 3.200) = 800 X 6 = **$ 4.800**. And $ 4.800 + $ 240 + $ 1.600 = $ 6.640.

3.1 The correct answer is c

The volume variance is (RV – BV) X BP (5.800 – 6.000) X 120 = - $ 24.000

3.2 The correct answer is a

The price variance is (RP – BP) X RV = ($ 132 - $ 120) X 5.800 = $ 69.600

3.3 The correct answer is b

The difference between budget and reality is (BV X budgeted profit margin) – (RV X real profit margin) = 6.000 X ($ 120 - $ 80) – 5.800 X ($ 132 - $ 80) = (6.000 X $ 40) – (5.800 X $ 52) = $ 240.000 - $ 301.600 = $ 61.600 of better profit margin with lower sales volume.

Solutions of the Exercise of Chapter 11

Methods to Calculate Profit and the Break Even Point

1.1 The correct answer is b

The full cost price is TFC (total fixed costs) : BV (budgeted volume) + variable costs= $1.200.000 : 24.000.000 = $ 0,05 + $ 0,20 = $ 0,25

1.2 The correct answer is c

Annual result in AC: turnover of	22 800 000 X $ 0.29 =	$6 612 000
Less full cost price,	22 800 000 X $ 0.25 =	-5 700 000
result of aggregate transactions		$ 912 000

Capacity variance is (RV-BV) X TFC

$$= 28 \text{ million} - 24 \text{ million} \times \$ 0.05 = \$ 200.000$$

Result for the period $1.112.000

1.3 The correct answer is a

The contribution margin and the result of the year are calculated as follows:

Turnover is 22 800 000 X $ 0.29	$6 612 000
Variable costs of this quantity 22 800 000 X $ 0.20	-4 560 000
contribution margin is	$2 052 000
total of fixed costs is	-1 200 000
result of the year is	$852 000

1.4 The correct answer is b

Turnover is 22 800 000 X $ 0.29	$6 612 000
Additional turnover is 4 000 000 X $ 0.23	920 000
total turnover is	$7 532 000
variable costs total: 26 800 000 X $ 0.20	-5 360 000
contribution margin is now	$2 172 000
total of fixed costs is	-1 200 000
result for the year $ 120 000 higher:	$972 000

2.1. The correct answer is c

Full cost price is ($ 875.000: 17.500.000) + $ 0,23 = $ 0.05 + $ 0,23 = $ 0,28

2.1 The correct answer is a

Result in the AC method. Turnover is 17 200 000 X $ 0.48		$8 256 000
Less full cost price 17 200 000 X $ 0.28		-4 816 000
result of aggregate transactions		$3 440 000
Capacity variance: (18 million – 17.5 million) X $ 0.05		25 000
result of the period		$3 465 000

2.3   The correct answer is c

Result in the VC method. Turnover is 17 200 000 X $ 0.48		$ 8 256 000
Less variable costs 17 200 000 X $ 0.23		-3 956 000
the contribution margin is		$4 300 000
total of fixed costs is		-875 000
result of the period		$3 425 000

2.2 The correct answer is b

Result in the AC method is $ 40.000 higher than in the VC method because unsold volume went to inventory at (18.000.000 – 17.200.000) X $ 0.05 of FCC (fixed costs component in the cost price) =$ 40.000. In the VC method the sold volume was 800.000 litres lower than planned. The unsold volume went to inventory at the variable costs of $ 0,23 = $ 84.000. In the AC method the 800.000 litres went to inventory at the full cost price of $ 224.000. The difference is 800.000 litres X $ 0.05 = $ 40.000. The $ 224.000 in the AC method are not considered as costs of the period but as part of the value of the volume in inventory and, thus, appears on the balance sheet. In a next period this sum will be considered as costs at the moment these 800.000 litres are sold.

2.3 The correct answer is a

Normal turnover is	17 200 000 X $ 0.48	=	$8 256 000
Additional turnover is	1 500 000 X $ 0.28	=	420 000
Total turnover=			$8 676 000
Cost price of turnover:	18 700 000 X $ 0.28	=	-5 236 000
Result of the transaction		=	$3 440 000
Capacity variance	(18.7 million-17.5 million) X $ 0.05		60 000
result of the period			$3 500 000

2.6 The correct answer is c

Normal turnover is 17 200 000 X $ 0.48	=$8 256 000
Additional turnover 1 500 000 X $ 0.28	=420 000
Total turnover	=$8 676 000
Variable costs 18 700 000 X $ 0.23	= -4 301 000
Contribution margin	= $4 375 000
Total fixed costs	= -875 000
Annual result	= $3 500 000

There is no difference in outcome between the AC and the VC methods because no unsold volume went to inventory.

2.7 The correct answer is b

The contribution margin is sales price – variable costs = $ 0,48 - $ 0,23 = $ 0,25. Breakeven point asks the question: how many times must $ 0,25 be earned to cover for total fixed costs: $ 875.000: $ 0,25 = 3.500.000 litres.

Check: 3.500.000 X $ 0,48	=$ 1.680.000
Variable costs 3.500.000 X $ 0,23	= 805.000
fixed costs earned back	= $ 875.000

6.2 The correct answer is b

Full cost price= variable costs $ 78 + ($ 4.800.000: BV of 384.000 kilograms) = $ 12.50, totals $ 90,50

6.3 The correct answer is c

VC method. 400 000 kilograms X $ 146	= $58 400 000
Variable costs are 400.000 X $ 78	= -31 200 000
Contribution margin	= $27 200 000
Total fixed costs	= -4 800 000
Result of the period	= $22 400 000

6.4 The correct answer is c

Full cost price for 400.000 kilograms= $ 78 + ($4.800.000:400.000)> 78+12 =$ 90

6.5 The correct answer is a

Breakeven point is= total fixed costs : total contribution margin per kilogram = $4.800.000 : ($ 146 - $ 78) = $ 4.800.000 : $ 68 = 70.588 kilograms

Check: 70.588 kilograms X ($ 146 - $ 78) = 70.588 X $ 68 = $ 4.800.000

6.6 The correct answer is b

Turnover 400 000 X $ 146	= $58 400 000
Full cost price 400 000 X $ 90.50	= -36 200 000
result of transaction	= $22 200 000
Capacity variance (RV –BV) X $ 12.50 FCC	
= (320 000 – 384 000) X $ 12.50	=-800 000
result of period =	$21 400 000

Solutions of the Exercises of Chapter 12

Pre-Calculation Methods for Investment Options

1.1 The correct answer is b.
Annual savings would be $ 110.000 less depreciation of $ 37.000 = $ 73.000. At 6% and 10 years the factor to be used for each year is 1) 1.06, 2) 1.1236 3) 1.1910 4) 1.2624 5)1.3382 6)1.4185 7) 1.5036 8) 1.5938 9) 1.6894 10) 1.7908.

The present value of the savings will be:

1. $ 73 000: 1.06 = $ 68 867.92	6) $73 000: 1.4185 =	$51 462.81
2. $ 73 000: 1.1236 = $ 64 969	7) $73 000: 1.5036 =	$48 550.15
3. $ 73 000: 1.1910 = $ 61 293	8) $73 000: 1.5938 =	$45 802.48
4. $ 73 000: 1.2624 = $ 57 826.34	9) $73 000: 1.6894 =	$43 210.61
5. $ 73 000: 1.3382 = $ 54 550.89	10) $73 000: 1.7908 =	$40 763.90
$307 507.15		+$229 789.95

Present value of the savings totals $537 297.10
The investment is - 380 000
net present value of investment $157 297.12.
Investment is a viable option.

1.2 The correct answer is c
To calculate the period to earn back the investment the future cash flows resulting from the investment are important. Annual growth of the profit will be $ 110.000 and the annual costs of depreciation will be ($ 380.000 - $ 10.000) : 10 = $ 37.000. Cash flows will be $ 110.000 + $ 37.000 = $ 147.000. After year 1 not yet earned back is $380.000 -$147.000 = $ 233.000. After year 2 not yet earned back is $ 233.000 - $ 147.000 = $86.000. In year 3 the investment will be earned back after ($ 86.000 : $ 147.000) : 12 months = 7 months. So: pay back period will be 3 years and 7 months.

1. The correct answer is a
Annual savings would be 30 X ($ 52.000 - $ 23.000) = 30 X $ 29.000 = $ 870.000. To calculate the present value of the annual savings these have to be divided by 1) 1.04 2)1.0816 3) 1.1248 4) 1.1698 5) 1.2166 6) 1.2653 7) 1.3159 8) 1.3685 9) 1.4233 10)1.4802. Present value is calculated:

1) $ 870.000: 1.04 = $ 836.538   6) $ 870.000: 1.2653 = $ 687.583
2) $ 870.000: 1.0816 = $ 804.363   7) $ 870.000: 1.3159 = $ 661.144
3) $ 870.000: 1.1248 = $ 773.470   8) $ 870.000: 1.3685 = $ 635.732
4) $ 870.000: 1.1698 = $ 743.716   9) $ 870.000: 1.4233 = $ 611.255
5) $ 870.000: 1.2166 = $ 715.107   10) $ 870.000: 1.4802 = $ 587.758

The total present value of the savings is $ 7.056.666. Part of that could be used by management to offer a voluntary farewell premium to the 30 older people.

Solution of the Closing Assignment
Chapter 1

The Investment Plan

The letters for the correct answers can be found in the investment plan at the end here below.

Since total investment cannot be established before we know which vendor of equipment and which vendor of the raw materials will be selected, we will postpone the choice for the building till the end of the solution.

What we do know already: the company will bring equity to a total of $ 550.000, which must be financing at least 40% of the assets to be invested. That means that total investments the company can afford amounts to ($ 550.000: 40) X 100 = $ 1.375.000 as a maximum.

First, we will have to find out the required equipment capacity. The chosen equipment must fill the needed annual quantities over the depreciation period.

When we calculate the startup quantity of production and add 10% on top of each previous year, we will find that in year 10 the quantity will be 353.692 pieces. Vendor A does not qualify since his equipment capacity is limited to 350.000.

To compare vendor B and C we not only should look at their price but rather at the annual costs involved, like we learned earlier by comparing motorcars.

	Vendor B	Vendor C
Annual depreciation	$ 30 000	$ 27 000
Costs of maintenance	- 7 000	- 6 000
Total costs	$ 37 000	$ 33 000

The obvious choice will be vendor C even if the capacity is more than needed. This is called **"rational excess capacity"**. So, we can put into the investment budget: $270.000

For the vendors of raw materials, the best way to compare is to calculate cost prices per battery:

	Vendor A	Vendor B	Vendor C
1 kilogram of carbon	$ 8.50	$ 8.80	$ 8.40
½ litre of battery fluid	- 3.00	- 2.70	- 2.80
total gross purchase price	$ 11.50	$ 11.50	$ 11.20
Less discount	3% - 0.345	7% - 0.805	5% - 0.56
total purchase price	$ 11.155	$ 10.695	$ 10.64
+ transportation	10% - 1.115	4% - 0.428	6% - 0.638
total cost price	$ 12.26	$ 11.12	$ 11.28

From this comparison vendor B wins the race. In the investment budget we will now put the quarterly quantity at cost price: (150.000 pieces. : 4) X $ 11.12 = $ 417.000 From the assignment we know: that warehouse racking will cost $ 125.000, that computers will cost $ 20.000 and that the company needs $ 50.000 in cash.

For the purpose of setting up an investment budget we also need to calculate the amount clients owe the company during their term of payment which we calculate as follows: (150.000 X $ 35) : 12 = $ 437.500

Total investments excluding the building would be $1.319.500

As we know, the total investment cannot be more than $ 1.375.000. The amounts for all of the investments excluding the building already totalling more than $ 1.300.000 make it clear that buying a building of which the buying price is $ 355.000 is not possible in view of the bank's demand that equity should account for at least 40% of the total of the financing. So, the company will have no other choice than to lease the building, leaving the future option to buy wide open.

We can now make the final investment budget:

FIXED ASSETS		correct answer letter	source of finance	
Building	0	a	-	
Equipment	$270 000	c	suppliers	$270 000
Racking and computers	-145 000	b	suppliers	$145 000
Total fixed assets	$415 000			
CURRENT ASSETS				
Raw materials	$417 000	c	suppliers	$417 000
Debtors	-437 500	a	equity	$437 500
Liquidity	-112 500	c	equity	$112 500
Total current assets	$967 000		credit from suppliers	$832 000
			Equity	$550 000
TOTAL INVESTMENT	$1 382 000		Total finance	$1 382 000

Since all of the suppliers are willing to extend a term of payment no loans are necessary to finance the assets. Only the outstanding receivables need financing by equity. The difference between the available equity and the outstanding receivables can be added to cash.

Solutions of the Closing Assignments Chapter 2

The Financing Plan

1. The correct answer is b.
   Fixed assets are: building of $ 300.000, cold room of $ 180.000, cool counter of $ 50.000, furniture and tooling for $ 12.000 and the cool van for $ 80.000, together totalling $622.000. Current assets are inventory of $ 15.000 and cash $ 20.000 is $ 35.000. Total $ 657.000

2. The correct answer is c
   Total investment is $ 657.000. His equity of $ 270.000 is 41,09 = 41,1% of the total. He will use the mortgage for 80% of the building = $ 240.000, the long-term loan for 50% of counter and cold room of a total of $ 230.000 = $ 115.000. Creditors will finance inventory of $ 15.000. He now can count on $ 370.000. He still needs a credit on current account of $ 17.000

3. The correct answer is a.
   Mortgage is 5% of $ 240.000 = $ 12.000, long term loan is 8.5% of $ 115.000 = $9.775 and credit in current account is 15% of $ 17.000 = $ 2.550. Totals $ 24.325

Solutions of the Closing Assignments of Chapter 3
The Balance Sheet

1.1 The correct answer is b

If a fixed asset proves to have a higher than book value (+ $ 300.000) it always must be recorded as **revaluation reserve** under equity (+ $ 300.000)

1.2 The correct answer is a

Equity belongs to the shareholders. So equity of $ 360.000: 200 = $ 1.800 per share

1.3 The correct answer is c

Obviously, the nominal value per share is $ 1.000 (200 shares = $ 200.000). Every dollar received in excess of $ 1.000 cannot be booked as shares. The item to be used is **additional paid-in capital**. So 40 X $ 1.000 = $ 40.000 under share capital, 40 X $1.500= $ 60.000 under additional paid-in capital (under the heading "equity"), Cash + is $ 100.000.

1.4 The correct answer is b

Depreciations are costs. If there is a profit clients must have paid those costs also. But in case of depreciation no flow of cash is caused. So profit + depreciation landed in the bank account of the corporation; therefore building - $ 40.000, equipment - $ 12.000 and furniture - $ 10.000. Cash is depreciation + profit = + $ 132.000. Net change on the debit side: $ 132.000 - $ 62.000 = $ 70.000. Exactly that figure comes under retained earnings.

1.5 The correct answer is c

Sales at cost price were $ 465.000 X 68% = $ 316.200. Monthly sales at cost price then, were: $ 316.200: 12 = $ 26.350. Inventory will last for ($ 100.000: $26.350) = 3,79 (3.8) months.

1.5 The correct answer is b

6% of $ 300.000 plus 8% of $ 100.000 plus 18.5% of $ 130.000 totals $ 50.050

1.6 The correct answer is b

The Golden Balance Rule applies because equity of $ 360.000 and the two long term loans of $ 400.000 are $ 760.000 in total, which is higher than fixed assets of $600.000 plus inventory of $ 100.000.

Solutions of the Closing Assignment of Chapter 4

THE P & L STATEMENT

Item	Dollars	percentage
turnover	$ 45 000 000	100
costs of raw material	- 34 255 284	76.12
profit margin on sales	$ 10 744 716	23.88
costs of personnel	- 4 587 840	10.20
costs of housing	- 380 000	0.84
marketing costs	- 1 300 000	2.89
office costs	- 140 000	0.31
costs of transportation	- 207 576	0.46
depreciation	- 790 000	1.76
TOTAL OF OPERATING COSTS	$ 7 405 416	16.46
OPERATING RESULT	$ 3 339 300	7.42
costs of financing	$ 189 300	0.42
NET PROFIT BEFORE TAX	$ 3 150 000	7.00

Solution of the Closing Assignment Chapter 5

LIQUIDITY PLAN

ACTION	January	February	March	April	May	June
Balance of cash	100 000*	-54 300	109 392	- 24 081	6 835	119 103
sales income	140 000*	600 000	600 000	600 000	600 000	600 000
other income			80 000		120 000 100 000	
TOTAL INCOME	240 000	545 700	789 392	575 919	826 835	710 103
purchases inventory	130 000*	130 000*	400 000	400 000	400 000	400 000
salaries and wages	150 000	150 000	150 000	150 000	294 000	150 000
office costs	8 000	8 000	8 000	8 000	8 000	8 000
purchase of assets				1 500		
interest: extra		3 258				
current account	2 700*	2 700	1 873	2 234	2 132	345
mortgage loan	2 000*	2 000	2 000	2 000	2 000	2 000
long term loan	0	3 750*	0	3 750	0	3 750
marketing costs	1 600	1 600 120 000	1 600	1 600	1 600	1 600 90 000
costs of maintenance		15 000	250 000			
other expenditures						
TOTAL EXPENDITURES	294 300	436 308	813 473	569 084	707 732	655 695
BALANCE	- 54 300	109 392	-24 081	6 835	119 106	63 408

* From balance sheet

1.2 The correct answer is c

1.3 The correct answer is a

For the mortgage loan a constant amount was paid monthly: 6 X $ 2.000 = $12.000 For the long-term loan payments were 3 X $ 3.750 =   11.250

For the current account debt there is a variation. January was   2.700

In February 1.5 % again on $ 180.000   2.700

In February 6% had to be paid extra because of the shortage of $ 54.300   3.258

February surplus was $ 109.392. Debt decreased to $124.908. 1.5% is   1.873

The March deficit of $ 24.081 increased the debt to $ 149.989 1.5% is   2.234

The April surplus of $ 6.835 decreased the debt to $142.154   1.5% is   2.132

The May surplus of $ 119.103 decreased the debt to $ 23.051   1.5% is   345

The June net income of $ 63.408 brought the current account in the black.

Total interest paid $ 38.492

1.4 The correct answer is c

Solutions to the Closing Assignment Chapter 6

The Closing Balance Sheet

1. CLOSING BALANCE SHEET

Building	$ 386 000	Share Capital	$580 000
Equipment -	534 000	Retained earnings -	106 150
Furniture -	232 000	Mortgage loan -	320 000
Inventory -	120 000	Long term loan -	400 000
Accounts receivable - 80 000		Provision maintenance - 60 000	
Cash -	354 150	Creditors -	100 000
		Current account credit -	140 000
TOTAL BALANCE	$ 1 706 150	TOTAL BALANCE $	1 706 150

1.2 The correct answer is c

Share capital increased by bonus shares of $ 80.000 issued from retained earnings to $580.000. Retained earnings of $ 120.000 decreased by the $ 80.000 of bonus shares of $ 80.000 to $ 40.000 and increased by the net profit after tax of $ 66.150 to $106.150

1.3 The correct answer is a

Cash started at $ 200.000 to which is added: the cash flow of $ 66.150 plus the depreciation costs of $ 108.000 is $ 374.150 in total, plus the provision for maintenance of $ 60.000 and from which is to be deducted the payments for equipment ($ 20.000) furniture ($ 40.000) and mortgage ($ 20.000) = $ 354.150

1.4 The correct answer is c

Share capital plus retained earnings on the opening balance sheet totalled $ 620.000. To be added is the net profit of $ 66.150 = $ 686.150. From retained earnings $80.000 was transformed into new shares. So, there are 580 shares now and the **intrinsic value** per share is $ 686.150 : 580 = $ 1.183

Solutions of the Closing Assignment of Chapter 7

Ratio Analysis of Annual Statements

1.1 The correct answer is c

For solvency the relation between equity and total liabilities is important. In year 1 equity was $ 1.728.000 and liabilities totalled $ 3.072.000. Total capital, therefore, was $ 4.800.000. Liabilities were 64% of the balance total and equity 36%. Every dollar invested in assets was financed by $ 0,36 of equity and by $ 0,64 of liabilities. Taking into account that current assets, when sold under pressure of time, never will earn 100% of their book value the ideal relation would have been: equity $ 0.70 and liabilities $ 0,30, or 70/30. So, where equity finances distinctly less of assets than liabilities do, the solvency becomes questionable.

1.2.2 The correct answer is b

Quick ratio in year 2 uses accounts receivables plus cash only: $400.000+$420.000 = $ 820.000: current liabilities $ 950.000 = 0,86. This is <1 and, therefore by far not solid enough to rest assured to pay off all of the current liabilities.

1.2 The correct answer is a

The golden balance rule does not apply here: long term financing sources (equity + long term liabilities) total $ 4.050.000. Fixed assets are $ 3.980.000. That leaves $70.000. This amount is not enough to also finance inventory, which shows at the balance sheet at $200.000.

1.3 The correct answer is b

Return on total capital is calculated by expressing the operating result in a percentage of the **average total capital** of the two years. This latter amount is: ($4.800.000 + $5.000.000) : 2 = $ 4.900.000. The operating result was $626.000 which is 12,78% of total capital.

1.4 The correct answer is c

Return on equity expresses net profit after tax in a percentage of equity. We need the average of equity of the two years: ($ 1.728.000 + $ 1.950.000) :2 = $ 1.839.000. Net profit after tax was $ 222.000 and that is 12.07% of this equity average.

1.5 The correct answer is a

Leverage effect occurs when the cost of financing is less than the yield on total capital. In this case interest costs were $ 330.000 which is 10.78% of the average of total liabilities of $ 3.061.000 of the two years. The operating return stems from operating income of $626.000, which is 12,78% of average total capital of the two years. The leverage effect is 12,78% - 10,78% = 2%. In simple words: every dollar invested yields $ 0,128 and costs $ 0,108. This narrow advantage certainly should not encourage to keep investing heavily in this company. We should remember that a balance sheet is a snapshot at one particular moment. A month later the snapshot could be quite different!

1.6 The correct answer is b

The turn of inventory is calculated by comparing average monthly sales at their cost price with inventory on the balance sheet to find out how many months this inventory will last. Divide 12 by this number of months and the result is the turn ratio. In this case total cost price of sales was $ 2.320.000, which is $193.333 per month. Inventory on the balance sheet is $ 200.000 which will last for slightly more than one month. Turn is $ 2.320.000: $ 200.000 = 11.6 which for a manufacturing company is very favourable, but for an ice cream saloon still too poor.

1.7 The correct answer is b

To find out how long it took clients to pay their bills we have to divide annual turnover by 12 and compare the outcome with the figure of accounts receivables on the balance sheet of year 2. $ 4.000.000 for the year is $333.333 per month. That should be the figure on the balance sheet if clients promptly pay after 30 days. In reality that figure is $ 400.000 which tells us that it took clients 1.2 months to pay their bills. (400: 333.33)

1.8 The correct answer is a

Working capital is found by subtracting all current liabilities of year 2 from the total of current assets of that year. $ 1.020.000 - $ 950.000 = $ 70.000. A positive working capital is a good sign for any company.

Solutions of the Closing Assignment of Chapter 8

Calculating The Full Cost Price

1. The correct answer is b

   This exercise is best be made along the following order: calculate total fixed costs, calculate the fixed costs per **piece**, then calculate the variable costs per **length** and then add fixed costs and variable costs.

   Total fixed costs are: depreciation of the building is $ 416.400: 30 = $ 13.880/yr. depreciation of equipment is ($ 350.000 - $ 40.000): 10 = $ 31.000, depreciation of the trucks is $ 300.000: 5 = $ 60.000, salaries amount to 12 X $ 23.760 = $ 285.120 and the office costs are $ 91.000. Total fixed costs are $ 481.000. Total volume in pieces per year is 1.300.000, each of which absorbing an equal part of the total fixed costs = $ 0.37. The variable costs are $ 0.08 per 10 centimetres. This means that total cost price per type length is 25: $ 0.37 + 2.5 X $ 0.08 is $ 0.20 > total $ 0.57; 35 cm is $ 0.37 + 3.5 X $0.08 is $ 0.28> total $ 0.65; 50 cm is $ 0.37 + 5 X $ 0.08 is $ 0.40> total $ 0.77

   2.1 The correct answer is b
   Before a cost price per hour can be calculated, we first have to know the annual costs of one consultant per year. In this case this is $ 30.000 X 129.6% = $ 38.880

   2.4 The correct answer is c
   To know what the cost price per hour is we first need to know how many billable hours a consultant has at his disposal. Gross number of working hours per year is 50 X 40 = 2.000 hours. To be deducted from this number are: 160 hours for seminars, 5 X 40 hours for holidays, 40 X 4 hours for meetings, 6 X 8 hours for sickness and 50 X 8 hours for office work which leads to a billable net number of hours of 1.032. This means that the variable costs per hour are $ 38.880: 1.032 = $ 37.67

   2.5 The correct answer is a
   When a company needs 30% of profit margin, then the cost price is 70% because the sales price always is 100%. When the cost price would be $ 56 then the sales price will have to be ($ 56 : 70) X 100 = $ 80 $ 80 - $56 = $ 24 profit margin which is 30%.

   2.6 The correct answer is b
   Total fixed costs per consultant are $ 185.400: 4 = $ 46.350. That is per hour $ 46.350: 1.030 hours = $ 45. Together with the variable costs of $ 32 per hour full cost price would be **$ 77** per hour. The hourly rate must be (77: 65) X 100 = **$ 118.46** (= 100%)

c. The correct answer is c

Cost price is calculated by dividing TFC by PV (planned volume): $ 900.000 : 60.000 = $15 and adding the variable costs of $ 14 = $ 29

Solutions of the Closing Assignment of Chapter 9

Cost Prices of Multiple Products and Services
=Activity Based Costing

1.1 The correct answer is c

First, we calculate total variable costs: (1.200 X $ 58) + (3.000 X $ 72) = $ 69.600 + $216.000 = $ 285.600. Then we calculate the cost-plus percentage: (Indirect costs: total variable costs) X 100% = ($ 380.000: 285.600) X 100% = 133.05322 %. Finally, we increase the individual variable costs by this percentage: $ 58 + 133.05322% = $135.17.

1.2 The correct answer is b

Total variable costs are (1.200 X $ 58) + (3.000 X $ 72) = $ 285.600. Indirect costs are 133.05322%. We apply this to be added to the variable costs: $ 72 + 133.05322% = $167.80.

2.1 The correct answer is $ b

Variable costs of the jugs are 150.000 X $ 9.40 = $ 1.410.000. Of all of the direct costs the following are to be allocated to the jugs: 40% of $ 120.000 (=$ 48.000) + 70% of the marketing costs of $ 260.000 (=$ 182.000) + 20% of $ 90.000 (=$ 18.000) + 45% of $430.000 (=$ 193.500) + 30% of $ 110.000 (=$ 33.000) + 50% of $ 172.000 (=$86.000) = $560.500. This portion of indirect costs makes 39.752% of the $ 1.410.000 = **the cost-plus percentage**. So, one jug has a cost price of $ 9.40 + 39.752% = $13.14

2.2 The correct answer is c

Variable costs of the tumblers are 230.000 X $ 11.60 = $ 2.668.000. The indirect costs are allocated to the tumblers as follows: 60% of $ 120.000 (=$ 72.000) + 30% of $ 260.000 (=$ 78.000) + 80% of $ 90.000 (=$ 72.000) + 55% of $ 430.000 (=$ 236.500) + 70% of $ 110.000 (=$77.000) + 50% of $ 172.000 (=$ 86.000) = $ 621.500. These indirect costs are 23.295% of the total variable costs of $ 2.668.000. We increase the variable costs per piece with this cost plus percentage: $ 11.60 + 23.295% = $ 14.30

2.3 The correct answer is a

total Indirect costs are:		$ 1 182 000
variable costs	(150 000 X $ 9.40) =	$ 1 410 000
variable costs	(230 000 X $11.60) =	$ 2 668 000
	TOTAL:	**$ 5 260 000**
These are covered by		
150 000 X $ 13.14		$ 1 971 000
+ 230 000 X $ 14.30		$ 3 289 000
		$ 5 260 000

3.1 The correct answer is b
A specialist costs $ 4.000 X 12 X 1.08 = $ 51.840: 1.950 hours = $ 26.58
A masseuse costs $ 2.800 X 12 X 1.08 = $ 36.288: 1.950 hours = $ 18.61

3.2 The correct answer is a

The specialists earn 4 X 12 X $ 4 000 x 1.08 =	$ 207 360
The masseuses earn 12 X 12 X $ 2 800 X 1.08 =	$435 456

Total variable costs	$642 816

3.3 The correct answer is c
Total indirect costs are $ 1.800.000. Variable costs total (4 X 12 X $ 4.000 X 1.08) = $207.360 of diet specialists plus (12 X 12 X $ 2.800 X 1.08) = $ 435.456 for masseuses = $642.816 in total. The cost-plus percentage is ($ 1.800.000: $ 642.816) X 100% = 280.02%. The variable costs per hour for a diet specialist are $ 4000 X 12 X 1.08 = $51.840 for 1.500 billable hours. So, the hourly variable costs are $ 51.840: 1.500 = $34.56. Cost plus percentage to be added: $ 34.56 + 280.02% = $ 131.33 per hour.

3.4 The correct answer is b
First, we calculate total salary costs per year and per hour.

	Salary	annual salary	total variable costs	hours	var. cost/hr
Specialist	12 X $ 4 000	X1.08 = $ 51 840	4 times = $ 207 360	$51840: 1 500 hrs	= $ 34.56
Masseuse	12 X $ 2 800	X1.08 = $ 36 288	12 times = $ 435 456	$ 36 288: 1 768 hrs	= $ 20.52

We know that of all of the direct costs $ 947.000 relate to specialists and $ 853.000 relate to masseuses. We now can fix the cost-plus percentage for the specialists: ($947.000: $207.360) X 100% = 456.69%. We add this to the hourly variable costs: $34.56 + 456.69% = **$ 192.39** And for the masseuses this is ($ 853.000: $ 435.456) x 100% = 195.9%. $ 20.52 + 195.9% = **$ 60.72**

Check: Fixed costs + total annual salaries = $ 1.800.000 + $ 207.360 + $ 435.456 = $2.442.816. These must be incorporated in the annual billable hours.

4 specialists X $ 192.39 X 1 500 =	$1 154 340
12 masseuses X $ 60.72 X 1 768 =	1 288 235.50

Total costs	$2 442 575.50.

The small difference was caused by working with decimal percentages.

3.5 The correct answer is c
When a profit margin is 35% the cost price must be 65%. The rate for a specialist will then have to be ($ 190: 65) X 100 = $ 292.31. For masseuses ($ 60: 70) X 100 = $85.71

Solutions of the Closing Assignments of Chapter 10

The Budgeting Process and Analysis of Variances

1.1 The correct answer is b

Budgeted Cost price is Fixed Costs Component per piece (FCC) + variable costs per piece. Total Fixed Costs: budgeted volume is FCC (fixed costs component per piece) = $108.000: BV of 7.200 pieces leads to a fixed costs component (TFC) of $15 per piece. Cost price according to budget is TFC of $ 15 + variable costs of $ 48 + $ 96 (3 hours per piece at $ 32 per hour) is

	$159
Real cost price was $ 108 000: 7 400 pieces is FCC of	$14.59
+ variable costs of materials: $ 340 400: 7 400 pieces	46.00
+ variable costs of labour: $ 594 000: 7 400 pieces	80.27=$ 140.86
Variance in cost price per piece is	$18.14

1.2 The correct answer is a

Sales price – cost price according to budget was $ 210 - $ 159 = $ 51. The real sales price was $ 1.626.400: 7.600 = $ 214. Sales price less real cost price of $ 140,86 is $ 214 - $ 140,86 is

	$73.14
Better profit margin minus budgeted profit margin is	$22.14

1.3 The correct answer is c

Efficiency variance of raw materials: (RV – BV) X BP = (7.400 – 7.200) X $ 48 = $ 9.600. When we look at the budget of 7.200 pieces these would require material costs of 7.200 X $ 48 = $ 345.600. In reality 7.400 pieces were made with a total of material costs of $340.400 = $ 46 per piece. Two dollars less per piece.

1.4 The correct answer is b

Price variance of raw materials: Gazelle spent $ 340.400: 7.400 = $ 46 in raw materials per piece. (RP – BP) X RV (real price minus budgeted price X real volume made). ($ 46 - $ 48) X 7.400 pieces = $ 14.800

1.5 The correct answer is c

Volume variance of sales: (RV – BV) X BP = (7.600 – 7.400) X $ 210 = $ 42.000

1.6 The correct answer is a

Price variance of sales: RP is $ 1.626.400: 7.600 = $ 214. Price variance formula is (RP – BP) RV = ($ 214 - $ 210) X 7.600 = $ 30.400

1.7 The correct answer is c

Efficiency variance in labour: (BV – RV) X BP in which BV is 3 X 7.200 = 21.600 hours. Real hours were 19.800. (19.800 – 21.600) X $ 32 = - $ 57.600

1.8 The correct answer is b

Price variance in labour: (BP – RP) X RV (budgeted price – real price X real number of hours) = $32 - ($ 594.000: 19.800) = – $ 30 = 2 X 7.400 = $ 14.800

1.9. The correct answer is a

Capacity variance was: (RV – BV) X ($ 108.000: BV) = (7.400-7.200) X $ 15 = $ 3.000

Solutions of the Closing Assignment of Chapter 11

Methods to Calculate Profit and the Break-Even Point

1.1 The correct answer is b
Variable costs of $ 0.15 + ($ 504.000: 4.200.000 bottles) = $ 0.15 + $ 0.12 = $ 0.27.

1.2 The correct answer is c

Turnover is 4 400 000 bottles X $ 0.38=	$1 672 000
Full cost price is 4 400 000 X $ 0.27=	1 188 000
result of transaction =	$484 000
Capacity variance 4.7 million – 4.2 million) X $ 0.12	$60 000 +
result of the period =	$544 000

1.3 The correct answer is a

Turnover is 4.400.000 X $ 0,38	=$ 1.672.000
Variable costs 4.400.000 X $ 0,15	= -660.000
contribution margin	=$ 1.012.000
total fixed costs	= -504.000
result of the period	= $508.000

1.4 The correct answer is b
The difference in profit between the two methods is $ 36.000. 300.000 unsold bottles return to inventory at full cost price of $ 0,27 in the AC method and at variable costs of $0,15 in the VC method. The difference is 300.000 X $ 0,12 = $ 36.000

1.5 The correct answer is c
Break even turnover is total fixed costs: total contribution margin > $ 504.000: ($ 0,38-$0,15) = 2.191.304 bottles. Check: 2,191.304 X $ 0,23 = $ 504.000

1.6 The correct answer is a
The order should be accepted, because the sales price per piece of $ 0,20 is higher than the variable costs of $ 0,15 so that there will be an additional contribution margin to cover more of the fixed costs by 350.000 X ($ 0,20 - $ 0,15) = $ 17.500

Solutions of the Closing Assignment of Chapter 12

Pre-Calculation of Investment Options

1.1 The correct answer is a

Wages per employee grow by 3% per year from $ 26.000 to $ 26.780 in year 2 to $27.583 in year 3 to $ 28.410 in year 4, and to $ 29.263 in year 5. Robot A can save labour costs of 3 people, robot B saves costs of 4 people. Depreciation costs per robot are A = $ 170.000: 5 = $ 34.000 and of B $ 40.000. Maintenance of A costs $ 8.000 and of B $ 10.000. Total costs of A per year: $ 34.000 + $ 8.000 = $ 42.000 and of B $ 40.000 + $10.000 = $ 50.000.

At an interest rate of 4% the annual savings must be divided by 1.04 (yr.1) – 1.0816 (yr.2) – 1.1248 (yr. 3) – 1.1698 (yr. 4) and 1.2166 (yr.5). The **present value** of the savings of robot A, saving 3 people and with wage increases of 3% per year:

Yr.	savings	costs	divide	= present value
1.	$ 78 000	- $ 42 000 =	$ 36 000: 1.04	= $ 34 615
1.2.	$ 80 340	- $ 42 000 =	$ 38 340: 1.0816	= - 35 447
3.	$ 82 750	- $ 42 000 =	$ 40 750: 1.1248	= - 36 338
4.	$ 85 232	- $ 42 000 =	$ 43 232: 1.1698	= - 36 956
5.	$ 87 789	- $ 42 000 =	$ 45 789: 1.2166	= - 37 636
			present value of the savings	= $ 180 892
			investment	= -170 000
			net present value	=$ 10 882

Robot B saving 4 people and with wage increases of 3% per year

Yr.	savings	costs	divide	= present value
1.	$ 104 000 -	$ 50 000 =	$ 54 000: 1.04	= $ 51 923
2.	$ 107 120 -	$ 50 000 =	$ 57 20: 1.0816	= - 52 810
3.	$ 110 333 -	$ 50 000 =	$ 60 .333: 1.1248	= - 53 638
4.	$ 113 643 -	$ 50 000 =	$ 63 643: 1.1698	= - 54 405
5.	$ 117 052 -	$ 50 000 =	$ 67 052: 1.2166	= -55 114
			present value of the savings	= $ 267 890
			investment	= - 200 000
			net present value	= $67 890

Conclusion: Robot B is more economical than robot A

d. The correct answer is c

The payback period can be calculated by reducing the investment sum by the annual savings expressed in cash flows.

The wages increase by 3% per year. The annual savings are as follows:

Robot A saves labour costs of 3 people from year 1 $ 78.000 and 3% more every year thereafter = 2: $ 80.340, 3: $ 82.750, 4: $ 85.232, 5: $87.789. Total: $ 414.111.

Robot B saves labour costs of 4 people= year 1: $ 104.000 and 3% more every year thereafter: 2: $ 107.120, 3: $ 110.333, 4: $ 113.643, 5: $ 117.052. Total $ 552.148.

Annual costs of A are depreciation of $ 34.000 + maintenance of $ 8.000 = $ 42.000 and B: depreciation of $ 40.000 + maintenance of $ 10.000. Cash flow is net profit + depreciation costs. Payback time can be calculated as follows:

	Robot A		**Robot B**
Investment year 1	$170 000		- $ 200 000
Cash flow year 1	$78 000		$ 104 000
	+ $ 34 000		+ $ 50 000
	-$ 8 000		- $ 10 000
	= $ 144 000		= $ 144 000
	---------------		-----------------
not yet earned back year 1	$66 000		$56 000
	$107 120		$ 80 340
	+ $ 50 000		+ $ 34 000
year 2	- $ 10 000		- $ 8 000
	= 147 120		= 106 340
	---------------		----------------
positive difference	$40 340	positive difference	$91 120
	($ 66 000: $ 106 340) X 12		($ 56 000: $ 147 120) X12
	= 1 year 7.4 months		**= 1 year 4.5 months**

Conclusion: Robot B offers the shorter payback period.

Indexes

Absorption costing 168, 170, 179
accounts receivables 118
acid test 118
Acid test 207
ACID TEST 114
additional paid in capital 102, 197
Additional paid in capital 64
Articles of Incorporation 28
assets 12, 14, 25
Assets 13, 29
authorized capital 32, 53
Authorized Shares 28
Average of total capital 208
average of total liabilities 230

balance sheet 13, 14, 30, 46
Bankruptcy 43
billable hours 210, 232, 235
bonus shares 58, 121
book value 63
borrowing capacity 42, 58, 93, 201
break even point 8
Break Even Point 172, 179, 216
budget 178, 222, 236, 237
budgeted volume 216, 236
buffer 42

Capacity variance 217, 219, 238
CAPITAL 42
cash flow 14, 30, 185
Cash flow 184
Cash flow method 184
cash management 14
Cash management 87
closing balance sheet 111, 204
CLOSING BALANCE SHEET 229
common stock 33, 34
contribution margin 168, 173, 175
Contribution margin 171
controllable costs 75
Controllable costs 78
Corporate solvency 115
corporate tax 100, 202
cost plus method 144, 146, 151

Cost plus method 149
cost price 231
costs of labour 153, 162, 181, 236
credit limit 41
creditors 87
Creditors 65, 66, 86
current account 46, 81
current assets 14, 37
CURRENT liabilities 50
CURRENT LIABILITIES 51
current ratio 119
Current ratio 207

Debt Ratio 115
debtors 14, 127
Debtors 24
depreciated value 31
depreciation 16, 56, 58
Depreciation 19, 20, 23, 67, 68, 105, 181
direct costs 146
Direct costs 148
DIRECT COSTS 143, 212
dividend 205
doubtful accounts 100
Doubtful accounts 101

Efficiency 236
Efficiency variance 236, 237
Efficiency Variance 162
emission of shares 25, 27
equity 11, 44, 50, 88, 127
Equity 48
equity value 32
excess capacity 15
EXPENDITURES 160

financial assets 102
financial costs 50, 100
financial statement 50
financing resources 50
fixed assets 116, 137
Fixed Assets 10
fixed costs 152, 161, 162
fixed costs component 217
Fixed Costs Component 236

241

full cost price 232, 238
Full cost price 219

general ledger 102, 105, 109
golden balance rule 112, 230
Golden Balance Rule 60, 225
goodwill 103
government bonds 110

incorporated 25
Indirect costs 234
installments 203
intangible assets 103
INTANGIBLE ASSETS 102
intangible fixed asset 195
intrinsic value 59, 229
inventory 52, 67
investment 62, 68
Investment 45
investment budget 24, 35

labour 240
Labour 214
landed cost price 13
legal entity 25, 28
leverage effect 124
Leverage effect 230
leverage in liabilities 122
liability 31, 55
limited liability company 27
liquidity 42
Liquidity 24
LONG TERM liabilities 50
LONG TERM LIABILITIES 39, 42
long term loan 109
Long term loan 96, 105, 106

market value 63
Market value 58
Mortgage 65, 66

net earnings 86
net present value 187, 239
net profit 168, 185, 190
Net profit 127, 230
NET PROFIT 83, 226
nominal value 52, 57

official stock exchange 25
operating costs 140, 168
Operating costs 123
operating loss 34
operating result 127, 161
OPERATING RESULT 169
operational costs 13

par value 121
pay back period 220
Personal Loans 40
planned volume 233
Preferred stock 28
present value 239
Price variance 236, 237
private capital 39
profit margin 132, 133, 134
Profit margin 108
provision 109, 120, 148
Provision 205, 229

quick ratio 127
Quick ratio 207, 230

ratio 80
Ratio 46
ratio capital: outside sources 18
ratio equity: liabilities 30
rational excess capacity 15, 222
reappraisal 58, 66
residual value 22
Residual value 20
retain ownership 40
retained earnings 191
Retained earnings 53, 57, 96, 192
Return on equity 230
Return on liabilities 127
return on total capital 208
revaluation 53, 58, 102, 191
revaluation reserve 225
Revaluation reserve 53, 102

share 84
Share 96
share capital 52
Share capital 39
shareholder 100
Shareholder 110
solvability 183
solvency 230
STOCKHOLDERS' EQUITY 42, 51

total fixed costs 238
Total Fixed Costs 236
Total variable costs 234
Turnover 108, 123

UNCONTROLLABLE costs 72

variable costs 232, 238
Variable costs method 169
variable costs of labour 136, 168

Variable costs of material 214
variances 163
Variances 236
VARIANCES 214
volume variance 165, 166, 215

Volume variance 236
working capital 13, 128, 172, 207
Working capital 231